JEWISH IDENTITY

Volume 48, Sage Library of Social Research

SAGE LIBRARY OF SOCIAL RESEARCH

JEWISH IDENTITY

A SOCIAL PSYCHOLOGICAL PERSPECTIVE

SIMON N. HERMAN

Foreword by **HERBERT C. KELMAN**

Volume 48
SAGE LIBRARY OF
SOCIAL RESEARCH

SAGE PUBLICATIONS   Beverly Hills   London

For information address:

SAGE PUBLICATIONS, INC.
275 South Beverly Drive
Beverly Hills, California 90212

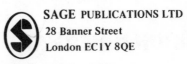

SAGE PUBLICATIONS LTD
28 Banner Street
London EC1Y 8QE

Printed in the United States of America

Library of Congress Cataloging in Publication Data

Herman, Simon N   1912-
  Jewish identity.

  (Sage library of social research ; v. 48)
  Bibliography: p. 251
  Includes index.
  1. Jews—Identity. 2. Jews—Politics and government—
1948-   I. Title.
DS143.H34   301.45'19'24   77-8605
ISBN 0-8039-0874-1
ISBN 0-8039-0875-X pbk.

FIRST PRINTING

To Segula
With Love

CONTENTS

FOREWORD

The concept of ethnic and national identity has become increasingly popular in recent years, both among social scientists and among political actors. It is an inherently social-psychological concept in that it refers to a state of mind shared by the members of a collectivity, formed through social interaction, and anchored in historical and social-structural processes. Yet there has been very little social-psychological work—conceptual or empirical—that has sytematically addressed itself to the analysis of group identity. Simon Herman's book thus represents a pioneering contribution to the study of ethnic/national identity, focusing on the special case of Jewish identity.

Professor Herman's book can best be characterized, it seems to me, as a fusion of two essays—one a conceptual and empirical contribution to the social psychology of national identity, the other a normative statement of what Jewish identity means to him and what form it ought to take. These two essays are not presented seriatim, but are interwoven in such a way that each argument enriches and illuminates the other.

The descriptive theme of the book identifies a set of dimensions and assumptions that provide a conceptual framework for analyzing group identity in all its richness and complexity. Professor Herman draws here on the work of his mentor, Kurt Lewin, whose insights remain fresh and valid thirty years after Lewin's death. The conceptual framework is applied specifically to the case of Jewish identity, which Professor Herman presents in its historical and comparative context. The historically unique features of the case—for example, the inextricable blending of religious and national elements in Jewish identity, the role of Jews' self-definition as a people in exile in shaping their identity, the central place of the Holocaust and of the creation of Israel in contemporary Jewish consciousness—do not reduce the contribution of the study to the analysis of national identity in general. Not only are the elements of the conceptual framework generally applicable, but—despite historical uniqueness—there are important continuities between this case and many others. To take just one example, religious elements play a central part in the identity of many ethnic groups, even though the precise mix between the religious and the national may vary. Moreover, the unique features of the specific case are often useful in highlighting some of the issues of national identity in general. For example, Professor Herman's extensive discussion of the relationship between Jewish and Israeli identity (particularly when we recall that a large majority of Jews are not Israelis and a sizeable minority of Israelis are not Jews) makes us aware of the ambiguities that are so characteristic of national identity.

Another special feature of this book is its comparative focus: It examines the elements, the evolution, and the meaning of Jewish identity among Israeli Jews, American Jews, and Jews in other parts of the world. In this connection, Professor Herman reports his empirical research with Israeli students, as well as Jewish students from the United States and elsewhere attending Israeli institutions. He has the special advantage of being able to compare the fresh data reported in this volume with findings from his earlier and extensive research on Israeli students (along with their parents and teachers) and on American students in Israel. To my knowledge, this is the only comprehensive empirical research program in existence that provides comparative data on Jewish identity.

In presenting his conceptual and empirical analyses, Professor Herman does not pretend to be a value-free social scientist—which brings me to the second or normative theme of this book. The author acknowledges the impossibility of a value-free stance in this area of investigation and states the value assumptions and biases that entered into his choice of conceptual categories and interpretation of empirical data. But he goes beyond this to develop his own perspective on Jewish identity and his own vision of its ideal dimensions. Readers need not have a personal concern about Jewish identity—nor share Professor Herman's particular perspective on it—in order to find this discussion illuminating. It enables readers to place the conceptually and empirically derived elements of Jewish identity in a coherent context and to identify the critical issues to which they give rise.

Thus, the discussion focuses attention on the relationship between Israel and the Jewish Diaspora, which is critical to an understanding of the identity of both Israeli and non-Israeli Jews, whether or not one shares the author's particular Zionist perspective on these issues. He provides a highly sympathetic and nondoctrinaire analysis of the situation of the non-Israeli Jews, who, as I mentioned above, form a large majority of world Jewry. (A similar analysis of the situation of non-Jewish Israelis—particularly the Arab minority within Israel—would be equally useful, but unfortunately it is outside the scope of Professor Herman's study.) Another critical issue on which the discussion focuses attention is the intermingling of religious and national elements in Jewish identity. The relationship between these two elements is essential to an understanding of the development and dynamics of Jewish identity, whether or not one subscribes to Professor Herman's maximalist bias. Finally, even those readers who do not share the author's profound commitment to Jewish survival, will derive important insights from his discussion of the role of the Holocaust in the formation of contemporary Jewish identity. These are some of the ways in which the normative context enriches and illuminates the conceptual and empirical contributions, while at the same time drawing upon them throughout.

June 1977   *Herbert C. Kelman*
Harvard University

ACKNOWLEDGMENTS

In the course of the preparation of this volume I enjoyed the benefit of consultation with colleagues at universities in the United States, England, and Israel. I gratefully render thanks to Bert Raven (UCLA), Joshua Fishman (Yeshiva University), Ben Halpern and Marshall Sklare (Brandeis University), Herbert Kelman and Israel Scheffler (Harvard University), Henri Tajfel (University of Bristol), Charles Liebman (Bar-Ilan University), Uri Farago and Ozer Schild (Haifa University), Charles Greenbaum and Shulamit Nardi (Hebrew University). I am particularly indebted to Professor Moshe Davis, head of the Institute of Contemporary Jewry at the Hebrew University, for the helpful advice and constant encouragement I received.

The empirical studies contained in this volume were conducted with the cooperation of Uri Farago and Ya'akov Harel in the Department of Psychology and the Institute of Contemporary Jewry under grants from the Memorial Foundation for Jewish Culture, the Levi Eshkol Institute, and the American Jewish Committee. Noam Stockman assisted in the preparation of the statistical tables.

The study was supported by a grant from the Paula and David Ben Gurion Research Fund established at the Hebrew University by the Federman family.

January 1977   *Simon N. Herman*
Hebrew University, Jerusalem

PART I

THE ELEMENTS OF JEWISH IDENTITY

Chapter 1

A SOCIAL PSYCHOLOGICAL PERSPECTIVE

The purpose of this volume is to bring the perspectives of social psychology to bear on the study of Jewish identity. While we shall draw upon the insights of the other social sciences as well, we shall be concerned primarily, in what is a study of social identity, with the contribution of social psychology as the discipline which deals with the individual in the group and with the fusion of the social and psychological processes.

We shall draw upon the relevant contributions to the subject from a variety of schools of thought among social scientists. At many points the insightful work of Erik Erikson in the field of identity has guided our exploration. The basic approach which we adopt, however, is largely in accordance with the field theoretical tradition established by one of the great psychologists of the century, Kurt Lewin. There have been few social psychologists who have grappled on so significant a level with the crucial human problems of our time.

Field theory is "more an approach to the scientific task than a theory about a realm of data."[1] Lewin posits as the basic tenet of a field theory that behavior has to be derived from a totality of coexisting facts and that these coexisting facts have the character of a "dynamic field" in the sense that the state of any part of this field depends on every other part of the field.[2]

The Practicality of a Good Theory

Many of the emphases contained in Lewin's approach, as he developed it in his pioneering work in the area of group dynamics, have served as guidelines in the present study.

(1) Lewin pointed to the limitations of an empiricism unguided by theory. In the absence of a theory, research tends to become a mere collection and description of facts with little, if any, predictive value. Turning to the work of the applied psychologist he observed that "there is nothing more practical than a good theory."[3]

(2) In order to understand or predict behavior, the person and his environment have to be considered as *one* constellation of interdependent factors. The life space (i.e., the person and the environment as it exists for him at a given moment in time) includes the relevant social groups to which the individual relates. Lewin became interested in the study of the group (a) as part of the "field"—the totality of coexisting, mutually interdependent facts—in which the individual moves, and (b) as a dynamic whole with attributes of its own transcending the sum total of its constituent parts.

(3) In his studies of group life he sought to reach beyond the level of description; the focus was on the forces which produce or resist change. As he saw it, the crucial questions of group dynamics are, "which forces are keeping up this type of group life, what forces would resist what changes, under what conditions would a change be permanent and when will group living bend quickly back to previous designs."[4]

(4) Lewin died on the very eve of embarking on a major project for the study of Jewish life, which he had been planning across the

years,[5] and he left behind only a few essays devoted exclusively to Jewish topics. Yet, at the time they were written in the early 1940s, these few essays had a profound effect on the thinking of Jewish intellectual circles in the United States (and in other countries as well). They constituted a scientific rationale for the Jewishness of these circles legitimized by an eminent social scientist. In a period when Jewish social scientists and others tended to emphasize the equality of the Jew as an individual no different from others, Lewin stressed that there could be no real equality for the individual Jew unless his Jewish group qua group was equal. When many social scientists of that period were inclined to slur over this group identification, Lewin pointed to its far-reaching implications in the life of the individual.

Lewin's approach to research in social psychology opened up new vistas, but in the years following Lewin's death, as has been pointed out by one of his former students, Morton Deutsch, the "interest in developing and applying a socially-useful social psychology largely disappeared from the main stream of American academic social psychology for about 15 to 20 years—the period of the nineteen fifties to the late nineteen sixties."[6] One of the reasons for this was that social psychologists, seeking to emulate the natural sciences, increasingly concentrated their research on the precise measurement of variables amenable to experimental control. This resulted in a neglect of the study of complex, not easily controllable issues and of social processes across time which could not be brought into the ambit of a laboratory experiment. While the report prepared by an international group of social psychologists participating in a conference on ethnic identity gives due credit to laboratory experimentation in social psychology as "the best possible way to advance knowledge in a major part of this field by small but reliable steps," it declares that "laboratory experimentation on small-scale social groups set in fairly artificial conditions does not, however, lend itself easily to the investigation of problems of identity, integration, ingroup and outgroup relations, in a large-scale social context." The report continues: "At the same time, many social psychologists are becoming increasingly and acutely aware that these problems—together with many other related ones pertaining to the psychological aspects of social change—are a challenge to their discipline which must be taken up."[7]

The challenge is indeed being taken up, and there has latterly been a promising resurgence of interest in a psychology which, while maintaining the canons of scientific rigor, wrestles with the significant social issues. The body of substantive knowledge which social psychological research has produced for the solution of social problems is still, however, very meager. What social psychology does more readily provide is a method of investigation and a perspective, a way of looking at the problem.

An Orientation to the Study of Contemporary Jewry

Social scientists, like all other men and women, have their biases, i.e., a priori beliefs and valuations about the phenomena to be studied. These beliefs and valuations, which shape the social scientist's approach to any social problem, often remain hidden—even to the scientist himself—and their operation is accordingly unchecked. It is not sufficient, then, that the conscientious researcher seeks out the facts with scrupulous honesty and care, that he distinguishes as well as he can between the facts and his opinions; it behoves him, in addition, to make explicit to himself and to his readers the underlying value premises on which the conclusions he presents are predicated.[8]

In our analysis of the nature of Jewish identity and of the forces which go into its shaping we shall focus on the factors calculated to preserve and strengthen that identity. Our approach reflects a survivalist as opposed to an assimilationist bias.

Our orientation to the study of contemporary Jewish identity proceeds from a view of the Jewish people as a continually changing organism to be studied as a totality in historical and in comparative perspective and in the setting of the majority cultures in which the larger part of this people is located.

AS A CHANGING ORGANISM

The Jewish people has been—and still is—a people on the move, called upon to adapt to the exigencies of new physical, social, and political environments. Not only has the demographic map altered radically but the expressions of Jewish life—particularly in the less restrictive settings—have become more diversified. In relation to such a people, static surveys serve only a limited purpose. It needs to be studied as the living, changing organism that it is, and the research should catch the reverberations of the changes.

"Their number is greater today than ever before in their history—nearly seventeen millions; but the perils which threaten their continued existence have grown even faster," wrote the pioneer sociologist of Jewish life, Arthur Ruppin, in October 1939 in the preface to an English edition of his book *The Jewish Fate and Future.* Referring to the studies that he had carried out since the beginning of the century, he observed: "All these books have the same purpose, to supply a survey of the contemporary social life of the Jews. But these works differ from one another, because the general political and economic background of the social life of the Jews has undergone fundamental changes since the beginning of the twentieth century."[9]

Ruppin could not have foreseen how profound would be the changes that would sweep over the Jewish people in the next three decades—the murder of six of the seventeen million, the establishment of the State of Israel, the "ingathering of the exiles," the evacuation of Jews from the Arab countries, and—more recently—the dramatic exodus of Jews from Soviet Russia.

AS A TOTALITY

Jewish life should be viewed in its totality, as one field, i.e., as a constellation of interdependent factors. While it may be necessary to concentrate on the exploration of one corner, the researcher should not lose sight of the relationship of that corner to the field as a whole. Thus, the problems of Jewish education in a community can only be properly understood if viewed within the framework of the forces making for greater or less Jewish identification in that community. And Judaism cannot be studied as something distinct from the Jewish people who are its carriers—as if it were a disembodied religious philosophy. It is knit into the life of the people, and the changes it undergoes are reflections of changes in that people's way of life.

Many of the problems facing a particular Jewish community can only be properly comprehended when placed within a global context which allows for an analysis both of the features of the problem common to a number of settings and those which are attributable to local circumstances. In his introduction to a study of American Jewish history, Moshe Davis writes: "The basic assumption of the study is that the internal development of the Jewish community in the United States is shaped principally by the developments in world Jewry, its cultural tradition and its historic continuity. This encompassing Jewish approach does not find sufficient expression in the majority of the historical and sociological studies of the American Jewish community."[10]

This criticism has special pertinence to studies of a subject—anti-Semitism—which over a period was the major concern of American social scientists at work in the Jewish field. Anti-Semitism occurs in a variety of cultures, and studies which see it as a purely local phenomenon present a limited view of a complex, worldwide problem. Some American studies have tended to regard it as merely a variant of the prejudice directed against minority groups in the American culture. In the course of a critical review of the studies of anti-Semitism in America, Lucy Dawidowicz observes: "Studying anti-Semitism as strictly an American phenomenon, without reference to its occurrence elsewhere in time and geography, strikes me as a highly provincial exercise. The specificity of anti-Semitism in America, to be sure, rests in indigenous political traditions and institutions, and it is important to know how these have affected certain forms of anti-Semitism, but the themes, images, and ideas from which anti-Semitism draws its force have throughout history been transnational and transcultural."[11]

Within the Jewish field, Israel, as the expression of the Jewish national collectivity, occupies an increasingly central position, and the study of any Jewish community needs to examine the role Israel plays in its life. And in turn the nature of Israel can only be understood if it is viewed in the context of the condition and aspirations of the Jewish people.

IN HISTORICAL PERSPECTIVE

Contemporary Jewish studies represent a departure from the tradition of past-oriented Jewish research (as exemplified by the Wissenschaft des Judentums—the study of Judaism as a scientific discipline which developed in Germany in the nineteenth century) which paid little, if any, attention to the present. The focus of these studies, as their designation indicates, is on the present—and its projection into the future. At the same time, the contemporary expressions of Jewish life have to be viewed in historical perspective.

While great changes have rocked the Jewish people, it is also been characterized by certain continuities across generations, and its condition at any moment has to be viewed in the perspective of continuity as well as of change. Researchers fail to grasp the peculiar nature of the Jewish group when they look at it as if it were a sociological phenomenon of contemporary origin. It is only when Jewish identity is studied in an historical context that the unique interweaving of religious and national components in that identity is properly understood. Nor can anti-Semitism be studied as just a contemporaneous phenomenon without reference to its historical development.

IN A COMPARATIVE CONTEXT

The worldwide distribution of the Jewish people provides intriguing possibilities for comparative studies. Jews are to be found in the democracies and in the totalitarian states, in societies with a cultural pluralism which allows them the free expression of their peculiar identity, and in societies where such expression is limited or regimented. Scattered as they are across the globe, the Jews adopt everywhere the language and customs of the majority cultures, but at the same time, despite the diversity, maintain a kernel of sameness which may be termed "Jewish." The study of the similarities and differences has gained enhanced interest with the establishment of the State of Israel. This allows for comparison between the Jewish majority society and communities which are in the position of minorities.

IN THE SETTING OF THE MAJORITY CULTURE

For a fuller understanding of its peculiar characteristics and development, a Jewish community has to be studied in the context of the Gentile environment in which it is located. The degree of acculturation will vary among different sectors of the Jewish community, but even the sector likely to be most strongly anchored in its own Jewish tradition—the Orthodox Jewish establishment—is subtly influenced at points by the prevailing norms of the majority culture.[12] A Jewish identity in the Diaspora bears the mark of its interaction with the majority national identity with which it is associated. The Jewishness of the American Jew can only be understood in the light of the impact on it of his Americanism, just as the identity of a French Jew cannot be studied in isolation from his French identity.

While placing the study of the Jewish community in this wider context, care has to be taken not to interpret Jewish life in terms borrowed from the Gentile world which are alien to its very nature. Judaism, for instance, is often misunderstood by being regarded as a "religion" analogous to Christianity.

The Structure of the Volume

We shall first look at Jewish identity in the wider context of the study of ethnic identities in general (Chapter 2). We shall then proceed to develop a conceptual framework for the study of Jewish identity. In elaborating the criteria for a Jewish identity, we shall not limit ourselves to a statement of principles but shall point to the form in which they find expression in contemporary Jewish life (Chapter 3). We shall refer to the changing emphases or variations, as well as the constancies, in a Jewish identity when it is viewed in historical and comparative context (Chapter 4). We shall discuss the definition of "who is a Jew" by Jews with special reference to the position of Jewish religious law, to the decisions of the Israel Supreme Court, and to the legislation of Israel's legislative assembly, the Knesset (Chapter 5).

There can be no proper understanding of contemporary Jewish identity without reference to the continuing impact of the memory of the Holocaust (Chapter 6). The other event which in this century profoundly influenced Jewish identity was the establishment of the State of Israel. We shall seek to analyze the role of Israel in Jewish life and discuss the difference between pro-Israel sentiment and Zionism viewed as an ideological force shaping contemporary Jewish identity (Chapter 7). We shall explore the part played by Jewish identity factors in the decision of Jews from a country of affluence, such as the United States, to settle in Israel (Chapter 8).

In our discussion of Jewish identity in the majority Jewish society of Israel, we shall report on an empirical investigation of a representative countrywide sample of Israeli high school students conducted in 1974. This study also serves to exemplify the application of the criteria for a Jewish identity developed in an earlier chapter. It replicates parts of a study conducted in 1965 on a similar population of students and allows us to obtain an impression of the direction in which changes have been occurring across the decade between the two studies (Chapter 9). We shall also report on studies of the attitudes of American Jewish students visiting Israel, their attitudes about the country and their interaction with Israelis, and we shall examine the impact of this sojourn on their American Jewish identity. We shall include for purposes of comparison some of the data derived from a survey of Jewish students from the Soviet Union who have settled in Israel (Chapter 10).

In the final chapter we shall look at social psychological problems arising in the aftermath of the Yom Kippur War, and in the light of the critical situation now confronting Jews, we shall examine the implications of the concept underlying the study—that of one Jewish people and one Jewish world (Chapter 11).

NOTES

1. D. Cartwright in foreword to K. Lewin, *Field Theory in Social Science* (London: Tavistock, 1952).

2. Ibid., p. 25.

3. Ibid., p. 169.

4. K. Lewin, "The Research Center for Group Dynamics at M.I.T.," *Sociometry* 8 (1945), 126-136, at p. 128.

5. Lewin planned the establishment of an International Jewish Research Foundation. Reference to his plans is contained in the biography by A.J. Marrow, *The Practical Theorist: The Life and Work of Kurt Lewin* (New York: Basic Books, 1969), p. 225.

6. M. Deutsch, "Introduction" in M. Deutsch and H.A. Hornstein, eds., *Applying Social Psychology* (New York: John Wiley, 1975), pp. 1-12, at p. 1.

7. H. Tajfel, "Aspects of National and Ethnic Loyalty," *Social Sciences Information* 9 (1970), 119-144, at p. 119.

8. For an illuminating discussion of biases in research, see, G. Myrdal, *An American Dilemma* (New York: Harper and Row, 1944), pp. 1035-1064. "There is no other device for excluding biases in social sciences than to face the valuations and to introduce them as explicitly stated, specific, and sufficiently concretized, value premises," p. 1043.

9. A. Ruppin, *The Jewish Fate and Future* (London: Macmillan, 1940).

10. M. Davis, *Beit Yisrael Be-Amerikah (From Dependence to Mutuality: The American Jewish Community and World Jewry)*, (Jerusalem: Magnes Press of the Hebrew University, 1970). (In Hebrew.)

11. L.S. Dawidowicz, "Can Antisemitism be Measured?" *Commentary* 50 (1970), 36-43, at p. 42.

12. S.M. Lipset, "The Study of Jewish Communities in a Comparative Context," *Jewish Journal of Sociology* 5 (1963), 157-166.

Chapter 2

THE NATURE OF ETHNIC IDENTITY

Despite the greatly increased interest in recent years in the problems of ethnicity, little has been done by way of systematic analysis of the structure and dynamics of any ethnic identity.[1] The social sciences have made important contributions to an understanding of the nature of ethnic group prejudice and of the factors calculated to promote intergroup cooperation. The studies of ethnic groups, however, rarely undertake a theoretical conceptualization of the identity with which they are dealing. This is markedly so in the case of the growing literature on Black ethnicity, and—with few exceptions—it holds true also for studies of the Jewish identity with which we are here concerned. The studies of the Jewish group—like those of Black ethnicity—are generally limited empirical explorations; their contribution is to our knowledge of specific questions only, and they are not a source for wider derivations. In the absence of a systematic conceptual framework, the various studies bear little relationship to one another; they do not "add up."

Almost any study of Jewish attitudes is pretentiously called a study of Jewish identity. A glance at most studies of Jewish communities in the Diaspora shows that they are at best studies of Jewish *identification.* They may deal with the process by which the individual comes to see himself a part of the Jewish group and the form the act of identification takes, or they may describe the extent to which and the circumstances under which the Jews in a particular community are prepared to stand up and be counted as such or prefer to throw in their lot with the majority. But very few of them are studies of Jewish *identity,* of what being Jewish means, of what kind of Jew and what kind of Jewishness develop in the majority culture.[2] In the Jewish majority society of Israel, where Jewish identification is taken for granted (unless there are indications to the contrary), studies move more readily into the field of Jewish identity.

Defining Ethnic Identity

Identity has been used by psychologists—often loosely—as a broad concept under which are subsumed a number of phenomena. They frequently fail to give it precise definition.

We shall adopt a conception of identity based on elements contained in definitions by Daniel Miller and Erik Erikson. Miller refers to identity as "the pattern of observable or inferable attributes 'identifying' a person to himself and others."[3] Erikson, who, despite his insightful studies of identity, admits to the difficulty of definition, states in his *Childhood and Society* that "the ego identity develops out of a gradual integration of all identifications."[4] Discussing elsewhere Freud's formulation of his own "inner identity" with Judaism, Erikson speaks of the reflection in the individual of "an essential aspect of a group's inner coherence."[5]

Identity reflects both likeness and uniqueness. To quote a popular phrasing of the fact: Every man is in certain respects

(1) like all other men (possesses universal human attributes),

(2) like some other men (shares certain attributes in common with specific social categories),
(3) like no other man (has unique personality of his own).[6]

Ethnic identity relates to that which the individual shares in common with some other men along with whom he is set off from still others by the possession of certain attributes. The question then arises as to what kind of attributes characterize an ethnic group, and on this question, as on the definition of identity, there is a lack of precision.

Otto Klineberg defines an ethnic group as one "which is set off from others by physical type (or 'race'), by religion, language, or national origin, or any combination of these."[7] A similarly wide definition is adopted in *A Dictionary of the Social Sciences,* which, in discussing the usages of the term, points out that it is "most frequently applied to any group which differs in one or several of its patterned, socially-transmitted ways of life from other groups, or in the totality of that way or culture."[8] Glazer and Moynihan observe that the usage of the term in recent years reflects the broader significance that ethnicity has acquired. Social scientists no longer limit the term to subgroups, to minorities, but apply it to all groups of a society "characterized by a distinct sense of difference owing to culture and descent."[9] It will be observed that Glazer and Moynihan introduce "descent" into what they regard as the now commonly accepted definition. We would submit that the emphasis should indeed be on the common origin; the common culture, as Frederik Barth has pointed out, should be more properly regarded as "an implication or result, rather than a primary and definitional characteristic of ethnic group organization."[10] This accords with Max Weber's definition which speaks of "groups that entertain a subjective belief in their common descent."[11]

A distinction has to be observed between the group identity and that identity as it is reflected in a particular individual who is a member of the group. As Herbert Kelman has pointed out: "Group identity is carried by the individual members of the group, but it is not coterminous with the sum of the conceptions of individual group members. For one thing, it has an independent existence in the form of accumulated historical products, including written documents, oral traditions, institutional arrangements, and symbolic artifacts. For another, different segments of the group differ widely in their degree of active involvement and emotional commitment to the group: various leadership elements and particularly active and committed subgroups are far more instrumental in defining the group identity than the rank-and-file members."[12] In accordance with this distinction, we shall use the term Jewish identity in different contexts to mean either: (1) the pattern of attributes characterizing the Jewish *group*; or (2) the relationship of the *individual* to the Jewish group and the reflection in him of its attributes.

Public Identity and Self-Identity

When we discuss an individual's identity as it is shaped in the course of social interaction it is useful to distinguish—as does Daniel Miller[13]—between objective public identity (a person's pattern of traits as they appear to others), subjective public identity (his perception of his appearance to others), and self-identity (the person's private version of his pattern of traits).

Turning first to public objective identity: A particular individual may be regarded as a Jew by members of the in-group (i.e., by other Jews) or by the out-group (by non-Jews) or by both. When we refer to the definition of "who is a Jew?" in Jewish religious law (the "halacha"), we are in the realm of public objective identity. According to this definition a person is regarded as a Jew if he has been born to a Jewish mother or has converted to Judaism according to the prescribed religious procedures. While this is a widely accepted definition in Jewish circles, it should be noted that some sectors of the Jewish in-group show greater latitude in their classification of individuals as Jews—they may regard as

Jews persons whose conversion has not been in strict accord with the prescribed procedures or persons born to a Jewish father and non-Jewish mother, or they may even classify as Jews all who feel themselves to be Jewish. The out-group, on occasion, may define as a Jew someone who is not regarded as such by Jews. Thus, the Nazi regime in its Nuremberg laws adopted a sweeping definition embracing even those who were no longer in the Jewish fold but who had a Jewish grandparent. On the other hand, an individual of "pure Aryan" ancestry who had converted to Judaism—and who was accordingly regarded as Jewish by Jews—was not classified as a Jew under the Nuremberg laws.

The individual's self-identity is influenced by subjective public identity, i.e., by the way he believes others see him. What is crucial here is not simply whether the individual sees himself classified as a Jew—this in most cases is not open to question—but how he believes others view the Jew and the value they attach to that identity. The question then arises as to whom the individual regards as the significant "others"— Jews or non-Jews. The answer will differ for a Jew in the majority Jewish society, which is Israel, and for Jews in a minority situation. While a Jew in Israel looks into a Jewish mirror, the member of a Jewish minority is influenced to a greater or lesser extent by the image of the Jew as reflected in what is often a distorting mirror held up by the majority. The extent will depend upon the individual's location in his group—a Jew seeking to be accepted into the majority will be more greatly influenced by the non-Jewish appraisal and the stigma attached to being Jewish than will an identifying Jew. For the latter the image projected in the non-Jewish mirror will be modified somewhat through the prism of his own Jewish subculture. But even on him it will leave some trace.

Exclusive and Inclusive Identities

An identity may be exclusive or inclusive of other identities. One of the problems facing particularly the developing countries in Africa and Asia is how to foster a more inclusive national identity which will integrate segmental tribal identities without suppressing them. The Nigerian-Biafran conflict illustrated the tragic results of failure on this score.

It has been maintained that the pluralistic conception of the American identity is "neither one of separatism—with or without equality—nor of assimilation but one of full participation combined with the preservation of identity."[14] But in practice cultural pluralism has meant "that immigrant communities, while adopting the dominant American culture, retained and contributed to America a form of subculture acceptable to the general consensus. The more superficial the cultural difference that immigrant groups brought with them the easier the naturalisation of these differences in America."[15] In the new ethnic climate American pluralism is being reexamined, and this may result in a lesser subordination of the minority cultures to the dominant majority culture while at the same time preserving the common American framework.

"The alternative to an exclusive totalism," Erikson has observed, "is the wholeness of the more inclusive identity." But in respect to the American Negro this, he points out, leads to another question: "If the Negro wants to find that other identity which permits him to be selfcertain as a Negro (or a descendant of Negroes) and *integrated as an American* what joint historical actuality can he count on?"[16]

The problem of integration in Israel has been facilitated by the strength of the overriding inclusive Jewish identity which has provided a wide enough spectrum allowing for the unquestioned maintenance of segmental identities such as the Ashkenazic and Sephardic. A "joint historical actuality" clearly exists. But with increasing diversification in the Jewish world there is not the same degree of consensus as to which are the legitimate segmental variations which may be integrated into a Jewish identity.

Empirical and Normative Definitions

A Jewish identity, like every other ethnic identity, relates to a particular people with a particular history. What constitutes such identity is not a matter of arbitrary definition, nor is it something which is created entirely anew. The study of Jewish identity cannot, however, confine itself to the investigation of just that part of the identity which constitutes a "given" or fixed datum. An identity does not exist as something completely preformed; as they make the choices in life which commit them to certain attitudes and courses of action, individuals and groups are engaged in a creative process of building up an identity. In drawing attention to the distinction between empirical and normative definitions of Jewish identity, Israel Scheffler observes:

> Insofar as a group is specifiable, one may investigate its characteristics empirically, and perhaps try to determine which are common and peculiar to it. But those who speak of finding or searching for an identity do not seem to be addressing themselves to such a cluster of empirical traits. Rather they seem to be raising a set of normative questions: what *to do* as a member of a given group, how the group *ought* itself to act, etc. ... The question is what we are to *make of* our historical group membership through our own deliberate choices, based upon an accurate awareness of our historical circumstances, and as reliable as possible an estimate of alternative possibilities open to us.[17]

This view closely corresponds to that expressed by Erikson when he writes that the pertinent question for the individual generally is not "who am I?" but "what do I want to make of myself—and—what do I have to work with?"[18]

In terms of this approach a Jewish education should concern itself not only with conveying what *being Jewish* means, but also what is involved in the process of *becoming* authentically Jewish and in the acting out of that Jewishness under the conditions of contemporary Jewish life.

The Need To Belong

The identity of the individual develops in the course of interaction between the innate characteristics with which he is born and the influences of his social environment. One set of influences derives from the ethnic group to which he belongs. While the ethnic identity—or more precisely, sub-identity—of the individual is just one of the subidentities which constitute the total identity, it may play a part of great importance in his life space.

Membership in a socially stigmatized minority group generally has far-reaching psychological implications.[19] This is particularly the case in regard to a group such as the Jews who occupy so singular a position in whatever society they are located. In a series of penetrating essays Kurt Lewin stressed how crucial in the shaping of the identity of the Jewish child is a clear sense of belonging and an acceptance of this belonging as positively meaningful. "One of the most important constituents of the ground on which the individual stands is the social group to which he belongs."[20] Uncertainty of belonging implies instability of the social ground and leads to instability of the person.

Some Jews may readily accept their membership and all that goes with it, regarding it as a mark of distinction even if it subjects them to certain difficulties. They know where they stand and their membership in what they regard as a desirable group bolsters their self-esteem. Other Jews may see the membership as a stigma and may develop inferiority feelings about their Jewishness. But they generally cannot escape it; they can only deny it by a formal act of conversion, and even then their Jewish origins will not always be forgotten by their Gentile neighbors (and will also be remembered by Jews in certain situations). In a sense such an individual is trying to reject a part of himself.

Jean-Paul Sartre has described the psychological plight of what he terms the "inauthentic" Jew. Unlike the "authentic" Jew, who seeks "to live to the full his condition as Jew," the "inauthentic" Jew denies it or attempts to escape from it. "Whenever he introduces himself in order to get away from Jewish reality, he senses that he has been accepted as a Jew and is at every moment regarded as a Jew. His life among Christians does not bring him the anonymity he seeks; rather, it is a perpetual tension."[21]

A Tunisian Jew, Albert Memmi, now resident in France, who, after personally tasting the bitterness of the plight Sartre describes, returned to his people, observes: "I discovered that one does not easily cease to be Jewish, and that self-rejection never solves anything. . . . The net result was, on the contrary, constant self-contradiction, a veritable and painful distortion of the whole being which isolated me, singled me out more surely than the accusation of others." He proceeds to tell of his decision: "I decided that henceforth I would tell others and myself: 'Yes, I am Jewish—what of it? Yes, to some extent and on several points I am *different* from my fellow citizens, from other men.'"[2 2]

In the life space of any minority group there are forces leading to positive identification with it on the part of its members and others which make for gravitation to the majority. Among those who gravitate strongly toward the majority will be persons who remain suspended between the two groups, the so-called "marginal men," who do not reconcile themselves to membership in the minority and at the same time cannot join the majority because of barriers in the way of their entry. Marginality is often accompanied by feelings of isolation and insecurity such as are reflected in the following words of a Russian Jewess (Larissa Bogoraz) alienated from the Jewish group and at the same time unable to feel herself Russian: "Who am I now? Who do I feel myself to be? Unfortunately, I do not feel like a Jew. . . . I am accustomed to the color, smell, rustle of the Russian landscape, as I am to the Russian language, the rhythm of Russian poetry. I react to everything else as alien. . . . And nevertheless, no, I am not Russian. I am a stranger today in this land. But I would not like this fate for my children and grandchildren."[2 3]

At times there is a search on the part of the marginal man for a substitute belonging. In his analysis of the attitudes of Benjamin Disraeli and of Karl Marx to their Jewish origins, Isaiah Berlin puts forward the thesis that

one of the sources of the vision of both Disraeli and Marx—what made the former see himself as a natural leader of an aristocratic elite, and the latter as the teacher and strategist of the world proletariat—was their personal need to find their proper place, to establish a personal identity, to determine in a world in which this question was posed much more insistently than it had ever been posed before, what section of mankind, what nation, party, class they properly belonged to. It was an attempt on the part of those whom history and social circumstances had cut off from their original establishment—the once familiar, safely segregated Jewish minority—to replant themselves in some new and no less secure and nourishing soil.[24]

Members of a minority, even when they clearly accept their group belonging, are sensitive to the reactions of the majority to their group. At times there is oversensitivity, and on occasion an individual may attribute failure because of personal deficiency to an act of discrimination against him because of his group membership.

The Peculiarity of Jewish Identity

The study of Jewish identity has to take cognizance of the peculiar interweaving in such identity of national and religious elements. Judaism is not just a religious creed analagous to Christianity. It is the religious civilization of one particular nation, it resides in the Jewish people and reflects its history. And the Jewish people is what it is because of this religious civilization. The Jewish prayers are suffused with references to the people and its land, the religious festivals are also national celebrations. Jews have indeed maintained throughout the centuries that there is an indisoluble connection between the Jewish people, the land of Israel, and the Torah. The Jewishness of even nonreligious Jews cannot be completely divorced from its religious associations. Although the term is used as a matter of convenience, there is strictly speaking no "secular" Jewishness.

In the Diaspora religious institutions such as the synagogue serve more than just a religious function in the Jewish community and affiliation with them is often an expression of Jewish identification rather than of religiosity. It is of interest to observe that a major occasion on which Jews in the USSR, most of them without the semblance of a religious background, demonstrate their Jewish identity is on "Simhat Torah" (the festival of the "Rejoicing of the Law") in and around the synagogue.

There have been Jews who have sought to see themselves as no more than Germans or Frenchmen of the Jewish faith while others have espoused a Jewishness based on the national element only. The two components are, however, so intertwined that they cannot be isolated without disturbing their essential character and distorting the nature of the Jewish identity.

NOTES

1. A recent contribution to the theory of ethnicity is N. Glazer and D.P. Moynihan, eds., *Ethnicity: Theory and Experience* (Cambridge, Mass.: Harvard University Press, 1975).

2. A good example of such study of Jewish identity is M. Sklare and J. Greenblum, *Jewish Identity on the Suburban Frontier* (New York: Basic Books, 1967).

3. D.R. Miller, "The Study of Social Relationships: Situation, Identity, and Social Interaction" in *Psychology: A Study of a Science*, S. Koch, ed., (New York: McGraw-Hill, 1963), Vol. 5, p. 673.

4. E.H. Erikson, *Childhood and Society* (New York: W.W. Norton, 1950), p. 213.

5. E.H. Erikson, "The Problem of Ego Identity" in M.R. Stein et al., *Identity and Anxiety* (Glencoe, Ill.: Free Press, 1960), p. 38.

6. Cf., C. Kluckhohn and H.A. Murray, eds., *Personality in Nature, Society, and Culture* (New York: Alfred A. Knopf, 1959), p. 53.

7. O. Klineberg, "The Multi-National Society: Some Research Problems," *Social Sciences Information* 6 (1967), 81-99.

8. J. Gould and W.L. Kolb, eds., *A Dictionary of the Social Sciences* (Glencoe, Ill.: Free Press, 1964).

9. Glazer and Moynihan, op. cit., at p. 4.

10. F. Barth, *Ethnic Groups and Boundaries: The Social Organisation of Cultural Difference* (Bergen, Norway: Universitetsforlaget, 1969), p. 11.

11. M. Weber, "The Ethnic Group," in T. Parsons et al., *Theories of Society* (Glencoe, Ill.: Free Press, 1961), Vol. 1, pp. 305-309. For additional definitions of ethnic identity, see A. Dashefsky, ed., *Ethnic Identity in Society* (Chicago: Rand McNally, 1976); and the study of American ethnic diversity by A.M. Greeley and W.C. McCready, *Ethnicity in the United States: A Preliminary Reconnaissance* (New York: John Wiley, 1974).

12. H.C. Kelman, "The Place of Jewish Identity in the Development of Personal Identity." A working paper prepared for the American Jewish Committee's Colloquium on Jewish Education and Jewish Identity, November 1974.

13. Miller, op. cit.

14. T. Parsons, "Full Citizenship for the Negro American? A Sociological Problem," in T. Parsons and K.B. Clark, eds., *The Negro American* (Boston: Beacon: The Daedalus Library, 1965), pp. 709-754, at p. 750.

15. B. Halpern, *The American Jew* (New York: Theodore Herzl Foundation, 1956), at p. 84.

16. E.H. Erikson, "The Concept of Identity in Race Relations: Notes and Queries," in *The Negro American*, op. cit., pp. 227-253, at p. 247.

17. I. Scheffler, "How Can A Jewish Self-consciousness Be Developed?" in S.N. Herman, ed., *The Study of Jewish Identity: Issues and Approaches* (Jerusalem: Institute of Contemporary Jewry, Hebrew University, 1971), pp. 1-2.

18. Erikson, "The Concept of Identity in Race Relations: Notes and Queries," op. cit., at p. 247.

19. Cf., E. Goffman, *Stigma: Notes on the Management of Spoiled Identity* (Englewood Cliffs, N.J.: Prentice-Hall, 1963); A. Kardiner and L. Ovesey, *The Mark of Oppression* (New York: W.W. Norton, 1951).

20. K. Lewin, *Resolving Social Conflicts,* G. Lewin, ed. (New York: Harper and Row, 1948), at p. 145.

21. J.P. Sartre, *Antisemite and Jew,* transl. by G.J. Becker (New York: Schocken, 1965), at p. 100. In his otherwise penetrating essay, Sartre exaggerates the role of the anti-Semite in defining the Jew. In the case of Jews other than the "inauthentic" Jew, the volitional element plays a greater part than would appear from Sartre's description of what constitutes the defining "situation."

22. A. Memmi, "Does the Jew Exist," *Commentary* 42 (1966), 5, 73-76, at p. 76.

23. L. Bogoraz, "Do I Feel I Belong to the Jewish People," in A. Voronel and V. Yakhot, eds., *I Am A Jew: Essays on Jewish Identity in the Soviet Union* (Academic Committee on Soviet Jewry and A.D.L., 1973), pp. 63-64.

24. I. Berlin, "Benjamin Disraeli, Karl Marx and the Search for Identity," *Midstream* 7 (1970), 29-49.

Chapter 3

CRITERIA FOR JEWISH IDENTITY

In developing a conceptual framework we shall focus on the relationship of the individual to his being and becoming Jewish, but in so doing we shall also keep the group indentity in sight. While our concern is here with Jewish identity, we would submit that the framework may be pertinent mutatis mutandis for the analysis of other ethnic identities as well.

An analysis of the Jewish identity of an individual must deal with:

(a) the nature of the individual's relationship to the Jewish group as a membership group; and

(b) the individual's perception of the attributes of the Jewish group, his feeling about them, and the extent to which its norms are adopted by him as a source of reference. This necessitates a consideration of the content of the Jewish group identity.

While it is useful to bear in mind the distinction to which we have alluded between "identification" and "identity", the two concepts will frequently intertwine in the analysis which follows.

Membership in the Jewish Group

An ethnic identity implies on the one hand alignment, a shared belonging with members of a specific group, and on the other hand a differentiation, a marking off, from members of certain other groups. We shall first discuss the marking off function, and will then explore the nature and implications of alignment with the Jewish group—the sources of such alignment, the sense of mutual responsibility which accompanies it, the temporal and spatial compass of the alignment.

MARKING OFF

Members of a minority—much more so than members of a majority—are conscious of being marked off. One of the most significant divisions of the world for members of a Jewish community is that between themselves and the non-Jews with whom they are in constant juxtaposition. Jews may be one of a number of minorities in a country, but there are occasions when they feel that the boundary line runs between Jews on the one hand and all non-Jews—whatever their specific affiliations—on the other.

Marking off is often accompanied by discriminatory action, but this need not necessarily be so. An acceptance of, and respect for, the differences between the groups which comprise it is clearly of the essence in a truly democratic and pluralistic society.

Among the members of the marked off group the boundary line evokes a variety of reactions. Jews seeking to leave the Jewish group would wish the lines of demarcation to be drawn differently or, at any rate, less sharply so that they might align themselves with those from whom they are now marked off. The strongly identifying Jews may wish to actively mark themselves off and maintain their distinctiveness in certain spheres where differences between groups are regarded as legitimate; at the same time they will resent being marked off in areas such as that of civic rights or of employment.

In the ghetto the Jews were clearly and sharply marked off. With the advent of the Emancipation the barriers were lowered in differing degrees in the various countries, but even where the entry of Jews into the social, cultural, and political life was least restricted, the boundary line was never completely erased. The Holocaust came as a grim reminder to Jews of their isolation in the non-Jewish world.

The Yom Kippur War, even more so than the Six Day War, emphasized the boundaries that exist between Jews and their non-Jewish neighbors. During the days and weeks they were anxiously following every development in the war situation, Jews found that it was only with their fellow Jews that they could share their anxieties. And more than ever they sought out the company of other Jews. As an American student studying in Israel, who had been on vacation in the States at the time of the war, expressed it: He felt himself "separated" from the world of his non-Jewish neighbors for whom the struggle was of little, if any, concern. While he was carrying about his transistor and agitatedly listening to every item of news from the Middle East, the Gentile friends he met were interested in the scores in some sporting contest. Any manifestation of anti-Semitism at this time served to emphasize the barriers.

A leader of French Jewry, Adolphe Steg, writes in similar vein about the psychological line of demarcation which the course of events drew between Jewish and non-Jewish intellectuals in France: "Jewish intellectuals could not dismiss a certain feeling of isolation and lack of empathy. Their anxiety for Israel found only a faint echo in their environment, and the silence of their colleagues during those terrible days was painful. Not only did their colleagues remain silent, but when appealed to, they could not help showing irritation with the problems of the Jews, which they defined as an obsession." And he points to the effect of their awareness of their nonconformity to the surrounding intellectual milieu on the Jewish consciousness of French intellectuals: "By obliging them to reflect upon this non-conformity of feeling and behavior in a milieu from which they thought themselves indistinguishable, and by uncovering the extent of the lack of comprehension shown by these circles to their deepest concerns, the Yom Kippur War may have slowed the rush towards assimilation in France."[1]

The constant juxtaposition in which they are placed with a non-Jewish majority heightens the salience, or awareness, of their Jewish identity for Jews in the Diaspora. Since in Israel Jews constitute the majority, the group from which they are marked off obtrudes less in their consciousness than it does in Jewish communities elsewhere. When Israelis do think of themselves as marked off as Jews, it is not so much in relation to any minority in Israel but as part of a Jewish people in the Gentile world; they place themselves in a global context.[2] The "marked off from" group is the general category of Gentiles, at times the Gentiles in countries from which anti-Jewish discrimination is reported. But these are Gentiles who are at a distance and of whose existence they do not have as constant a reminder as do Jewish minorities in the Diaspora.

It would seem that events after the Yom Kippur War (the continued isolation of Israel, the ovation accorded to the terrorist leader, Yasser Arafat at the U.N., the resolution condemning Zionism as "racist") have sharpened in the minds of Jews in both Israel and the Diaspora the sense of a line of demarcation. The tendency has grown for Jews to see themselves as "a people dwelling alone."

BASES OF ALIGNMENT

Alignment may be based on a perception of similarity or a feeling of interdependence or both.

Kurt Lewin stressed the importance of looking at the social group as a dynamic whole based on the interdependence of the members or subparts. He observed that a group with a very high degree of unity may contain very dissimilar parts. "Not similarity but a certain interdependence of members constitutes a group."[3]

Jewish society has become increasingly diversified since the Emancipation. The migrations of the latter part of the nineteenth and in the twentieth century, and the consequent socialization of Jews in settings so different politically, culturally, and socially, have accelerated this process. If we compare the two major communities—in Israel and in the United States—we find that they are much less alike now than they were at the beginning of the century. At that time both American Jewry and the Jewish community in Eretz Israel (the "Yishuv") were to a large extent composed of Yiddish-speaking immigrants from Eastern Europe who had taken different routes. Since that time two new generations have grown up, socialized in the different environments and speaking different languages; and at least half of Israel's Jewish population is not from Europe but from the countries of the Middle East and North Africa. Dissimilarities develop not only between communities but also between Jews inside each community.

Confusion often exists among Jews as to how the Jewish group should be defined and what their relation is to other Jews whom they see as dissimilar from themselves in so many respects. On the other hand, the facts of Jewish existence, particularly since the Holocaust, are such that a feeling of interdependence can be more easily invoked. When we speak here of interdependence we are using the term in the sense of a change in the state of any part affecting all the other parts. In the context of Jewish life this means that whatever happens to Jews qua Jews anywhere has implications for Jews everywhere. When interdependence is recognized as the basis of belonging, even Jews who see themselves as dissimilar from other Jews regard themselves as belonging to the Jewish group. The feeling of interdependence, of a common fate, represents the widest minimal basis, the common denominator, of Jewish belonging in our times.

There are, of course, kinds of interdependence as well as degrees of interdependence. There is the promotive interdependence which results from cooperation in the pursuit of a common goal as well as the interdependence in the face of an external threat.[4] The cooperative effort on the part of Jews throughout the world in making possible an "ingathering" of Jews in Israel contains both elements. It would seem, however, that in the situation in which they find themselves, the external threat weighs most heavily on Jews.

Despite the growing diversification of Jewish life, a core of similarity—the common origin, the common religious tradition—always remains. While the feeling of interdependence represents the widest and almost readily invocable basis for Jewish belonging, the role of similarity should not be ignored. It is the similarity which often gives rise to interdependence.[5]

SENSE OF MUTUAL RESPONSIBILITY

Social psychological experimentation has demonstrated that a concomitant to the feeling of interdependence is a sense of mutual responsibility.[6]

Our studies of Israelis and visiting students from the United States and other countries in Israel show a widespread recognition of the mutual obligations of support between Israel and Jews abroad. In time of crisis, as during the Six Day War and the Yom Kippur War, Jewish communities throughout the world have rallied spontaneously and unreservedly to the aid of Israel. This sense of responsibility exists not only between Israel and Jews abroad but between Jews wherever they are. It is summed up in the Hebrew phrase, *"kol Yisrael arevim ze lazeh,"* all Jews are guarantors one for the other. In the long history of persecutions and migrations, Jews always knew that they could turn to their fellow Jews for help. And Jewish communities do not make the aid contingent on the Jewish loyalties of their fellow Jews—as witnessed by the assistance accorded to assimilated Jews compelled to leave Poland after the purges of 1968.

Our studies of Israeli students show that they feel particularly close to Jews who are under attack; such discrimination or persecution underlines the element of common fate and activates the sense of mutual responsibility. They have felt this sense of closeness and responsibility in recent years to the Jews of Soviet Russia and of Syria, whom they regard as the most threatened of the Jewish communities. "To work for the ingathering of Jews from the golah" ranks highest among what are considered by Israeli students as the characteristics of "a good Jew" in Israel.[7]

ALIGNMENT ACROSS TIME

The alignment with an ethnic group implies a relationship to the group beyond a given moment in time—to its past and future as well as its present. It points to the individual's link with "the unique values, fostered by an unique history, of his people."[8] The identity of the group itself reflects the impact of the traditions and experiences of the past and also of the hopes and aspirations for the future.

An analysis of the relationship between historical time perspective and ethnic identity requires a breakdown of the concept of time perspective into its various dimensions. The relevant dimensions in the study of identity are those which relate to past, present, and future orientation, to scope, to differentiation, to structuration, to probability of locomotion, to selectivity, and to continuity. We shall observe that time perspective has implications for morale as well as for identity.

The orientation of a group may be primarily to the past, the present, or the future, or it may have a more balanced view embracing the three time sequences. A people may tend to dwell on the glories of its past and disconsolately see no relation between the past, a bleak present, and an unpromising future. Conversely, it may find in the past a source of inspiration for the planning of a brighter future, the hope of which in turn makes tolerable the hardships of the present.

In referring to the past, the group may find in it circumstances analogous to those with which it is confronted in the present. It may feel that it can face them as it faced them before. Again, the past may be the source of a tradition of conduct running through the present into the future.

Scope refers to the range, or span, of the time perspective. It may be narrowly limited to events which occurred only a short while ago or which are immediately impending, or it may be broad, stretching extensively into a more distant past or future. When Israeli students in our studies were asked what historical events had influenced them personally, the majority quoted events from recent history. But a number of the more religious students referred to the Exodus from Egypt and the Giving of the Law on Mount Sinai.

There may be instances in which members of a group find solace in hopes which may be realized only in an indeterminate future—as do some deeply religious Jews waiting patiently for the coming of the Messiah—but generally morale is low where there are no clear boundaries to the scope of the future time perspective. This brings us to a consideration of further dimensions which are concerned with the structure and with the clarity of the boundaries in the time sequences.

Differentiation relates to the division of the past or the future into a series of distinguishable segments. The number of segments determines what is known as the density of the time perspective. There will obviously be a relation between familiarity with a history of a particular period and the degree of its differentiation.

Structuration refers to the organization of the segments. The time perspective is said to be structured when there is an understanding of how the past has led into the present, or, in regard to the future, when there is some vision of the paths that lead to the hoped-for goals, or how and when the aspirations can be realized. The clarity of the structure of the future time perspective and the anticipated attainability of a meaningful goal within a reasonable time (the perceived "probability of locomotion") have an important bearing on morale.

Selectivity is concerned with the differential attitudes which may exist toward the segments of the past. The memories affect the orientation to the present and to the future, but the interpretation of the events of the past is influenced by the needs and moods of the present and the hopes and aspirations for the future. Some events are singled out for glorification, others are obscured; some are referred to with pride, others with shame. In references to the Jewish past in the Diaspora, the focus may be on events reflecting the precariousness of such Jewish existence, or prominence may be given to centers of Jewish creativity which flourished in that past. In the treatment by Israelis of the period of the Holocaust, the intitial emphasis was on the acts of resistance, but a broader perspective has developed in recent years.

Most basic of all these dimensions for the study of identity is that of continuity, the perceived interrelatedness of past, present, and future. Is a particular event—such as the destruction of European Jewry—relegated to the limbo of the historic past, or is it seen as representing a continuing influence through the present into the future? In the study of Israeli Jewish identity it becomes important to enquire whether Israelis perceive themselves as an inseparable part of the Jewish people or as a new people. Related to this is the question whether the State of Israel is seen as a continuation of the Jewish history of all periods or whether there is an attempt to obliterate the memory of the Diaspora and leap across the centuries of dispersion, "skipping" them in order to establish a direct link with the period before Jews were exiled from the Land of Israel.

A past cannot be "adopted." It is only when it consists of memories still playing a part in the lives of men and impinging on their present life-space that it properly contributes the development of an ethnic identity. Just as it cannot be adopted, so the actuality of the past cannot be artificially erased. A Jew anywhere is what he is because of the centuries of Diaspora existence experienced by his people.

The Jewish people is a group with a particularly long memory, and this has contributed in no small measure to the preservation of its distinctiveness across the centuries. It has been characterized through the vicissitudes of time and place by a sense of continuity. An obvious example is the way in which on Passover, when celebrating the Exodus from Egypt, the Jew is enjoined to regard himself as personally involved in that event, as if he himself were among those liberated from Egyptian bondage. And many Jews—even if they have never seen Jerusalem—could with sincerity state about their own lives what the Israeli writer S.Y. Agnon said so succinctly in his speech in Stockholm when accepting the Nobel Prize for literature: "As a result of the historic catastophe in which Titus of Rome destroyed Jerusalem and banished Israel from its land, I was born in one of the cities of the Exile. But always I regarded myself as having been born in Jerusalem."

ALIGNMENT ACROSS SPACE

Alignment with so widely dispersed a people as the Jews has to be across space as well as time, and has to bridge other differences as well. Some Jews think in terms of "one Jewish people," of "klal Yisrael," and see themselves aligned with all Jews irrespective of differences in geographical location or communal background or ideology, while there are others whose relationship is primarily with the local community or confined to some particular segment of it with little concern for Jews elsewhere.

Even where a sense of alignment extending across space exists, there may nonetheless be differences in the degree of closeness experienced towards various sections of the Jewish people. Similarity is one of the factors playing a part in determining the degree of closeness. Thus, while religious students in Israel align themselves with all Jews wherever they are, they feel closer to Jews elsewhere who are religiously observant like themselves than they do towards the nonreligious.[9] The other factor is interdependence. The fact that a particular Jewish community is under attack influences the feeling of closeness experienced towards it.

The relationship of an individual to the Jewish group may be one of wider or more limited scope in terms of space and time. In the light of our discussions of the criteria so far listed, we would submit that a *relationship to the group in full compass* requires that the individual

(a) regards himself aligned with, and responsible for the welfare of all Jews wherever they are; and
(b) sees himself linked not only to the Jews of the present but to generations past and those still to come.

The Content of a Jewish Identity

An ethnic identity implies more than the mere fact of affiliation with the group. The additional questions which arise are:

(1) On the cognitive level: How does the individual perceive the attributes of the group, and which of these attributes does he see as inhering in himself? Furthermore, in what situations is the group membership a salient factor in his consciousness, and how central a position does it occupy in his life-space?
(2) On the affective level: How does he feel about the group, its members, and its attributes? What attracts him (positive valence) and what repels him (negative valence)?
(3) On the behavioral level: To what exist does he adopt its norms, i.e., to what extent does the membership group serve also as a source of reference? Is his self-definition as a Jew purely classificatory, with possibly an affective element, or is it seen also to include obligations to action?

PERCEPTION OF THE GROUP'S ATTRIBUTES AND ITS POSITION IN THE LIFE-SPACE

Religious and national components. In the consideration of the individual's view of the attributes of his group, particular importance attaches to the question whether he perceives his Jewish identity in its full compass as a blend of religious and national elements inextricably interwoven. With this goes the question as to what extent the attributes are reflected in his own identity.

A weakening in any one of the two components leads to a weakening in the Jewish identity as a whole. Our studies of

Israeli youth demonstrate the extent to which religious observance is a crucial variable in a Jewish identity.[10] The
religiously observant students rank highest on all criteria—not
only, as might be expected, in regard to the content of their
Jewishness, but in their relationship to Jews everywhere. And
American studies have similarly indicated the stronger Jewish
identity of the religiously observant.[11] A secular Jewishness
has severe limitations, and its durability across generations is
questionable. There are limitations also to a strictly religious
Jewishness of the kind which endeavors to strip Judaism of
its national component and sees in it only a religious creed
analogous to Christianity. It artificially restricts the scope of
the Jewishness of the Jewish group, minimizes the cultural
differences between Jews and their neighbors, and, as historical experience has shown, leads to the erosion of the Jewish
identity.

The individual's perception of the nature of the Jewish
group will be reflected in his relationship to other Jews. The
Jew who sees it as only a religious entity is more likely to
limit his interest to the local community although he may
also come to the aid of his "coreligionists" further afield; he
who perceives it as a religio-national group will generally have
a stronger feeling of kinship and a greater concern for the
fate of his "fellow Jews" everywhere.

Salience and centrality. The central regions in the life-
space have been described as "the more intimate, personal
regions" in which the individual is more sensitive than in the
peripheral.[12] The centrality of a region is related to the
proximity of that region to other regions within a whole. The
more central a region, the more readily does it influence
other regions and the more readily is it influenced by them.[13]
Centrality may thus be said to correspond to breadth or
extensity of influence.

An individual's ethnic identity may affect the main
spheres of his life or may have only limited implications for
him. Membership of an underprivileged minority generally
has repercussions in many spheres although there will be

differences between the members in the degree of the group's centrality for them. Centrality is a major component of what is termed the individual's "involvement" in a group.[14]

Salience refers to prominence in the perceptual field, the "figure" against the "ground," the extent to which an object or activity captures the person's attention at a given moment.[15]

Certain behavior settings,[16] such as the synagogue, will bring to the fore, i.e., enhance the salience of the Jewish identity of the person in Israel or in the Diaspora. Again, the Jew in the Diaspora may be reminded of his Jewishness in a particular situation by an anti-Semitic remark, or by some form of discrimination. The frequency of these reminders in a wide variety of situations contributes to the centrality of the Jewish identity. There is indeed a relationship between salience and centrality, although at the same time the distinction between the two should be observed. "Salience is a short-term phenomenon, i.e. a function of the immediate situation; centrality refers to a much more durable interest on the part of the individual in certain kinds of objects, with these objects remaining important for him in many different, specific situations."[17]

VALENCE OF JEWISHNESS

The extent to which an individual adopts the norms of the Jewish group will depend in no small measure on the likes and aversions he has for the various facets of Jewish life. Many Jews, while accepting the fact of their Jewish belonging and recognizing the religio-national character of the group, may reject some religious customs or may be completely antireligious. At times the aversions may be such as to lead the individual to conceal his membership in the group or to seek to reject it. In encounters with non-Jews he may be very sensitive at any hint of his Jewishness. Severe tension results in situations where the salience of Jewish membership is high but the valence negative.

When the individual rejects his Jewish group, it becomes at times a negative reference group, i.e., he demonstratively indicates the severance of the connection by adopting norms contrary to those of the Jewish group, which now serves him as a yardstick for what he should not be and should not do.

An individual may, however, be critical of a particular characteristic he attributes to his group, but the group as a whole may nevertheless have positive valence for him. The imputation of such a negative trait may on occasion be found among Jews who identify strongly with their group. Studies show that where the individual imputes a negative trait to the group, he generally does not regard this trait as attaching to himself personally.[18]

THE ADOPTION OF JEWISH NORMS: A QUESTION OF DISTINCTIVENESS

In the majority Jewish society of Israel the Jewish group can more easily serve as a source of reference as well as membership. In the Diaspora the Jew is immersed in the majority culture whose norms may run counter to those of the Jewish group. And even when they are not at odds, the norms of the Jewish group lose their specific Jewish quality when they become submerged in the dominant culture. Writing about the image which the Jew in the suburban community he studied (termed "Lakeville") had of what constitutes a "good Jew," Sklare commented: "The 'mitzvot' he prized most were often identical with virtuous acts enjoined by the general American culture. In other words, though the Lakeville Jew borrowed the traits that made up his model of the good Jew from traditional Judaism, he borrowed so selectively that the model came out more standard American than Jewish."[19] Daniel Bell has pointed to the loss of distinctiveness involved in accepting the ethical content of Judaism while rejecting the ritual: "The ethical view is fundamentally syncretistic, drawing on all faiths, for to be valid, an ethical precept must be binding on every man and applicable to all men. . . . The ethical dissolves the parochial, and takes away from individuals that need for the particular identification

which singles them out and shapes their community in distinctive terms: terms which make possible a special sense of
belonging shared by a group."[20]

Reviewing the position among American ethnic groups,
Glazer and Moynihan observed that "the cultural *content* of
each ethnic group in the United States seems to have become
very similar to that of others, but the emotional significance
of attachment to the ethnic group seems to persist."[21] But,
as Barth emphasized, "ethnic groups only persist if they
imply marked differences in behavior i.e. persisting cultural
differences."[22]

It is precisely the content of their Jewishness which constitutes a problem for the third generation of American Jews,
grandchildren of the immigrants who came at the time of the
mass migrations from Eastern Europe. There are indications
that the third generation—unlike some of the second-generation parents—are not in revolt against their Jewishness. But
while they may quite readily accept their Jewish affiliation,
the content of this Jewishness has been considerably diluted
for many of them. They look upon themselves as Jews, they
are looked upon by others as such, their social contacts
generally are mainly with Jews, but "each new generation is
in part the product of its inheritance,"[23] and the homes of
their second-generation parents already had less Jewish content than those of their immigrant grandparents. The problem of members of this third generation is thus not so much
one of identification with the Jewish group as of giving
distinctiveness to their identity as Jews. As Tajfel has pointed
out, "A social group will ... be capable of preserving its
contributions to those aspects of an individual's social identity which are positively valued by him only if it manages to
keep its positively valued distinctiveness from other
groups".[24]

The Jewish cultural environment in which some of the
communities in Eastern Europe once lived allowed for the
development of an intensive Jewish identity. The American
and other Diaspora milieus do not provide the conditions for
the sort of Jewish living conducive to the production of such

identities. In the great centers of Jewish culture in Europe
before the Holocaust, an important expression of a Jewish
identity, and one which gave it distinctiveness, was a specific
Jewish language—Yiddish.[25] The overwhelming majority of
Jews in the Diaspora now know only the languages of the
country in which they dwell. Although Hebrew is firmly
entrenched in Israel, it has not succeeded as yet in becoming
the second language of Jews in the Diaspora.

A language reflects a people's cultural cast of mind. The
fact that Jews in the Diaspora no longer know their own
language and use only the language of the majority culture
constitutes a step on the road to assimilation.

The process of secularization has further contributed to
the erosion of Jewish identity. The religiously observant Jew
knows, and in the daily conduct of his life gives expression
to, what sets him off from others in the non-Jewish society in
which he lives. The secular Jew, constantly exposed to the
pervasive influences of the majority culture, becomes en-
gulfed by these influences unless specific Jewish content is
introduced into his life. The increasing secularization of the
majority Christian culture facilitates the acceptance of its
norms by the Jew. There is no ideology of assimilation in the
United States—as there was in Europe—but there is a process
of Jewish cultural attrition from generation to generation.
The situation lends cogency to the contention of those who
urge that only the more intensive forms of Jewish education
are likely to provide the distinctive content.

In Soviet Russia, where Jews are denied the possibility of
even the most elementary Jewish education, many Jews, as
one of them has observed, "have no choice but to see
themselves through the eyes of others. They have no re-
sources of self-knowledge. They have been deprived of their
literature, their history and their art. Dispersed among the
nations, they think in the categories accepted among those
nations."[26]

In Israel the problem is not one of distinctiveness in the
sense of setting apart in order to avoid submergence in a

non-Jewish culture. It is rather a question of giving meaningful content to the Jewish identity of the various segments of Israeli society. While the majority readily accept their affiliation with the Jewish people, there are significant differences between the "data'im" (religiously observant), the "mesorati'im" (traditionalists), and the nonreligious in regard to the content and scope of their Jewish identity. The following are typical statements expressing these differences:

> My entire way of life is determined by my Jewishness. It influences my way of thinking and conduct. I am a Jew all the time and cannot even imagine myself being anything else.
>
> (a religious student)

> What is important is to feel oneself Jewish, to consider oneself part and parcel of the people and to observe at least some of the Jewish customs which symbolize the special character of the Jewish people.
>
> (a traditionalist)

> I think very rarely about Jewish affairs, mainly only when something happens to the Jews abroad and also at the time of the holidays.
>
> (a nonreligious student)

We may now summarize our discussion on the content of the Jewish identity by stating that the extent to which the group identity will be reflected in a particular individual will depend upon whether

(a) he perceives the Jewish group as being both a national and a religious entity, and not just exclusively one or the other;
(b) the Jewish group occupies a position of centrality in his life-space;
(c) being Jewish has high positive valence;
(d) the Jewish group serves as a source of reference in significant spheres of his life;
(e) he acts—more particularly in the daily conduct of his life—in accordance with norms of the group which have a distinctive Jewish stamp.

These propositions allow for the construction of a continuum along which identities may be ranged in terms of intensity. At one end of the continuum would be an assimilated Jew who views the Jewish group as a religious entity only, does not himself observe any of the religious practices, avoids association with Jews, and seeks to escape from a group which has no attraction for him. At the other end would be an orthodoxly observant Jew who is also a Zionist.

Interaction with Other Subidentities

A Jewish identity exists nowhere in isolation as the sole ethnic identity of an individual. The Jewish identity of an American Jew can only be understood in the context of his Americanism, just as the Jewishness of an Israeli Jew has to be seen in relation to the Israeliness with which it is associated and with which it interacts.

The relationship of the two ethnic subidentities can best be analyzed by regarding the individual (e.g., the Israeli Jew or the American Jew) as being in overlapping situations, i.e., as subject simultaneously to influences from two or more psychological situations. An analysis of the properties of overlapping situations would lead us to examine

(a) the extent of the overlap between the subidentities, i.e., their pertinence to identical regions of the person's life-space;

(b) the degree of compatibility between them, i.e., the extent to which the two situations are seen as giving rise to psychological forces moving in the same or in opposite directions;

(c) the relative salience: which identity in a given situation is in the forefront of the individual's consciousness;

(d) which is the more central in his life-space;

(e) the relative valence: which is the more attractive; and

(f) the relative potency: which identity determines attitudes and behavior in a given situation.

In comparing the relationships between the Jewish identity and the various other identities with which it is associated, what is of particular interest are the differences in overlap and compatibility. The degree of perceived overlap and also compatibility is greatest between the Israeli and Jewish identities. Our studies show that a substantial majority of Israelis indicate that when they feel more Israeli, they also feel more Jewish, and that when they feel more Jewish, they also feel more Israeli. Only a minority feel that the two are not interconnected, and a very small percentage indicate that there is incompatibility. The sense of overlap is strongest among the religious sector, many of whom see their Israeliness as an extension of their Jewishness.[27] The boundaries between the Jewish and the Israeli subidentities are not sharply demarcated; they are permeable, and Israeliness and Jewishness may be said to constitute what Erikson has termed a "wholeness."[28]

There are situations in which an individual's Jewishness will be salient, and others which increase the salience of his Israeliness. Their valence and relative potency will differ for different individuals. In our study some students declared that they were first and foremost Israelis, while others designated themselves as first and foremost Jews. But what was found to be of primary importance was whether they saw the two as *interrelated.* The students who see them as interrelated—and they are the majority—have both the stronger Jewish and the stronger Israeli identity. Where—as with the minority—the two are separated and compartmentalized, the Jewishness is generally weaker, and the Israeliness also less rooted.[29]

The studies of visiting American students in Israel show that the majority see their Jewishness and their Americanism as things apart; only a minority regard them as interconnected and compatible. Although no systematic inquiry has been carried out on a representative sample of the American Jewish population, it seems reasonable to assert that in most of his activities the American Jew acts as an American and only on special occasions as a Jew. This means that in the United States being Jewish occupies specific, delimited re-

gions of the life-space whereas in Israel it is far more pervasive. The restriction of Jewishness to specific regions is in
keeping with the prevailing American ideology of strict sepa-
ration between the religious and secular spheres of life. In the
secular spheres the majority culture occupies a dominant
position, placing its stamp on most activities, and the Jewish
identity accordingly becomes constricted.

The limited degree of overlap with the other identity is
characteristic of all Jewish identities in the Diaspora. In a
study we conducted of students who had come to Israel from
the United States, USSR, South Africa, and Argentina, the
students were asked to indicate how their feeling about their
other identity was affected when they felt more Jewish. These
students are not representative of their communities in the

Table 3.1: Perceived overlap between subidentities
(A comparison between students from five countries)

	Israel	USA	USSR	South Africa	Argentina
When I feel more Jewish, (1) I also feel more Israeli, American, Russian, South African, Argentinian	75	4	6	5	15
(2) There is no relation- ship between my feeling Jewish and my feeling Israeli, American, Russian, South African, Argentinian	23	68	46	45	60
(3) I feel less Israeli, American, Russian, South African, Argentinian	2	28	48	50	25
Total %	100	100	100	100	100
N	1,856	270	428	42	52

country of origin, but their responses are suggestive of the kind of relationship which may exist between the identities in their community. Their responses should be compared with those of Israeli students (see Table 3.1).

There are differences from one culture to another in the extent of the inclusiveness or exclusiveness of the majority identity. While their Americanism and their Jewishness are seen by the majority of students as pertaining to different regions, and while "the melting pot never did happen,"[30] they nevertheless regard their American identity as an inclusive one, embracing, to a greater or lesser degree, the minorities in American society. In the case of South Africa, the concept of "South Africanism" has been slow in developing, and in viewing the white sector of the population the emphasis is on three distinct ethnic elements, Afrikaans-speaking, English-speaking and Jews. The students from the USSR see their "Jewish nationality" as something distinctly separate from the Russian and other nationalities. The students from Argentina find little in common between their Jewishness and their Argentinian identity, which is not seen as an overarching identity as is the American identity.

The mutually reinforcing relationship between Jewishness and Israeliness and the almost complete absence of feeling that they are incompatible constitute a major distinction between Jewish identity in the Jewish state and Jewish identities in the Diaspora.

Outside the general consensus in Israel are the ideologies represented by two very small fringe groups—at opposite poles from one another—based on a complete sundering of Israeliness and Jewishness. The one group are the so-called "Canaanites," who wish to see an Israeliness divorced from the Jewish people and from the Jewish past in the Diaspora. The other group are the ultra-Orthodox "Neturei Karta" ("Guardians of the City"), who isolate themselves from Israeli society, see themselves only as Jews and not as Israelis, and do not recognize the existence of the "profane" State of Israel.

In a recent case before the Israel Supreme Court—George Tamarin v. the State of Israel—the petitioner, who had been registered as a Jew in the population register under the item "le'om" (literally nationality, but here equivalent to ethnic affiliation or peoplehood), asked that the registration "Jew" be deleted and "Israeli" be substitued. The petition was disallowed, the court holding that an Israeli Jew could not be regarded as belonging to an Israeli ethnic group as an entity distinct from the Jewish ethnic group.[31]

NOTES

1. A. Steg, "France: Perspectives," in M. Davis, ed., *The Yom Kippur War: Israel and the Jewish People* (New York: Arno Press and Herzl Press, 1974), pp. 206-213, at p. 212.

2. See Chapter 9 of this volume.

3. K. Lewin, *Field Theory in Social Science*, D. Cartwright, ed., (London: Tavistock, 1952), at p. 147.

4. M. Deutsch, *The Resolution of Conflict* (New Haven, Conn.: Yale University Press, 1973), at p. 20.

5. See the discussion of the concepts by Lewin, op. cit., pp. 146-148. Cf., Wittgenstein's definition of similarity in L. Wittgenstein, *Philosophical Investigations,* transl. by G.E.M. Anscombe (Oxford: Blackwell, 1963), pp. 31-32.

6. L. Berkowitz and L.R. Daniels, "Responsibility and Dependency," *J. of Abn. and Soc. Psychol.,* 66 (1963), 429-436.

7. See Chapter 9 of this volume.

8. E.H. Erikson, "The Problem of Ego Identity," in Stein et al., *Identity and Anxiety,* op. cit., p. 38. See also Erikson, "The Concept of Identity in Race Relations: Notes and Queries," in Parsons and Clark, *The Negro American,* op. cit.: "Identity also contains a complementarity of past and future both in the individual and in society; it links the actuality of a living past with that of a promising future." (p. 243). For further discussions of time perspective, see R. Kastenbaum, "The Structure and Function of Time Perspective," *J. of Psychological Researches* 8 (1964), 1-11; Y. Talmon, "Pursuit of the Millenium: The Relation between Religious and Social Change," *European J. of Sociol.* 3 (1962), 125-148; L.K. Frank, "Time Perspectives," *J. of Social Philosophy* 4 (1939), 293-312; K. Lewin, "Time Perspective and Morale;" in *Resolving Social Conflicts,* op. cit.

9. See Chapter 9 of this volume.

10. Ibid.

11. Sklare and Greenblum, *Jewish Identity on the Suburban Frontier,* op. cit.

12. Lewin, *Resolving Social Conflicts,* op. cit., p. 20.

13. Lewin, *Field Theory in Social Science,* op. cit., p. 123.

14. S.N. Herman, Y. Peres, and E. Yuchtman, "Reactions to the Eichmann

Trial in Israel: A Study in High Involvement," *Scripta Hierosolymitana* 14 (1965), 98-118.

15. For a fuller discussion of salience, see S.N. Herman and E.O. Schild, "Ethnic Role Conflict in a Cross-Cultural Situation," *Human Relations* 13 (1960), 215-228.

16. For a given milieu a certain pattern of behavior is perceived as fitting. The milieu together with the pattern of behavior perceived as fitting has been termed a "behavior setting": R.G. Barker and H.F. Wright, *Midwest and Its Children: The Psychological Ecology of an American Town* (Evanston, Ill.: Row, Peterson, 1954), pp. 7-10.

17. T.N. Newcomb, R.H. Turner, and P.E. Converse, *Social Psychology* (New York: Holt, Rinehart and Winston, 1965), p. 59.

18. M. Zavalloni, "Social Identity: Perspectives and Prospects," *Social Sciences Information* 12 (1973), 65-91, at p. 85.

19. M. Sklare, J. Greenblum, and B.B. Ringer, *Not Quite at Home* (New York: Institute of Human Relations Press, A.J.C. Pamphlet Series, No. 11 (1969), at p. 47.

20. D. Bell, "Reflections on Jewish Identity," in P.I. Rose, ed., *The Ghetto and Beyond* (New York: Random House, 1969), pp. 465-476, at. p. 468.

21. Glazer and Moynihan, *Ethnicity: Theory and Experience*, op. cit., at p. 8.

22. F. Barth, *Ethnic Groups and Boundaries: The Social Organisation of Cultural Difference* (Bergen, Norway Universitetsforlaget, 1969).

23. Sklare and Greenblum, *Jewish Identity on the Suburban Frontier*, op. cit., at p. 331.

24. H. Tajfel, "Social Identity and Intergroup Behaviour," *Social Sciences Information* 13 (1974), 65-93, at p. 72.

25. M. Weinreich, "Yidiskayt and Yiddish: On the Impact of Religion on Language in Ashkenazic Jewry," in J.A. Fishman ed., *Readings in the Sociology of Language* (The Hague: Mouton, 1968), pp. 382-413; M. Samuel, *In Praise of Yiddish* (New York: Cowles, 1971).

26. A. Voronel, "The Social Pre-conditions for the National Awakening of the Jews in the U.S.S.R.," in A. Voronel and V. Yakhot, eds., *I Am a Jew: Essays on Jewish Identity in the Soviet Union* (Academic Committee on Soviet Jewry and A.D.L., 1973), at p. 31.

27. See Chapter 9 of this volume.

28. E.H. Erikson, *Insight and Responsibility* (New York: W.W. Norton, 1962), at p. 92. In the case of Israeli Arabs there is a strict compartmentalization between "being Arab" and "being Israeli." S.N. Eisenstadt and Y. Peres, "Some Problems of Educating a National Minority," mimeographed research report, U.S. Office of Education Project No. E-6-21-013.

29. See Chapter 9 of this volume.

30. N. Glazer and and D.P. Moynihan, *Beyond the Melting Pot* (Cambridge, Mass.: M.I.T. Press, 1963), in preface. See also, M. Novak, *The Rise of the Unmeltable Ethnics* (New York: Macmillan, 1973).

31. In the Supreme Court sitting as Court of Civil Appeals. Before the President (Justice Agranat), Justices Berinson and Kahn. Dr. George Tamarin, Appellant, v. State of Israel, Respondent. (C.A. 630/70). Judgment delivered by Justice Agranat, January 1972. As an extension of this judgment, it would follow that also in the case of Israeli Arabs, there is no Israeli ethnic identity as an entity distinct from the Arab identity.

Chapter 4

CONSTANCIES AND VARIATIONS

Although elements of quintessential sameness characterize the Jewish identity in different climes and periods, significant variations also appear around the constant core. For the proper understanding of these differences, a Jewish identity must be viewed in historical and in comparative perspective.[1]

The Historical Perspective: Jewish Identity in a Changing World

There are variations in Jewish identity which flow from the peculiarities in the historical development of various communities, from the need to adjust to changes in the Jewish situation in the non-Jewish world, from the impact of political and social movements, both of a Jewish and general character, on Jewish life.

It is not our purpose here to discuss the character of these historical variations but rather to underline that Jewish identity as we know it today is the product of historical evolution. We shall at the same time refer to some of the forces which are continuing to shape Jewish identity.

Jewish identity after the Emancipation (which removed the civic disabilities of the Jews and opened the way for their participation in the political and social life of the country) differed from that which typically developed in the seclusion of the ghetto where the boundaries separating Jew from non-Jew were unmistakingly clear and insurmountable. The exodus from the ghetto did not, however, result—as some had hoped—in a complete absorption of the Jews into the surrounding society. The Jews in the countries of Emancipation became "a novel and singular social entity, and at the same time, a thoroughly changed but recognizable variation of the ancient Jewish community."[2] The transformation in Jewish life, moreover, did not take place simultaneously nor to the same degree in the various communities. Emancipation came first to West European Jewry and reached the Eastern parts only later and in attenuated form. While the immigrants who came to the United States brought with them their historical memories and their ideologies, the American Jewish community as such developed as a post-Emancipation community without the direct experience of passing through the crucible of Emancipation and having to grapple with the problems which followed in its wake.[3]

The Haskalah movement (the Jewish Enlightenment movement which began to spread in the latter part of the eighteenth century) made deep inroads into the traditional patterns of Jewish life, but more so in some communities than in others. There were Jews who believed that they could and should partition off their Jewish identity from the rest of the self and limit it to the private precincts of their lives in accordance with the then current maxim coined by Yehuda Leib Gordon: "Be a Jew in your tent, and a man outside." But there were others who reacted as did Rabbi Israel Salanter when he declared: "Haskalah is bent upon drawing me into the world outside. Accordingly, I will look deeper into myself. Haskalah is out to make me less of a Jew, and more of a man, but I want to be more of a Jew, because that will also make me more of a man."[4]

The various ideologies of Jewish life—such as Zionism (or to a lesser extent Diaspora nationalism, Bundism, or Territorialism in their time) on the national level, doctrines of Orthodoxy, Conservatism, and Reform on the religious level—all left their mark. These ideologies affected some parts of the Jewish world more than others. Thus, the political controversies around Zionism in European Jewry hardly reverberated among the Oriental Jewish communities, although they too shared the Zionist aspirations. The Jewish identity of a "hasid" in the Ukraine expressed itself differently from that of a "mitnagged" in Lithuania. "Lithuanian Jewry produced the Vilna Gaon, the pure intellectualist; Ukrainian Jewry produced the Baal Shem Tov, founder of Hasidism, and mystic lover of this life. For the former, the hard bench of the hungry scholar; for the latter, joyous prayer made up of song and wine."[5]

Jewish migrations during the last hundred years have been on so vast a scale that the great majority of Jews have been resident for no more than three generations in the countries in which they now live. The generations represent different stages of acculturation, and the grandchildren rarely know the language in which their immigrant grandparents were socialized. The family histories of many immigrants from South Africa now living in Israel provide an illustration of the nature of Jewish wandering. Their parents came to South Africa from Lithuania, their mother tongue was Yiddish; they were born in South Africa, their mother tongue was English; their children born in Israel are Hebrew-speaking. Three generations, three countries, three languages.

The winds of modernity and of secularism continue to blow in varying degrees through sectors of the Jewish community. The trend towards secularization has had particularly serious consequences for Jewish identity in which the factor of religious observance plays so important a role. Changed relationships between parents and children and between the sexes have affected the Jewish family—the nuclear cell in Jewish identity formation. Assimilation has appeared in Jewish life in various guises, and marginal Jews have sought to cast their Jewishness into whatever mold was perceived by them as likely to render it acceptable to the majority group. The growing rate of out-marriage in the United States and in many other countries, particularly in some of the smaller European Jewish communities, has far-reaching implications for the Jewish identity of these communities. In many cases, the Jewish partner in such marriages drifts away from the community; in others, the non-Jewish spouse seeks—with or without conversion—to enter the Jewish fold.

In various periods the general political and social movements current at the time have had a marked influence on the attachment of Jews to their own group. Some ideologies—such as Communism, with its universalistic orientation—have alienated Jews from their particularistic Jewish identification; in regard to other ideologies, Jews have sought—as in the case of Zionist Socialism—to develop a synthesis, or some form of coexistence, between elements in that ideology and their Jewishness. The radical movements which swept across the American campuses in recent years have estranged some of the Jewish students from the Jewish group and have brought others to seek new forms of Jewish identification consonant with the ideology they espouse.

In the past three decades, Jewish identity has been profoundly affected by two events—the *Holocaust* and the establishment of the *State of Israel.*

The Holocaust tragically changed the face of Jewish life. Except for a saving remnant, this was the virtual end of an influential, largely Yiddish-speaking Diaspora with its great institutions of Jewish learning. The center of gravity in the Diaspora shifted more markedly to an English-speaking American Jewry, which, along with the Hebrew-speaking Israel, now determines the main patterns of contemporary Jewish life. At the same time, the memory of the Holocaust still exercises a continuing influence on the Jewish identity of a generation born after that devastating tragedy. The Eichmann trial and events associated with the Six Day War and the Yom Kippur War have reactivated a memory which was always present, if only in latent form, in Jewish consciousness. There can be no adequate understanding of the view Jews have of their own collective existence and of their relationship to the non-Jewish world, unless full consideration is given to the deeply significant background factor which the memory of the Holocaust constitutes in the minds of Jews. It is because of the long shadow which the Holocaust continues to cast that Jews view with particular apprehension the current worldwide resurgence of anti-Semitism and react more vigorously to any threat to the existence of a Jewish community.

Israel is woven into the Jewish historical time perspective. Through the centuries of their dispersion, Jews have never ceased to regard themselves as a people in exile. The peculiar relationship between their people and the Land of Israel has been an integral part of their conception of a Jewish identity. Increasingly since the establishment of the State—and in particular after the Six Day War, which made Israel a focus of world attention—Jews everywhere find it necessary to define their Jewish identity with reference to Israel. (Even for the small minority of anti-Zionists it serves as a reference point, although a negative one.) Obviously the role of Israel in Jewish identity differs from country to country and varies with changing conditions. For some of the Jews in Soviet Russia, who have been cut off from the wellsprings of the Jewish cultural tradition and who are desperately seeking to leave for what they regard as the homeland of the Jewish people, Israel constitutes a focal point in their Jewish identity. For many American Jews it is mainly a source of pride and inspiration, but for others it means much more. During the Yom Kippur War there were those who declared that they saw in the threat to Israel a threat to their very existence as Jews. The awareness of Israel's meaning had grown since the Six Day War, and the new threat brought to those Jews a stark realization of how dark the world would be for them without Israel. This does not always mean that they

have adopted a Zionist ideology—indeed only few have a
Zionist conception of Jewish life—but it does mean that they
have advanced beyond the stage of just being pro-Israel to a
measure of involvement in Israel whereby it is seen as inti-
mately related to the central regions of their own lives.

Although there are divisions of opinion among their membership about the centrality of Israel, all three religious
denominations, Orthodox, Conservative, and Reform, stress
the significance of Israel for the American Jew. Of particular
interest is the pro-Israel orientation of the Reform movement
and its affiliation to the World Zionist Organization, dramati-
cally reflecting the change which has taken place in that
sector of American Jewry over the years. Ideologically the
Orthodox remain closer to Israel than the non-Orthodox,[6]
and their proportionate contribution to the number of
"olim" is also greater.[7]

For the secular Jew, who in his American environment has
few occasions, apart from consorting with other Jews, to
express the specific Jewish facet of his identity, activity in a
variety of forms on behalf of Israel has become one of the
most concrete demonstrations of his Jewishness. The number
of Jews who visit Israel is considerable, and a study period in
Israel has complemented the Jewish education of many
students. Our research has shown that such a study visit
deepens the inner Jewish staunchness of these students.[8]

Among recent events which have influenced the Jewish
consciousness everywhere has been the dramatic assertion of
their Jewish identity by Jews in the USSR, and the participation of Jews throughout the world in the struggle on behalf
of their right to leave for Israel.

The changes in Jewish identity in these three decades
reflect the cumulative impact of the interacting factors to
which we have referred—the destruction of European Jewry,
the haunting memory of the Holocaust, the establishment of
the State and the War of Independence, the "ingathering of
the exiles," the struggle of Russian Jewry, the Six Day War,
the Yom Kippur War and its aftermath (in addition to factors
of a general, not specifically Jewish character).

The Comparative Perspective:
The Influence of the Majority Culture

Jewish identity in the Diaspora has to be viewed in the context of the Gentile society in which it is located and with which it interacts. As Lipset has pointed out, "The comparative study of the Jew must be linked inseparably with the comparative study of the Gentile."[9]

The study of the similarities and differences in the identity of Jewish communities spread across the globe—adapting themselves to the many diverse environments in which they are located and yet everywhere maintaining, despite the divergencies, a kernel of sameness which can be termed "Jewish"—constitutes a subject of unusual interest to the social scientist engaged in cross-cultural research. Jewish identity inevitably assumes different forms in a pluralistic society such as that of the United States, from those it assumes in an antireligious totalitarian society such as that of the USSR; and the Jewish majority society in Israel provides the milieu for the fuller expression of a Jewish identity not available to Jewish communities in a minority situation constantly exposed to non-Jewish influences.

Jewish identity is, as we have observed, a peculiar blend of religious and national elements inextricably interwoven. On what component a particular Jewish community in the Diaspora places the emphasis will be determined in substantial measure by the prevailing conception about group differences in the majority culture. In the countries of the West, where the legitimate differences were seen as confined to religious faith, the accent after Emancipation was on the religious component in Jewish identity, whereas in the countries of Eastern Europe, with their multiplicity of nationalities, the emphasis was on the national element. In the United States the most legitimate source of difference has been on the religious level, and American Jews readily accept a division of Americans into Protestants, Catholics, and Jews. In fact, those Jews who are marginal and anxious to be identified primarily as Americans will maintain that they differ from other Americans by virtue of religious affiliation only and will adopt this basis of classification even if they themselves—as is often the case—are not religious. Other American Jews recognize the presence of a national component, but they, too, generally see in the religious facet an important constituent of their Jewishness.

The expression of the religious element in the Jewish identity among American Jews bears the mark of the American culture. Whereas in Israel the emphasis is on religious *observance*, American Jews pay greater attention (members of the Reform movement more so than Orthodox adherents) to expressions of *faith*. The national component gained in strength with the establishment of the State of Israel, and it has been further influenced in recent years by the new ethnic climate stimulated by the assertion of Black identity. But the basically religious orientation of American Jewry to differences between themselves and other groups still persists.

When we turn to students from another Jewish community, South Africa, included in the comparative study of students from different countries, we find that it is not religion but rather national origin which serves as the major differentiating factor in the white sector of the South African society of which they are a part. At the same time, religious affiliation is widespread in the society at large, and so, too, among the Jewish community. The Jewish community in South Africa is mainly of Lithuanian origin and continues a Lithuanian Jewish tradition.

While differing emphases exist, the students from the United States and South Africa—as well as the Israelis—see a Jewish identity as including both the religious and national components. Thus, the great majority of Israeli students together with a majority of students from the United States and South Africa defined the Jewish group as "both a people and a religious group." On the other hand, a majority of students from Argentina and the USSR limited the definition to "a people" only (see Table 4.1).

In defining their position inside the majority society, the Argentinian students saw themselves closer to, and able to

Table 4.1: Definition of Jewish group by students from different
            countries ("How do you define the Jewish group?")

	Israel	USA	South Africa	USSR	Argentina
As a religious group	5	3	0	4	0
As a people	14	16	30	56	67
As both a people and a religious group	81	71	63	40	33
Another definition	—	10	7	—	—
Total %	100	100	100	100	100
N	1,845	271	40	442	51

identify with, the secular sector in a Catholic country, and
because of this and other reasons, they tend to take up a
nonreligious stance. Their position in Argentinian society in
this respect seems analogous to that of Jews in France, who
have been placed by French history, as Lipset observes, "in
the anti-clerical or, if you will, the non-Catholic community
which regards all religious adherence as out-moded. Hence,
French Jewry has also been extremely irreligious; in effect,
most native born French Jews have behaved religiously like
the rest of the non-Catholic half of France."[10]

The students from Soviet Russia saw themselves as a "nationality" parallel to the Russian and other nationalities but
without a territorial base possessed by those others. They were
now returning to Israel, the homeland of the Jewish people
and the territorial base of their Jewish nationality.

There were differences in the Jewish background and outlook of students from different regions in the Soviet Union.
The students from Georgia had come from an enclave which
had preserved Jewish traditional practices and, although they
too subscribed to the general conception of Jews as a nationality, they were more conscious than the others of the
religious component in their identity. The Jewishness of the
students from other parts of the USSR bore the impress of
the antireligious climate in which they had grown up, even if
they did not wholly succumb to its influence. While a num-

ber of the students from the Baltic countries (Lithuania, Latvia, Estonia), incorporated in the USSR during World War II, had received some elements of Jewish tradition in transmission from parents and grandparents, those from Moscow, Leningrad, and other cities in the interior had little, if any, possibility of access to the sources of their Jewish heritage. They, in particular, had been the victims of a Soviet policy which officially designated them as Jews, but did not allow them to develop their own Jewish culture. A student of Soviet Jewish affairs, Zvi Gitelman, has succinctly summarized the situation of these Russian Jews: "Since their internal passports designate them officially as Jews, and since Soviet society, which places great emphasis on ethnic identity, regards Jews as such, they are in the curious and uncomfortable position of being culturally Russian but legally and socially Jews."[11]

The Jewishness even of the nonreligious Jew in the Western world is suffused with elements of Jewish tradition. For many of the students from the Soviet Union, being Jewish meant being part of a Jewish people whose Bible they had not read and of whose traditions they were almost completely ignorant. In Israel they have the opportunity of *becoming Jewish*, in the fuller sense, by integrating into their identity the missing traditional strands. To the extent that they succeed in doing so, they may overcome what is a serious weakness in the scope and strength of their Jewish identity.

Even if the immigrants from the USSR succeed in incorporating the traditional Jewish strands into their identity, their Jewishness will always vary in some respects from that of the immigrants from other countries. An immigrant can never completely shed the traces in his Jewishness of the culture of his country of origin. Nor is he required to obliterate such influences, which are the products of a long process of socialization, if they do not conflict with the essence of his Jewish being. At the same time, the fact that the many variegated groups of immigrants have in common the core elements of an inclusive Jewish identity facilitates their successful integration into the life of Israel.

NOTES

1. Cf., M. Davis, "Centres of Jewry in the Western Hemisphere: A Comparative Approach," *The Jewish J. of Sociol.* 5 (1963), 4-26; M. Davis, *The Jewish People in Metamorphosis* (Syracuse University: The B.G. Rudolph Lectures in Judaic Studies); D.J. Elazar, "The Reconstitution of Jewish Communities in the Post-War Period," *The Jewish J. of Sociol.* 11 (1969), 187-226.

2. For an analysis of the changes brought about by emancipation, see, J. Katz, *Out of the Ghetto* (Cambridge, Mass.: Harvard University Press, 1973); C.S. Liebman, *The Ambivalent American Jew* (Philadelphia: Jewish Publication Society of America, 1973).

3. N. Rotenstreich, "Emancipation and its Aftermath," in D. Sidorsky, ed., *The Future of the Jewish Community in America* (New York: Basic Books, 1973), pp. 46-61; D. Sidorsky, "Judaism and the Revolution of Modernity," in D. Sidorsky, ed., op. cit., pp. 3-21; B. Halpern, *The American Jew* (New York: Theodore Herzl Foundation, 1956).

4. A. Kariv, *Lithuania, Land of My Birth* (New York: Herzl Press, 1967), at p. 73.

5. S. Levin, *The Arena,* transl. by M. Samuel (London: Routledge, 1932), at p. 17.

6. C.S. Liebman, "Israel in the Ideology of American Jewry," *Dispersion and Unity* 10 (1970), 19-26.

7. C. Goldscheider, "American Aliya: Sociological and Demographic Perspectives," in M. Sklare, ed., *The Jew in American Society* (New York: Behrman, 1974), pp. 335-384.

8. S.N. Herman, *American Students in Israel* (Ithaca, N.Y.: Cornell University Press, 1970).

9. S.M. Lipset, "The Study of Jewish Communities in a Comparative Context," *The Jewish J. of Sociol.* 5 (1963), 157-166.

10. Ibid.

11. Z. Gitelman, "Patterns of Jewish Identification and Non-Identification in the Soviet Union." Paper prepared for the continuing seminar on "World Jewry and the State of Israel," convened by the President of the State of Israel, Jerusalem, July, 1975.

Chapter 5

WHO IS A JEW?

In Chapter 3 we discussed the criteria for gauging the compass and the intensity of the self-identity of a Jew. We now turn to the question as to who is regarded as a member of their group by Jews, i.e., the public objective identity in Jewish eyes. The definition by Jews does not necessarily coincide, as we have indicated, with the non-Jewish perception of who is a Jew.

A discussion of definitions must begin from that provided by Jewish religious law (the "halacha"). This is the definition accepted not only by Orthodox Jews but also in wider tradition-minded circles throughout the Jewish world. It represents a constant standard amid the variations in Jewish life and serves as the reference point in the consideration of other definitions; there is inevitably reference to the measure of their approximation to, or divergence from, the halachic definition.

The Definition of Religious Law

According to the halacha a person is a Jew if he was born to a Jewish mother or converted to Judaism in accordance with the prescribed procedures. A mere declaration of faith or of the feeling of belonging does not make a person a Jew. Nor does a person cease to be a Jew because of either lack of faith or of a sense of belonging.

The halachic definition is not—as some of its critics would make it out to be—"racist." Membership of the Jewish group is determined not only by descent; it is open to all who are prepared to accept the tenets of Judaism and convert according to the prescribed procedures.

The definitions current in some sections of the Jewish community may diverge from the halachic definition on the question of descent (the progeny of a Jewish father and a non-Jewish mother may be designated as Jews) or on the subject of conversion (the requirements may be less demanding than the halachic procedures), or there may be a complete disregard of both descent and conversion and anyone expressing the feelings of belonging may be regarded as a Jew.

In Israel certain matters of personal status, such as marriage and divorce, have been placed by the Knesset within the domain of religious law subject to the jurisdiction (in regard to Jews) of the rabbinic courts. (It should be observed that Israel is not—as is sometimes mistakenly supposed[1]—a theocratic state; the rabbinic courts, as well as the religious courts of the Moslem and Christian minorities, derive their authority from the secular legislature, the Knesset.) The problems which have arisen relate to the definition of the term "Jew" in matters outside the jurisdiction of the rabbinic courts.[2] Any decision taken in Israel about the question "who is a Jew" is seen as bound to have implications for Jewish life everywhere, and particular care has accordingly been taken by responsible Israeli leadership to avoid definitions that may be divisive.

The Responsa of the Jewish Scholars

In 1958 the Prime Minister of Israel, David Ben Gurion, addressed a letter to forty-five leading Jewish scholars—significantly, to those in the Diaspora as well as in Israel—asking for their opinion on a matter relating to the registration of children of mixed marriages with a view to the formulation of procedures "in keeping with the accepted tradition among all circles of Jewry, orthodox and non-orthodox of all trends, and with the special conditions of Israel, as a sovereign Jewish state in which freedom of conscience and religion is guaranteed and as a center for the ingathering of the exiles."[3] (The immediate occasion of the problem at the time was the arrival of immigrants from Poland with non-Jewish wives. The parents wished to register their children as Jews without their having to undergo the conversion procedures.) The question referred to the scholars was whether a child could be registered as a Jew on the basis of the expression of the desire of the parents and their declaration in good faith that the child did not belong to another religion, or whether any further ceremony was required.

The majority of the scholars objected to any departure from the halachic rules, and a number of them pointed to the dangerous schism which might result between Israel and the Diaspora from the adoption of different criteria in designating a person as "Jewish."[4]

The Case of Brother Daniel

In recent years the Israel Supreme Court has been called upon to decide who is a Jew for the purposes of the population register and of the Law of Return, which affirms the right of all Jews to settle in Israel without need for special application.

The subject received incisive treatment in 1963 in a judgment of the Supreme Court in the case of Oswald Rufeisen v. the Minister of the Interior.[5] The petitioner, Oswald Rufeisen, known since his conversion as Brother Daniel, was the son of Jewish parents in Poland and was educated as a Jew. During the Nazi occupation he, on a number of occasions and at great personal risk, rescued Jews from death at Nazi hands. Pursued by the Nazis he found refuge in a convent and during this time converted to Christiantity. Despite his conversion he continued to regard himself as belonging to the Jewish people, and eventually came to Israel as a member of the monastic order which he had entered at the end of the War. The question before the court was whether he could be considered a Jew in terms of the Law of Return.

In the main judgment Justice Silberg pointed out that according to religious law, the fact of Brother Daniel's conversion did not obliterate his Jewishness. He could still be regarded as a Jew for certain purposes.[6] "A Jew, even when he has sinned, still remains a Jew," according to a well-known Talmudic dictum. But the judgment went on to state that in the Law of Return, the term "Jew" had a secular meaning, that is, "as is usually understood by the man in the street . . . by the ordinary, plain and simple Jew." The answer given by the court was "that a Jew who has become a Christian is *not* deemed a Jew."[7] By the act of joining an antithetical group, he had severed his connection with the Jewish group.

Looking at Jewish identity in an historical perspective, Justice Landau in his concurring judgment stressed the inseparability of the religious and national components:

> The meaning of this law cannot be severed from the sources of the past from which its content is derived, and in these sources nationalism and religion are inseparably interwoven. A Jew who, by changing his religion, severs himself from the national past of his people, ceases therefore to be a Jew in the national sense to which the Law of Return was meant to give expression. . . . He has denied his national past, and can no longer be fully integrated into the organized body of the Jewish community as such. By changing his religion, he has erected a barrier between himself and his brother Jews.[8]

The court divided four to one. The dissenting judgment of Justice Cohn was a harbinger of differences of opinion still to come between members of the Supreme Court. He observed:

> In the absence of an objective test provided by the Law itself, there is no alternative, in my opinion, but to assume that the Legislature intended to content itself with the subjective test, that is to say, that the right to return to Israel belongs to any person who declares that he is a Jew returning to his homeland and wishes to settle there.[9]

The Shalit Case

Seven years later the differences that exist around the definition of who is a Jew were sharply reflected in a ruling of the Israel Supreme Court as well as in the controversy which followed the court's decision and which culminated in the Knesset's legislation on the subject. In the case of Benjamin Shalit v. the Minister of the Interior, the petitioner, a Jew, asked that his children, born to his non-Jewish wife (who had not converted), be registered as Jews in the population register under the item "Le'om." The court, sitting as a full bench of nine judges, divided five to four on the issue, the majority holding that the children should be registered as Jews in accord with the declaration of the petitioner.[10]

The majority of the court held on formal grounds that the question of who is a Jew and whether the petitioner's children are Jewish or non-Jewish did not arise for decision by the court. The registration officer is bound to effect registration in accordance with the notification of the declarant, unless he has reasonable grounds for assuming that the declaration is not correct. In the circumstances of the Shalit case, the majority held that this rule applied and the the registration officer was bound to register the children as Jewish in accordance with the notification of the declarant. At the same time, some of the judges, in the course of their judgments, gave expression to their views on the substantive issue, and these views are found to be widely divergent. Thus, one of the judges, siding with the majority, stated:

Here before us is the wife of a Jew faithful to the State. Though not herself Jewish by religion (or rather being irreligious), she has immigrated with her husband out of identification with the Jewish people, and bound her fate with that of the people of the State of Israel. They rear their children like other Israeli children. Should we refuse to recognize these children as members of the Jewish nation for the purposes of their registration in the Population Registry, and leave them nationless in the State of Israel?[11]

But one of his fellow judges, siding with the minority, saw it differently:

Which criterion should the Court select when determining the Jewish nationality of a person—the usual objective test of the Halacha, which regards Jewish motherhood or conversion as the sole identification mark of the Jew, or all the subjective tests chosen by the petitioner, which regards as the Jewish national identification mark a person's attachment to Israeli Jewish culture and its values?[12]

And he added later: "What is significant is that even the free Reform communities acknowledge that one cannot join the *people* of Israel without accepting the *religion* of Israel."[13] He proceeded to state the merits of the halachic test:

The Halachic test is a very easy and simple one for determining the nationality of a Jew. It is clear-cut and readily applicable to every Jew, whether from North Iceland, or from South Yemen, whether he is one of the righteous of the world, or a hardened sinner. This seems paradoxical, but looking at it more closely we shall see that Judaism has dealt most justly and most wisely with its children, in not demanding of them either inner recognition or observance of the Torah and its precepts in order to be called a Jew. Thus it has avoided the forsaking of Jewry, the final, eternal rupture of the bond between the individual and the community.[14]

The Knesset Resolution

The decision gave rise to heated public debate, and a bill was submitted to the Israel Knesset in February 1970 and passed by a substantial majority to define as a Jew for the purposes of the Population Registry Law and the Law of Return "a person born to a Jewish mother, or who has converted, and who is not a member of another religion." At the same time, in order to facilitate immigration of families of mixed marriages, the benefits accorded by the Law of Return are extended to the members of the family of a Jew—to his spouse and children and even grandchildren.

It is noteworthy that in the discussion around the Shalit case the proponents of the differing views found it necessary to stress that their particular proposal was best calculated to avoid a rift between Israel and Diaspora Jewry. But wide divergences of view existed about the form "the act of identification" with the Jewish group should take—from opinions that a mere declaration of belonging should suffice to an insistence (with all manner of gradations in between) on the strict halachic requirement of conversion according to prescribed requirements. Reflected in some of the definitions proposed in the debate is an ahistorical view of the Jewish group as if it were a sociological phenomenon of contemporary origin; against this are the definitions which look at the group within the framework of an historical time perspective. Basic differences of conception appear about the structure of Jewish ethnic identity; some participants in the debate sought to separate out the "religious" and the "national" components, while others maintained that they could not be disentangled. While it was widely agreed that there needed to be—in the case of so dispersed a people as the Jews—a commonly accepted criterion (applicable alike in Israel and in the Diaspora) as to who is a Jew, questions arose about the extent to which it was feasible to speak of "a Jewish *identity*" existing everywhere as a uniform entity; it was argued by some that the variations which had developed around the quintessential common core were such as to make it more appropriate to think in terms of a pluralistic Jewish society allowing for a diversity of "Jewish *identities*."

The Knesset resolution requires an act of conversion from a person not born to a Jewish mother who wishes to be registered as a Jew. While the resolution in no way departs from the halachic definition, it does not specifically state that the conversion should be according to the halachic procedures required by the Orthodox rabbinate. Soon after the passage of the resolution, the controversy took a further turn when the Ministry of the Interior refused to register as a Jew a woman who had been converted by a Reform rabbi in Israel. In this particular case the controversy was ended when the woman concerned, Helen Seidman, withdrew her petition to the Supreme Court and sought conversion by an Orthodox rabbi according to the requirements of the halacha. But the question left unanswered by the Knesset resolution has not yet been resolved. At the time of writing a committee of cabinet ministers appointed to examine the issue still has to submit its recommendations.

The debate around who is a Jew is likely to remain on the agenda of Jewish life. Indeed in some quarters regret has been expressed that it has been found necessary to undertake an act of formal definition instead of allowing the process of historical evolution to produce its own definitions.

NOTES

1. In a survey conducted in 1971 by the French Institute of Public Opinion on a sample of 619 French students, 83 percent described Israel as a theocratic state. *The Image of Israel in the Eyes of French Students*. A report published by the Information Department of the Israel Office of Foreign Affairs, Jerusalem, June 1971. (In Hebrew.)

2. With the ingathering of Jews from all parts of the world in Israel, questions of personal law have arisen requiring decisions by the rabbinic courts as to whether certain scattered tribes long removed from the mainstream of Jewish life, such as the Bne Israel of India, still fell within the boundaries of the Jewish group. But here the definition itself is not in question. Vide M. Elon, *Chakikah Datit* (Religious Legislation), (Tel Aviv: Hakibbutz Hadati, 1968), 174-177. (In Hebrew.)

3. B. Litvin and S.B. Hoenig, *Jewish Identity: Modern Responsa and Opinions on the Registration of Children of Mixed Marriages* (New York: Feldheim, 1965).

4. Ibid.

5. Oswald Rufeisen v. Minister of Justice. In the Supreme Court sitting as the High Court of Justice. Before Justices Silberg, Landau, Berinson, Cohn, and Manny. Judgment delivered 1962. Published in A.F. Landau and P. Elman, eds., *Selected Judgments of the Supreme Court of Israel,* special volume, Ministry of Justice, Jerusalem, 1971.

6. Ibid., pp. 3-10. The wide interpretation given by Justice Silberg to the contexts in which a convert to another religion would still be regarded as a Jew under religious law has been questioned. Elon, op. cit., pp. 52-53, points out that a convert does not retain *all* the privileges of a Jew. He expresses doubts as to whether under religious law such convert would be regarded as a Jew entitled to the privileges extended by the Law of Return. At the same time, he questions the correctness of a decision not to turn to the halachic definition in matters relating to the Law of Return.

Almost a decade later, the Knesset resolution, which came in the wake of the Shalit case, expressly stated that a convert to another religion is not entitled to the privileges of the Law of Return. Referring to this resolution, Elon points out that it is in conformity with the halacha: "A Jew converted to a different faith remains a Jew as regards his personal status and all this entails—such as the need for him to grant a divorce to his Jewish wife—but he is deprived of various religio-social rights and is not numbered as a member of the Jewish community (i.e., he cannot be counted toward 'minyan' and so on); for this reason he is also deprived of the rights of a Jew under the Law of Return." *Encyclopaedia Judaica* (Jerusalem: Keter, 1971) Vol. XII, p. 147.

7. Landau and Elman eds., *Selected Judgments,* op. cit., p. 11.

8. Ibid., p. 22.

9. Ibid., pp. 116-117.

10. Benjamin Shalit and others v. Minister of the Interior and another. In the Supreme Court sitting as the High Court of Justice. Before Justices Agranat, Silberg, Sussman, Landau, Berinson, Witkon, Cohn, Manny, and Kister. Judgment delivered January, 1970. Published in Landau and Elman, eds., *Selected Judgments,* op. cit.

11. Justice Berinson, ibid., p. 188.

12. Justice Silberg, ibid., p. 51.

13. Ibid., p. 58.

14. Ibid., p. 59.

PART II

CONTEMPORARY EXPRESSIONS OF JEWISH IDENTITY

Chapter 6

IN THE SHADOW OF THE HOLOCAUST

There can be no proper understanding of contemporary Jewish identity without consideration of the profound and continuing impact on it of the memory of the Holocaust. "The memory of the Holocaust stirs to the depths the heart of every Jew," remarked the judges in the Eichmann trial in Jerusalem. It is a constant background factor—moving from time to time into the foreground—affecting the way Jews see themselves and the way they perceive their relationship to the non-Jewish world. The elapse of three decades has not dimmed the memory of the Holocaust. It seems rather that there is now less of a tendency to repress the memory, and that a greater readiness exists for a conscious confrontation with the implications of the Holocaust for Jewish life and for Jewish-Gentile relationships. But only gradually—as perspective comes with the passage of years—is a fuller comprehension emerging of the awesome implications of this devastating tragedy.

In the three decades that have passed, it has become increasingly apparent how the annihilation of European

Jewry has impoverished Jewish life everywhere. Gone forever are the great centers of Jewish mass settlement from which came the immigrants who built up, and for years vitalized, communities throughout the world. No longer are the ranks of Jewish leadership replenished by the personalities shaped in that intensive Jewish environment. The face of the Jewish state would have been different, its Jewish roots would have been deeper, if it could have drawn from the reserves of Jewish energy which were destroyed. The massacre of the six million Jews, including more than a million children, sapped the vitality of the Jewish people for generations to come.

The nineteenth century witnessed the remarkable demographic growth of the Jewish communities of Eastern and Central Europe. Towards the end of the century, the great migrations began to America and other countries, but until World War II the majority of the Jewish people still remained in Europe. After the Holocaust the center of gravity of Jewish life, which had been shifting to the American continent and to Israel, moved with tragic decisiveness to those countries. In Poland, for example, eight thousand Jews are all that remain of the once great community of three million Jews.

The shadow which the Holocaust casts over the relationship between Jews and the non-Jewish world has lengthened across the years. This is not only because of the haunting memory of the atrocities committed by the Nazis and their collaborators. As research uncovers more of the facts about the period and they become more widely known, Jews realize with increasing dismay how even the Western democracies—with but few honorable exceptions—looked on with indifference and did little to stop the destruction and rescue the Jews. It had been known how cold-heartedly country after country shut its doors in the face of Jewish refugees, and the additional revelations about the failure of even the democracies to act as the campaign of extermination progressed have sharpened the sorrow and the indignation.

Writing at the beginning of 1942, the eminent Christian theologian, Reinhold Niebuhr, warned: "The problem of what is to become of the Jews in the post-war world ought to engage all of us, not only because a suffering people has a claim upon our compassion, but because the very quality of our civilisation is involved in the solution. It is, in fact, a scandal that the Jews have had so little effective aid from the rest of us in a situation in which they are only the chief victims. The Nazis intend to decimate the Poles and to reduce other people to the status of helots; but they are bent upon the extermination of the Jews."[1] The admonition went largely unheeded.

For a while at the end of World War II there were stirrings of conscience. The feelings of shame, guilt, and compassion aroused by the reports of the horrors of the Holocaust, the plight of the survivors in displaced persons camps and their insistent plea to be allowed to proceed to the Jewish homeland, contributed in no small measure to the resolution adopted by the U.N. in November, 1947, in favor of the partition of Palestine and the establishment of a Jewish state. With the passage of the years, however, such twinges of conscience as existed seem to have abated. Moreover, after the Six Day War Jews began to be seen as victors—and presented by their detractors as "aggressors"—rather than as victims to be pitied. The revulsion produced by the enormity and fiendishness of the Nazi atrocities had created an atmosphere which restrained the more blatant expressions of anti-Semitism in some countries. With a lessened fear of public opprobrium, anti-Semites have now become emboldened in the expression of anti-Semitism even if at times they still feel the need to issue a disclaimer that a statement or action is anti-Semitic and to present it under a more "respectable" label as anti-Israel or anti-Zionist. The worldwide resurgence of anti-Semitism—which now finds its most virulent expression in Soviet Russia and in the Arab countries—has made Jews conscious of the fact that the world has not set its face against another Holocaust.

Outbreaks of anti-Semitism are viewed more seriously against the background of the Holocaust, and whenever a threatening situation develops, the thought that there may be a recurrence of the Holocaust is frequently present. This accounts in no small measure for the alarm expressed for the future of Soviet Jewry and Syrian Jewry.

Among the Jews who during World War II were in the United States and other free countries there is an sense of guilt that they did not act with sufficient alacrity and bold- ness on behalf of European Jewry. This persisting sense of guilt intensifies the feeling that they dare not now be silent about the treatment of Soviety Jewry, of the Jews in the Arab countries, and wherever else danger may lurk.

The Eichmann Trial

Among the events that have served to reactivate the mem- ory of the Holocaust three stand out: the Eichmann trial, the Six Day War, and the Yom Kippur War.

In capturing Eichmann and bringing him to stand trial in Jerusalem, Israel gave dramatic expression to its peculiar link with Jews the world over—not only with the living, but also with the dead, "the six million accusers" in whose name the prosecutor in the trial spoke. The historical significance of the trial was stressed by Prime Minister David Ben Gurion in his Independence Day address in 1961:

> This is not an ordinary trial, nor only a trial. Here, for the first time in Jewish history, historical justice is being done by the sovereign Jewish people. For many generations it was we who suffered, who were tortured, who were killed—and we who were judged. Our adversaries and our murderers were also our judges. For the first time Israel is judging the murderers of the Jewish people. It is not an individual who is in the dock at this historic trial, and not the Nazi regime alone, but anti-Semitism through- out history. Only the independence of Israel could create the necessary conditions for this historic act of justice.[2]

Ben Gurion saw in the Eichmann trial an occasion to unfold to Israeli youth the tragic story of the Holocaust. "The importance of Eichmann's capture and trial in Israel," he wrote, "resides in the fact that the entire story of the

Holocaust can now be laid bare in an Israeli court so that the youth in this country—which grew up after the Holocaust and has heard only faint echoes of this atrocity unparalleled in history—and world opinion as well, will know and remember."[3]

A chapter of history was projected with peculiar intensity, from the past into the present, as the story of the destruction of European Jewry was retold—and in a sense relived—by its survivors. It may be, at any rate for those who were not in Europe at that time, that the impact of the Holocaust, seen in the perspective of the trial, was stronger than that of the stories which filtered through piecemeal soon after the events. Not only was there initially high interest in the trial, but over a period of months the trial was, day in day out, a main feature in all the newspapers, and parts of the evidence were reported in full detail. Kol Yisrael, Israel's only broadcasting service, relayed some of the sessions from the court-room, and a survey showed that 60 percent of the Jewish population had listened in to at least one of the sessions of the radio broadcast from the court-room on the first day of the trial, on April 11, 1961. Throughout the months the radio continued to devote considerable time to the trial in its new bulletins, and each evening at the peak listening hour it broadcast a newsreel with recorded excerpts of the evidence. The trial became a main topic of conversation, an inescapable part of the social interaction of almost every citizen. Indeed, insofar as the individual was amenable to influence, it would seem that it was the contact with this climate of opinion— and not just the content of a specific broadcast or report in a newspaper—that was the main source of influence. Questions relating back to the period of the Holocaust were discussed intensely, often heatedly, as if they were the questions not of yesteryear but of this day.

A study of reactions to the Eichmann trial shows that while there were differing degrees of involvement in the Holocaust, and accordingly in the trial, on the part of different sectors of the population—from survivors of the Holocaust to members of the younger generation who had been born after the Holocaust and whose families had not been in Europe at the time—the impact of the trial and the atmosphere around it extended to all sectors.[4] There were reverberations among Jewish communities throughout the world, although not comparable to the impact in Israel. The trial had a wide press coverage throughout the world, but a study undertaken in the United States showed that its influence was limited to a small minority of the non-Jewish population.[5]

The Six Day War

The events preceding and following the Six Day War sharpened the memory of the Holocaust. Despite the fact that the Israel War of Independence was fought only a few years after the Holocaust, and the Six Day War twenty years later, the indications are that the consciousness of the Holocaust was even more strongly present in 1967 than it was in 1948, conceivably because of the directness of the threat of destruction posed by the Arab states in the weeks prior to the outbreak of the war. In interviews carried out with soldiers and members of kibbutzim after the war, there are numerous references to the profound influence of the memory of the Holocaust as a background factor in their reactions to the threats of the enemy.[6] It steeled their determination to show their mettle as free Jews in their homeland and to hurl back an enemy bent on their destruction. This theme runs through a number of the interviews with the soldiers and finds poignant expression in a letter written by a paratrooper, Ofer Feninger, who later fell in the battle for Jerusalem. He describes graphically how after a visit in the Museum of the Holocaust at Kibbutz Lochmei Ha'Ghettaot (the Kibbutz of the Ghetto Fighters), he was haunted by the picture of inmates of a concentration camp, "those abysmal eyes behind the electrified fence," and he concludes with the resolve the Jews must be "strong and proud, never to be led again to slaughter."[7]

A study of American Jewish students who were in Israel during the Six Day War shows how the crisis reactivated for them the memory of the Holocaust.[8] The following quotations from interviews are typical of the feelings expressed at the time: "Whenever Jews are threatened, the Holocaust comes into your thoughts"; "feeling that we can't and we won't let it happen again"; "we have to be strong and depend on ourselves—we've been the world's scapegoat for too long. The Six Day War has caused me to believe that strongly. The Holocaust should have and did show me this, but the Six Day War and its preceding and post-war days gave me an example I would see before my eyes."

At the same time these students were impressed by the contrast between the position of a beleaguered, but self-reliant state and a powerless European Jewry. The consciousness of the Holocaust also accounts in no small measure for the swiftness and spontaneity of the unprecedented aid extended by world Jewry when danger threatened Israel. Indeed, Arab threats aroused greater anxiety among Jews outside of Israel than among the Israelis who were on the whole confident of their capacity to resist.

Commenting on the reactions of American Jewry, Lucy Dawidowicz writes: "The moods, feelings and spontaneous and organized actions of American Jews testified to their sense of Jewish solidarity and their commitment to Jewish survival." And she observes:

American Jews, like Jews elsewhere in the world outside Israel, experienced a trauma, perhaps best diagnosed as a reliving of the Holocaust in an eerie awareness of once again being put to the ultimate test. . . . It is generally agreed that the Holocaust was the underlying catalyst. American Jews have been afflicted with a deep sense of guilt. With the passage of time, their very survival, when millions of other Jews were murdered, and even worse, their failure to rescue more than a miniscule number of European Jews, have increasingly tormented them.[9]

The Yom Kippur War

In contrast to the trepidation experienced in May 1967 by world Jewry, there was confidence at the time of the Yom

Kippur War in the capacity of Israel's Defence Forces to repel the attack of the Arab states. But the attack nonetheless was seen as a threat to Israel's survival and as such a threat to Jewish existence. Furthermore, the isolation of Israel, the severance of diplomatic ties on the part of a number of countries, the refusal of certain countries to allow the passage of arms, Britain's refusal to supply the equipment already purchased—all these reminded Jews, both in Israel and in the Diaspora, of the attitude of the non-Jewish world to European Jewry at the time of the Holocaust. (In studies carried out by us in 1974 on Israeli students and on American students visiting Israel this factor is mentioned with great frequency by the students as reminding them of the period of the Holocaust.)

The events following in the wake of the war—such as the abject surrender of so many countries to Arab demands because of their dependence on oil and the ovation accorded to the terrorist leader, Yasser Arafat, at the U.N.—have heightened the feeling that Jews now, as at the time of the Holocaust, have to contend with a world which in large part is either inimical or indifferent. It is in this frame of mind that Jews reacted to the resolution adopted in the U.N. assembly stigmatizing Zionism as "racist." The parallel was drawn between this resolution and the initial stages of the Nazi campaign for the extermination of the Jews. The U.N. resolution was seen as part of a continuing war against the Jews, conducted at this time by the Arab and Communist blocs in association with a number of subservient African states. On this occasion Jews derived some encouragement from the repugnance expressed at the U.N. resolution by the United States and other democracies. The U.S. ambassador to the U.N., Daniel P. Moynihan, minced no words: "A great evil has been loosed upon the world. The abomination of anti-Semitism—as this year's Nobel Peace Laureate Andrei Sakharov observed in Moscow just a few days ago—the abomination of anti-Semitism has been given the appearance of international sanction. The General Assembly today grants symbolic amnesty—and more—to the murderers of the six million European Jews." While welcoming the support extended by non-Jewish circles, Jews continue, however, to feel that in the ultimate resort they have to depend upon themselves. Viewing the U.N. resolution and other manifestations of anti-Semitism in the mirror of the tragic Holocaust experience, they see in them an ominous portent of things that may still come.

The Attitudes of Israeli Youth

There has always been a problematic side to the attitudes of Israeli youth to Jewish communities in the Diaspora. Concern about the attitudes of the youth to the Jews of Nazi-occupied Europe was expressed as far back as 1944 by one of the cultural leaders of the Yishuv, Berl Katznelson. Speaking to a gathering of youth, he observed that there were youngsters who were able to identify with the Jews in their revolt but not in their suffering. And he adds: "Even if there was no revolt in the ghetto I would not utter a word of criticism against the Jews of the ghetto, and I could not demand such resistance from them. When people are attacked by a wild beast of this kind, you cannot demand of them to revolt, when it is known beforehand that there is no hope. People generally are prepared to revolt when they have the belief that they will emerge victorious on the morrow." And he concludes his talk with a troubled question: "Is there in the soul of the youth of Eretz Yisrael the capacity and the need to share the feeling of a common Jewish destiny, to experience a kinship with the Jewish people?"[10]

The Eichmann trial served to focus attention strongly on the question. The trial which across a number of months became an overwhelmingly salient fact in the lives of the Jews of Israel, old and young, evoked no small measure of heart-searching among them. It uncovered some of the deeper recesses in the attitudes of Israelis to Jews the world over, and afforded additional glimpses into the tortured inner dilemma of sections of Israeli youth about their relationship to their people's past in the Diaspora. While on the whole the trial produced a deeper understanding of, and identification with the Jews of Europe, it gave rise to expressions of perplexity on the part of some young Israelis that the Jews in Europe should have gone meekly to their doom "like sheep to the slaughter"—for so it seemed to these Israelis viewing the past from their particular vantage point.

In terms of historical time perspective, Israeli youth are in an unusual psychological position. They have grown up in independence as members of a majority in their own sovereign state, but their Jewish past is to a considerable extent the annals of a dependent Jewish minority in the Diaspora. They have no difficulty in relating themselves to the warriors led by Bar Cochba at the fortress of Masada, or even much further back to the Jews of the earliest Biblical days. But there is an understandable problem in identifying with the long period of Jewish minority existence so different from the conditions of their own life. The way they feel about the different periods is generally determined by two criteria which reflect the tenor of their own lives: first, the extent to which it is one of Jewish activism and not of passivity; secondly, the extent to which it is characterized by efforts at the maintenance of the Jewish identity, and not its surrender.

In the years following the Eichmann trial, increasing emphasis was placed by educators and others on the Warsaw ghetto revolt and other instances of resistance. Such acts of resistance Israelis readily admire. In the studies we conducted in 1965 and 1974 on representative countrywide samples of eleventh-graders, we found that the great majority expressed a feeling of pride when they looked at the behavior of Jews during the period of the Holocaust. But feelings of ambivalence still occurred in a minority who admitted to a sense of shame (see Table 6.1). Pride in the behavior was found to be associated with a stronger, and shame with a weaker, Jewish identity. Whereas the nonreligious students found the occasion for pride mainly in the active resistance of European Jews, the religious students also made frequent mention of acts of passive resistance and maintenance of Jewishness ("Kiddush Ha'Shem," "Sanctification of the Name" in their

Table 6.1: Attitude to the behavior of Jews in Europe during the Holocaust

	All Respondents		Religious*		Traditionalists		Nonreligious	
	1974	1965	1974*	1965	1974	1965	1974	1965
Pride	73	73	85	77	76	74	64	70
Neither pride nor shame	10	5	4	7	10	4	14	5
Shame	16	21	10	14	13	20	21	25
Lack of knowledge	1	1	1	2	1	2	1	0
Total %	100	100	100	100	100	100	100	100
N	1,800	767	461	168	622	247	717	352

Table 6.3: Duty of Jews to see themselves as survivors of the Holocaust—differences according to religious observance and communal background
("Do you agree with the statement, 'Every Jew in the world should see himself as if he is a survivor of the Holocaust'?")

	All Respondents		Religious		Traditionalists		Nonreligious	
	Ashkenazi*	Oriental	Ashkenazic*	Oriental	Ashkenazic	Oriental	Ashkenazic*	Oriental
I agree completely	53	46	74	64	49	43	44	36
Only those from Europe	10	12	5	8	13	15	12	8
Only those who themselves suffered	22	24	13	14	23	27	27	31
No, don't agree at all	15	18	8	14	15	15	17	25
Total %	100	100	100	100	100	100	100	100
N	1,078	635	279	134	232	358	567	143

martyrdom; faith in God; observance of "mitzvoth," religious commandments, under conditions of direst stress).

The emphasis on resistance, however, represents only a partial approach to the tragedy—even when it removes mis-understandings about the behavior of the Jews and produces feelings of pride. What of the relationship of Israel's youth to Jews who did not—and often could not—resist at all? Do they identify with European Jewry as it was and for what it was?

The great majority—88 percent—do indeed identify with the suffering of the Jews in Europe (see Table S6.2). But do they see the Holocaust just as a tragic event belonging to a now receding Jewish historical past, or do they go beyond this and see its implications as extending to the Jewish present and future? What seemed particularly crucial to examine was the presence or absence in this generation of young Israelis of a degree of identification with European Jewry which brings them to see themselves as being in the position of survivors and accordingly charged with the re-sponsibility of ensuring the Jewish future. Such identification reflects a recognition of the historic continuity which links the generations.

In our 1974 study approximately 50 percent of the students endorsed the statement that every Jew should see himself as if he were a survivor of the Holocaust. Since these were all students born after the Holocaust, we regarded the percentage of agreement as not insubstantial. The conscious-ness of being in the position of survivors is one of the strongest expressions of the sense of interdependence, and the data of our studies confirmed that it is associated with an intensity of Jewish identity. The statement is endorsed by a greater percentage of religious than nonreligious students. (see Table 6.3).

Statements such as, "This was the tragedy of the entire Jewish people"; "The Holocaust imposed the duty which is perhaps the justification for our existence—to save whatever has remained and to prevent a repetition of what has hap-pened"; "It affects every Jew wherever he be," recur in comments by students explaining their endorsement of the thesis. The interviews with these students showed that the memory of the Holocaust was deeply embedded as a potent background factor in their Jewish consciousness, even though it did not have the keen edge it possessed for their parents. A number of them were sons and daughters of families of survivors, and the families of many others had lost relatives. But even students whose families were not among the six million murdered had a sense of involvement in the Holocaust. While, as could be expected, the higher measure of involvement was to be found in the Ashkenazic (European) sector of Israeli society, the students of families in the Oriental sector showed a substantial sense of involvement as well. Fifty-three percent of students from Ashkenazic families endorsed the statement, and 46 percent of those from the Oriental communities did so.

But there were also the students of the other half of the sample who did not endorse the statement. In most cases they indicated that only the Jews who had been in Europe or families who had suffered could legitimately be regarded as survivors. A few asserted that it was best to forget and not to be weighed down by the tragedy of the past. There is, thus, still a section of the youth which is impervious to the implications of the Holocaust, and much remains to be done to foster a proper understanding of the tragedy. But the impression gained in our studies is that the consciousness of the Holocaust is more widespread than is commonly supposed.

When the students were asked which historical events influenced them the most personally, the events which most frequently appear in combination are: the establishment of the State of Israel, the Six Day War, the Yom Kippur War, and the Holocaust.

A majority of the students stated that they saw a repetition of the Holocaust as a possibility in at least some countries. The countries in which this contingency is seen as most likely are the Arab countries and the USSR. (see Table 6.4).

The memory of the Holocaust continues to exercise a pervasive influence on the perception of the students of

Table 6.4: Possibility of recurrence of Holocaust
("Do you think that a Holocaust is possible in the future?")

(1)	Yes, in all countries	22
(2)	Yes, but just in some countries	58
(3)	No, in no country	20
	Total %	100
	N	1,812

Jewish-Gentile relationships. They do not place much reliance on Gentile goodwill, although they have less of a distrust of them than have their parents. Comparing our 1965 and 1974 studies, there is more of a tendency now to see the Gentile world—at least, part of it—as anti-Semitic.[11] The students tend to speak of Gentiles in general terms, as a broad universal category from which they are marked off as Jews. At the same time, they also, when occasion demands, make a differential evaluation of different parts of this world. Among the factors which determine this evaluation an important part is played by the treatment accorded in a particular country to the Jewish minority—during the period of the Holocaust, as well as at the present time. Thus, the students accord the highest measure of esteem to the Danish people; the story, highlighted during the Eichmann trial, of how the Danes had rescued the Jews of Denmark from annihilation by the Nazis had engraved itself in their minds. And when they speak of "righteous Gentiles," they refer in particular to Gentiles in the various countries who rescued Jews during the Holocaust.

Reactions in Different Parts of the Jewish World

There are variations in the strength of the memory of the Holocaust in different countries. For the remnants of the communities in what was once Nazi-occupied Europe, there can be no forgetting. In the case of communities outside the continent of Europe, a number of factors determine the extent to which the memory of the Holocaust is evoked—the intimacy of the links which existed with the European Jewry from which they originated, the number of survivors who reached their shores and their place in the life of the community, the intensity of the Jewish consciousness of the community, the educational measures taken to perpetuate the memory of the Holocaust.

ISRAEL

To Israel came by far the greatest number of survivors, and members of the generation born after the Holocaust are in contact with them, or at least aware of their presence. Among the first representatives of the Yishuv (the Jewish community of what was then Palestine) to meet the survivors were the members of the Jewish Brigade who fought alongside the Allies in World War II. How deeply stirred they were by this meeting is reflected in the words of a member of the Brigade who wrote:

> It was only in June 1945, when we reached the Austro-Italian border, and for the first time met face-to-face with people who had left the concentration camps, when we saw their pyjamas, the tatooed numbers, the terrified eyes, the stricken souls, the children who had grown up wild, the thunder of another planet—only then something happened also to us. It seems to me that for the young "tzabarim", the members of my generation, this was the first Jewish experience.[12]

All who live in the Jewish state, and certainly all who have passed through its educational system, learn about the Holocaust. In hundreds of schools pupils have "adopted" communities destroyed in the Holocaust, have interviewed the survivors, and have prepared exhibits and publications on all that they can ascertain about the leading personalities, the organizations and cultural life of the communities. The education branch of Israel's army issues special material on the Holocaust and has arranged seminars on the subject. The Hebrew University in its Institute of Contemporary Jewry has a special division devoted to Holocaust studies, and the subject is included in the curricula of other Israeli universities as well. A very large proportion of Jews in Israel have visited one of the Holocaust memorials, such as that set up by statute of the Knesset at Yad Vashem in Jerusalem, at Kibbutz Lochamei Ha'Ghettaot, and at Yad Mordechai, a kibbutz named after a leader of the Warsaw ghetto revolt, Mordechai Anilewitz. The references to the Holocaust are frequent in the public life of the country. One of the candidates for the presidency of Israel in 1973, in describing his approach to various issues, remarked: "I am the son of parents who perished in the Holocaust and the father of a son who fell in defence of this country." And the prime minister of Israel, in discussing the dangers of assimilation in the Diaspora, pointed to the fact that a people which has lost six million of its members cannot afford to lose more through assimilation.

Holocaust Remembrance Day in Israel is a day of national mourning; all places of entertainment are closed, the sirens sound, and the entire country pauses in silent tribute. The press gives the day special attention, the radio and television programs are devoted to subjects relating to the Holocaust, memorial ceremonies are held throughout the country addressed by leaders of the state.

The associations connected with the word "German" still arouse considerable antipathy in certain sections of the Israeli public, and the signing of the reparations agreement and the establishment of diplomatic relations with the Bonn government were preceded by intense emotional debate. But since relations have been established, and in the light of the help accorded by West Germany to Israel, particularly during the Six Day War, there is an increasing tendency to differentiate between Nazis and the liberal elements that have emerged in Germany. The heads of both states have exchanged visits. At the same time, there is general agreement that the past cannot be forgotten, and that accordingly there cannot be a complete "normalization" of the relations between the two peoples. Such comprehension of the continuing role of the past found expression in the words of the Chancellor of West Germany, Willy Brandt, on arrival in Israel on an official visit in June, 1973: "I think I should say this, coming from the Federal Republic of Germany; we cannot undo what has been done. The sum of the suffering and of the horror cannot be removed from the consciousness of our people. Cooperation between our two countries remains characterized by the historical and moral background of our experiences." When in 1975 Prime Minister Rabin visited West Germany his first act was to proceed to the Bergen Belsen concentration camp site to pay homage to the memory of the Jews who had been murdered.

THE UNITED STATES

Survivors of the Holocaust reached the shores of the United States, albeit in limited numbers. The GIs who had fought in Europe in World War II brought back the tale of horror unfolded when as liberators they entered the concentration camps. But the memory of the Holocaust was never as salient in the United States as in Israel.

Universalistic reactions were also more common than they are in Israel. The Holocaust was frequently described as an instance of "man's inhumanity to man" or as an example of what happens in a totalitarian society. The stress was on the need to point out the dangers for mankind, to strengthen democratic or anti-Facist or anti-Nazi forces. Some of the proponents of the universalistic approach have tended to obscure the specific Jewish elements in the tragedy.

Although the Eichmann trial had an impact, its influence was much less direct and powerful than it was in Israel. The Six Day War served to reactivate the memory of the Holocaust. Since 1967 the Holocaust has become a more salient factor in the consciousness of American Jews, and the reactions, while they are yet more universalistic than in Israel, have tended to contain particularistic elements with greater frequency.

An examination of publications dealing with American Jewry shows that during the 1950s and 1960s limited attention was given to the memory of the Holocaust as a factor in Jewish life. The Eichmann trial focused attention on the Holocaust for a short while, but in the years that followed it again receded into the background. The Six Day War brought about a dramatic change. In what is the major study of a Jewish community (Sklare's Lakeville study) carried out in 1957, there are only a few references by the residents of Lakeville to the Holocaust. But when Sklare returned to Lakeville after the Six Day War, he observed that the memory of the Holocaust came to the fore at the time of the war, and it is against the background of this memory that the reactions of Lakeville's Jews can be understood. So he wrote: "It seems to us that the response of May-June was not a response to Israel in the conventional sense, but rather a response to the events of Jewish history from the 1930s onwards. . . . The crisis brought to the forefront of consciousness the possibility of a repetition of that history—the possibility of another Holocaust."[13]

Teachers at American universities report on the special interest of students in courses on the Holocaust. Comparing American students visiting Israel across the years 1965 to 1974, we find an increased consciousness about the Holocaust. Like the Israeli students they see the possibility of a recurrence of the Holocaust, and regard the Arab countries and the Soviet Union as the main danger zones. In discussing the period of the Holocaust they make less frequent reference than do Israeli students to the question of active resistance. It is a reasonable surmise that this would also hold for the reaction of the American Jewish community at large.

SOVIET RUSSIA

Two and a half million Russian Jews perished in the Holocaust. The survivors saw how readily the local populations in the Ukraine and elsewhere joined the Nazis in perpetrating the slaughter. The much vaunted "fraternity of peoples" proved to be a hollow slogan. And despite the magnitude of their sacrifice and their participation in the ranks of the Soviet Army, the Jews did not obtain the relief which they hoped the victory would bring. Anti-Semitism continued unabated, and the memorials erected spoke of the victims of Nazism and Fascism, but never was there mention of the Jews who had been massacred.

In interviews carried out with students from Soviet Russia who had arrived in Israel, we found—as could be expected from descendants of a European Jewish community directly affected by the Holocaust—that for a number of them the memory of the Holocaust was a background factor of considerable significance in the arousal of their Jewish consciousness. "It represents for us the crystallization of the precariousness of Jewish minority existence," remarked a student from Riga. And a girl, a member of an assimilated family from Moscow, whose Jewish consciousness was aroused in her late teens, observed: "We didn't know Jewish history. Our only knowledge was of the Holocaust. Every family has its story about this catastrophe, and this was our starting point in Jewish history."

Responding to a question on the subject in a survey conducted on students from the USSR in Israel, 72 percent indicated that a close member of the family had suffered during the Holocaust and a further 10 percent stated that a distant relative had suffered.

SOUTH AFRICA

While there was an awareness on the cognitive level of how tragic an event the Holocaust was in the history of the Jewish people, the memory of the Holocaust evoked less emotional reaction among students from South Africa who were interviewed in our study.

The origins of South African Jewry, which is considered one of the most staunchly Zionist communities in the world, are in Lithuania. The South African government's Quota Act of 1930 virtually put an end to immigration from Eastern Europe. A few thousand refugees from Germany slipped through a loophole in the Act before immigration from that country too was stopped. Thus, South African Jewry has been cut off from its European source for more than forty years; very few survivors reached its shores. This accounts in no small measure for the lack of vibrant Jewish cultural life in South Africa, and for the lesser intensity of the consciousness of the Holocaust among the grandsons and granddaughters of the Jewish immigrants from the Lithuania whose Jewry was destroyed in the Holocaust.

Emphases in the Jewish Reaction

While the implications of the Holocaust have received increasing attention in recent years, differing emphases are reflected in the treatment of the subject. We proceed to indicate where we believe—in terms of our orientation to the study of contemporary Jewry—the emphases should be placed.

(1.) *The catastrophe has to be seen in the perspective of Jewish history* and what it tells of the condition of Jews in a Gentile world. The road leading to the Holocaust was paved by the anti-Semitism preceding it, and this endemic anti-Semitism found expression not only in the Nazi atrocities, but also in the indifference of the world which did not halt the slaughter. The Holocaust, however, cannot be treated as just another, though more terrible, link in the long chain of anti-Semitic outbursts and persecutions. Attention has to be given to what lifts it far and beyond other tragedies which have befallen the Jewish people. As the historian J. L. Talmon has expressed it:

> Even if we agree that antagonism to the Jews is an unchanging element, a primary factor, continuous and identical from Hellenistic times until today . . . —even then we shall be obliged to recognize a multiplicity of formulations, expressions, methods of implementation, modes of incitement, types of accusation, all dependent on place, time, political and socio-economic conditions, moral and spiritual values and psychological factors. In short, anti-Semitism may be an autonomous whole, more exactly a primary phenomenon, but in one way or another it is a function of external factors. Anti-Semitism is part of a wider context.[14]

While the specific Jewish focus should not be obscured, the forces which led to the Holocaust have to be viewed in their broad historical context.

(2.) *There are very obviously universalistic implications to the Holocaust*, and they must not be forgotten, neither by Gentile nor by Jew. But is is questionable whether Jews, the descendants of the victims, are the proper address for the exhortations often directed to them to bend their efforts to change society as part of the lessons to be learned from the Holocaust. They certainly would not wish to see the recurrence of the social and political conditions which allowed the Nazis to come to power, and if they are conscious of what brought about the Holocaust, they, probably more than many others, can be relied upon to strive for a just and democratic society. But this cannot be the primary admonition to them. While not ignoring the universalistic implications, it is more proper to focus their attention on the particularistic Jewish implications of what was a tragedy of the Jewish people.

A tendency also exists, particularly in the United States, to equate the Holocaust with other tragedies, such as Hiroshima and Biafra. But the analogy obscures that which differentiates the Holocaust from all other tragedies and gives it its unique character. Never in the annals of mankind was there so diabolically systematic and relentless an effort—unrelated to the exigencies of war—to exterminate an entire people, to destroy all Jews, men, women, and children, wherever they were and whatever their beliefs.[15]

(3.) *We dare not forget. Whom must we remember?* We need to remember, first of all, the survivors in our midst whose lives were maimed and who continue to mourn the families they lost.

At the time of the Eichmann trial there were some who ventured the opinion that for the survivors of the Holocaust the trial would reopen wounds which had barely healed; others thought it would provide a helpful catharsis. In any event, it became apparent that the vast majority of survivors welcomed the trial—and not simply because one of the principal villains had been brought to justice. For many of them it had been a source of deep distress to feel that the world around them—even the Jewish world around them—seemed to have forgotten. The trial restored the period of the Holocaust to the position of a salient fact of contemporary Jewish experience, and for the survivors who had been carrying their sorrow with them, often in loneliness, there were some solace and perhaps easing of pain in the Jewish people's remembrance of the tragedy. Among the numerous letters Attorney General Hausner received there were many expressions of gratitude from survivors. "Thank you," wrote one woman, "for having liberated the tears which remained welled up in me since the day in 1942 when, as a girl of nine, I was separated from my parents, never to see them again."

The survivors must be able to feel that even with the passage of years, the Jewish communities among whom they live remain cognizant of, and share in their sorrow.

We dare not forget the communities which perished. We need to remember how they lived, what they stood for, and how they died. We need to recall how Jews sacrificed their lives in acts of heroic resistance—both active and passive resistance ("Kiddush Ha'Shem," "Sanctification of the Name"). At the same time, we must not forget how the masses of Jews, despite the intolerable agony of their existence, gave expression to a determination to hold onto life. This striking phenomenon of "Kiddush Ha'cha-yim," "Sanctification of Life," (a term first used by Rabbi Nissenbaum, of the Warsaw ghetto) has been described by one of the ablest historians of this period, Shaul Esh, who stressed that this was not simply an urge on the part of the Jews to continue living but also to preserve the Jewish character of their lives.[16]

(4.) *There has been much questioning across the years about the extent of Jewish resistance,* and this has included at times critical statements that Jews went meekly to their dorm. Historical research has been providing increasing information and a fuller perspective on the subject. It has helped to clarify how strong was the disbelief that the worst would happen, how limited were the opportunities for resistance by Jews and how they nonetheless resisted more than other groups. The facts as far as they can be ascertained should be provided, irrespective of whether they reveal weaknesses or strengths.

While the questions are legitimate, it would be immoral for those who were not there to serve as judges on this matter. Certainly we dare not point an accusing finger against the Jews who perished. An accusing finger can be pointed not merely against the Nazi murderers and their accomplices, but against the countries of the free world who did so little to rescue even a part of the stricken European Jewry. And an assessment of the role of Jews in the free countries shows that it fell far short of the needs of the catastrophic situation.

The indications are that the "passivity" of European Jewry is ceasing to be the subject of critical reference in discussions of the Holocaust. While when specifically questioned a minority of Israelis still expressed such an opinion, the interviews with them indicate that even they speak less critically about the subject. They have in recent years seen—in tragic cases such as that of the murder of the Israeli athletes at Munich and of school children at the border village of Ma'alot—how powerless unarmed civilians can be when assailed by armed terrorists.

(5.) *Some educators fear that the discussion of the Holocaust may inculcate feelings of hate in the Jewish youngster.* To them it may be said that there certainly is no need, psychological or moral, to repress feelings of hate against the persecutor. Such feelings are often the basis for constructive action, though special care has to be taken that these feelings are not generalized into groundless group prejudices.

But the arousal of the feeling of hatred, while it is a natural concomitant of a discussion of the Nazi atrocities, is not the purpose of education about the Holocaust. Far more important is the stimulation of a sense of identification with the Jewish past as reflected in the life and fate of European Jewry, and the development of a sense of responsibility for the Jewish present and future.

(6) *While some Jews have sought to flee from their Jewish belonging, many more throughout the world have been moved by the Holocaust to a reaffirmation of their Jewishness.* Those already at the center of the Jewish group have intensified their identification, many of those at the periphery have moved closed to the center. Emil Fackenheim has given striking expression to the Jewish reaction: "Jews are forbidden to grant posthumous victories to Hitler. They are committed to survive as Jews, lest the Jewish people perish."[17]

A people can think back to a tragedy in its past but look upon it so disconsolately that it does not spur them to action. The reaction to the Holocaust has been—and must continue to be—a stiffening of the determination to strengthen Jewish life, to consolidate the Jewish state and actively change the conditions under which such a tragedy could occur.

(7.) *The establishment of the Jewish state is a striking expression of the Jewish will to live,* and no one can understand the significance of Israel unless he sees it in the perspective of the Holocaust. The Holocaust, the plight of the survivors in the displaced persons camps, and their insistent plea to be allowed to proceed to the Jewish homeland strengthened the demand for a Jewish state. It aroused stirrings of conscience in parts of the non-Jewish world who gave support to the demand.

Israel, however, cannot—and should not—be regarded, as some tend to do, as a recompense for what was lost. Norman Lamm has properly observed that "never, never must there be an attempt to make a metaphysical equation, to assert or even imply, that the State is, in some measure, a compensation for the anguish of the Holocaust."[18] Ben Gurion has stressed that "it is a very grave mistake to think that the Nazi Holocaust resulted in the creation of the State in 1948." He has pointed out what a difference it would have made had the martyred six million remained alive after World War II, they "who needed and aspired to it [the Jewish State] with all their hearts, and who were qualified and prepared to build it."[19]

Education and Memorialization

Not all historical events are deeply imprinted in the life of a people. It would seem that much depends on the centrality of the event to the people, its relevance to the conditions of their present and to their strivings for the future, and also on educational measures taken to perpetuate the memory of such an event in a way which emphasizes its continuing pertinence for the present and future.

The Holocaust is an example of such a traumatic event, central in the history of the Jewish people, a persisting memory which has been further sharpened by the constellation of happenings around the Six Day War, the Yom Kippur War and its aftermath. No study of Jewish identity and of relationships between the Jewish and other groups can ignore the profound impact of this event.

Serious thought is now being given to the proper presentation of the Holocaust in programs of Jewish education attuned to the different age levels. But much still remains to be done—in Israel as in other countries—to give the Holocaust the place it must occupy in the Jewish education of every generation.

There is also need to give thought to the proper memorialization of the tragedy. While Holocaust Remembrance Day is a deeply moving experience, it still has to find the fitting form and content which will weave it fully into the life of the people—not only in Israel, but in Jewish communities everywhere, as part of Jewish traditional observance. Across thousands of years the exodus from Egypt has been celebrated in Jewish homes, and in each generation Jews see themselves as if they were personally liberated from bondage. And on Tisha Be'Av (the fast on the ninth day of the month of Av) Jews through the centuries have continued to mourn the destruction of the Temple. The Holocaust, too, must become part of the Jewish calendar and be perpetuated in the Jewish historical consciousness.

NOTES

1. R. Niebuhr, "Jews After the War," *The Nation*, Feb. 21, 1942.

2. D. Ben-Gurion, *Israel: A Personal History* (New York: Funk and Wagnalls, 1971), p. 599.

3. Ibid., p. 574.

4. S.N. Herman, Y. Peres, and E. Yuchtman, "Reactions to the Eichmann Trial in Israel: A Study in High Involvement," *Scripta Hierosolymitana,* XIV (1965), 98-118.

5. C.Y. Glock et al., *The Apathetic Majority* (New York: Harper and Row, 1966).

6. N. Near, ed., *The Seventh Day* (London: Deutsch, 1970).

7. Ibid.

8. S.N. Herman, *American Students in Israel* (Ithaca, N.Y.: Cornell University Press, 1970).

9. L.S. Dawidowicz, "American Public Opinion," in *American Jewish Year Book* 69 (1958), 198-229, p. 203.

10. B. Kaznelson, "Youth and Jewish Faith," *Molad* 10 (1949), 226-229. (In Hebrew.)

11. See Chapter 9 of this volume.

12. Hanoch Bartuv in the newspaper *Ma'ariv.* The role of the Jewish Brigade in rescue operations is recounted in Y. Bauer, *Flight and Rescue: Brichah, The Organized Escape of the Jewish Survivors of Eastern Europe 1944-1948.* (New York: Random House, 1970).

13. M. Sklare, "Lakeville and Israel: The Six Day War and Its Aftermath," *Midstream* 14 (1968), 1-19, p. 18.

14. J.L. Talmon, "European History as the Background to the Holocaust," in *Hasho'ah Vehatekumah* (The Holocaust and the Revival). Proceedings of a Symposium. (Jerusalem: Yad Vashem, 1975), 11-48. (In Hebrew.)

15. How relentless was the campaign of extermination is documented in L.S. Dawidowicz, *The War against the Jews 1933-1945* (New York: Holt, Rinehart and Winston, 1975).

16. S. Esh, *Studies in the Holocaust and Contemporary Jewry* (Jerusalem: Institute of Contemporary Jewry, Hebrew University, Yad Vashem and Leo Baeck Institute, 1973), pp. 238-252. (In Hebrew.)

17. E. Fackenheim, "Jewish Faith and the Holocaust," *Commentary* 46 (1968); 30-36, p. 32.

18. N. Lamm, "Teaching the Holocaust," *Forum* 24 (1976), 51-60, p. 54.

19. D. Ben-Gurion, op. cit., p. 840.

Chapter 7

ZIONISM AND PRO-ISRAELISM:

A DISTINCTION WITH A DIFFERENCE

While the wound inflicted by the Holocaust can never be healed, the establishment of the State of Israel in 1948 reinvigorated a people which might otherwise have remained broken and demoralized. No Jew can remain impervious to the existence of the Jewish State; he is inevitably required to take up a stand. Support for Israel is widespread throughout the Jewish world; on no other issue is there a broader consensus. The question that needs to be asked is whether and to what extent this pro-Israel sentiment is integrated into a Zionist ideology, for on this depends, in our view, the depth of its influence on the identity of the Jew and on the quality of Jewish life everywhere. Zionism means more than pro-Israel support in the Diaspora and more than Israeli patriotism in Israel.

Zionism was for many years the guiding, inspiring idea in Jewish life, even though only a minority of Jews were affiliated with Zionist organizations. It united a dispersed people in pursuit of a common goal, canalized its energies and served as a beacon of hope across years of travail. The establishment of the State of Israel was a triumph for Zionism. Some saw it, indeed, as the fulfillment of Zionist aspirations, but others understood that this was just a step—albeit a most important one—along the road to Jewish redemption.

The dramatic quality of the building of the Jewish State in the face of constant attack from its Arab neighbors and the magnitude of the task of the "ingathering of the exiles," have made the state the focus of attention. An understandable anxiety not to antagonize the non-Zionist circles which extend their support to Israel (in fund-raising campaigns and otherwise) has caused Zionists to slur over ideological issues, and to present Zionism as little more than a safely noncontroversial pro-Israelism.

With the exacerbation of the Arab-Israeli conflict, Zionism has increasingly become the object of a fierce onslaught from the foes of Israel and of the Jewish people. In November 1975 a majority in the general assembly of the United Nations, composed of the Arab and Soviet blocs and including a number of African and South American states, passed a resolution stigmatizing Zionism as "racist." Jews everywhere saw the attack on Zionism as directed against the Jewish people, against the very existence of Israel, and against the essence of their Jewish being. There was an impressive demonstration everywhere of support for Zionism. At the same time, while the word "Zionism" is more freely invoked than ever before, the sentiments which were aroused could be described as pro-Israel rather than as reflections of a renewed interest in Zionist ideology. Such pro-Israel sentiment is important in itself, but much of the enthusiastic support may evaporate unless it takes the more enduring form of a clear Zionist ideological commitment.

In the face of the anti-Zionist onslaught, attention is being properly given to the exposition—which is best when it is unapologetic—of the true nature of Zionism for those who are prepared to listen, in non-Jewish as well as Jewish circles.

Our concern in this chapter is with Zionism as a specific expression of Jewish identity, with its role *from the internal Jewish standpoint*—what contribution it can make in providing coherence and direction to contemporary Jewish life, particularly so in a period of stress and confusion.

Reinterpreting Zionism

The classical Zionist theories of Pinsker, Herzl, Achad Ha'am and others were based on an analysis of the Jewish situation of their time and had special pertinence to the countries of Europe in which the bulk of Jewry was located. The developments in Jewish life have confirmed the validity of their basic theses, and much of what they wrote still applies to the Jewish condition. But cognizance has also to be taken of major transformations in that condition. While maintaining its fundamental principles, Zionism has to adapt itself to meet the changing Jewish needs. Otherwise it will become an abstract, out-dated ideology unrelated to the fate and future of the Jewish people. The Holocaust, the demographic shift to new centers in the West, the establishment of the State of Israel—all these render essential a continuing process of reinterpretation.

In this process of reinterpretation, Zionism also cannot ignore the ideologies in the world around it which now impinge on Jewish life. In relation to some of these ideologies it will need to show how and why it differs, in relation to others it may show how it accords. Just as it should not fear to do battle where it differs, so where it accords it should not fail to indicate the peculiarly Jewish quality which enters into its own ideology. Thus, in keeping with the temper of the times, Zionism is nowadays frequently described as a movement of national self-liberation. It is such a movement, but a simplistic equation of it with other similar movements in the contemporary world is misleading if there is no reference to its special distinguishing features—the persistent longings and strivings of a dispersed people across centuries to return to a homeland from which it saw itself as exiled, the way in which the relationship to a distant homeland became part of the very texture of Jewish life. It is also a movement which has to be viewed against the background of centuries of unending discrimination and persecution culminating in the unique and terrible tragedy of the Holocaust.

While the fundamentals of Zionist ideology apply to Jewish life everywhere, there will be variations reflecting the character and the needs of particular communities. The renascent Zionism of Jews in the Soviet Union expresses the need they feel for a homeland allowing for the unhampered expression of their Jewish nationality and its culture. Zionism in the United States bears the mark of its development in a democratic, culturally pluralist society. American Zionists have always been at pains to stress the compatibility of their Zionism with the ideals of the society of which they are a part. The Zionist in Israel has to look outward in the direction of his fellow Jews in the Diaspora, and his Zionism furthermore bears the impress of the ever-present tasks of immigrant absorption and of defense.

While for Jews in distress in countries of anti-Jewish persecution Zionism represents the hope of immigration—if and when they are allowed to leave—to a homeland which welcomes them, there is no clear understanding of what Zionism implies for Jews of the free democracies of the West nor indeed what its meaning as an ideology is for the Jew in Israel. Our discussion will concern itself with Zionism in the largest of the free democracies, the United States, and with Zionism in Israel.

The Absence of an American Zionist Ideology

The immigrants to the United States at the turn of the century brought with them the Zionist ideologies which prevailed in Europe. The Zionism which developed in the American climate, however, had a pragmatic quality, and, while it propagated the conception of a Jewish people and its relation to an ancestral homeland, it was not sharply distinguishable from support for Jewish settlement in Palestine. After the establishment of the State, as pro-Israel sentiment became widespread, the distinction between Zionists and pro-Israel Jews became even less apparent. The more general acceptance of the conception of Jewish peoplehood removed a further point of difference between Zionist and non-Zionists.[1]

A recent report drawn up by an American Jewish Committee task force, composed of leading American Jewish scholars, maintains that the classical Zionist theories do not provide a framework for the interpretation of developments in American Jewry. "Zionist theory has had no ideological framework in terms of which it understands or interprets the dynamic processes which have been taking place on the communal and individual level in the American Jewish community."[2] While it refers to the inapplicability of the classical Zionist theories, the report does not point to any indigenous version of Zionist ideology adapted to the needs of American Jewish life. It notes that "the focusing of Diaspora energy on the shoring up of Israel's position and achievement has made Israel a *center* of concern, although in a way different from that which Ahad Ha'am predicted. This process, has, however, charged American Jewish life with a sense of responsibility for Israel, and has often made Israel the substance of Jewish program and activity."[3] This statement seems to us to summarize the nature of the relationship of a large section of American Jewry to Israel. It is pro-Israelism but not Zionism.

There is no comprehensive study of the attitudes to Israel and Zionism of a representative sample of the American Jewish community. Such empirical studies as have been conducted on specific sectors of the population show that the great majority support Israel, but only a minority designate themselves as Zionists, and only a very small number are prepared to consider settlement in Israel.[4]

David Sidorsky has expressed the position as follows: "Support of Israel in a non-ideological way, that is, without a

philosophy of Jewish history or a coherent set of principles
but with a sense of moral purpose and pragmatic policies, has
become a major aspect of the American Jewish consensus.
The obvious question to put to the thesis is whether the
distinction between a pro-Israel consensus and a Zionist
ideology is a distinction without a difference."[5]

The Difference Between Zionism and Pro-Israelism

Wherein the difference between pro-Israelism and a Zionist
ideology? It is often maintained that the difference between
the pro-Israel Jew and the Zionist is to be found in the
latter's decision to immigrate to Israel. In the minds of many,
Zionism and aliya are coterminous. But while the decision to
immigrate represents the apex of a Zionist development, it
does not exhaust the scope of a Zionist ideology. Nor is every
oleh a Zionist—there are cases where this practical step may
be taken for reasons unconnected with Zionist ideology.
Moreover, while the recognition of the central role of aliya
and the obligation to encourage it are essential elements in a
Zionist ideology, it is debatable whether the term "Zionist"
should be limited—as was urged at one time by David Ben
Gurion and by others—only to those who feel themselves
personally obligated to immigrate. In the case of American
Jewry—and, indeed, in the case of most Jewries in the
Western world—it would mean that only a small fraction of
the community would be entitled to call themselves Zionists.
There seems to us to be cogency to the contention that the
appellation "Zionist" should be accorded also to those who
when joining a Zionist organization are still at the beginning
of a process which may eventually lead to a fuller acceptance
of a Zionist ideology and to aliya.

Our submission, then, is that Zionism is more than the
expression of a positive attitude to Israel (although, of
course, it is this too), and it also connotes more than aliya
(although aliya occupies a central position in the Zionist
conception). The view we are advancing is that a Zionist

ideology represents an all-encompassing approach to the problems of the Jewish people. Presented in these terms, Zionism is more likely to be seen by Jewish communities everywhere as designed to meet their needs. We would contend that a Zionism of this kind could give direction to Jewish life, could result in increased support for, and heightened involvement in, Israel, and could ultimately lead to an increased aliya.

We shall seek to elaborate the contituent elements of such a Zionist ideology on the basis of a reading of the writings of Zionist thinkers[6] and the resolutions of the Zionist congresses, the supreme legislative body of the World Zionist Organization. The analysis of the ideological issues and of the validity of differing viewpoints will inevitably reflect the Zionist bias of the author. In recent years social scientists have given increased attention in their studies to the place of Israel in Jewish life, but there has been little reference to the role of a Zionist ideology, actual or potential. And so the social psychological analysis we undertake moves in what is largely an uncharted field.

The essential constituents of a Zionist program are contained to a large extent, although not in completeness, in the resolutions of the twenty-seventh Zionist congress held in Jerusalem in 1968. These resolutions, termed the Jerusalem Program, state the aims of Zionism as follows:

The unity of the Jewish people and the centrality of Israel in Jewish life;

The ingathering of the Jewish people in its historic homeland, the Land of Israel, through aliya from all countries;

The strengthening of the State of Israel which is based on the prophetic vision of justice and peace;

The preservation of the identity of the Jewish people through the fostering of Jewish and Hebrew education and of Jewish spiritual and cultural values;

The protection of Jewish rights everywhere.

The propositions stated in this form are likely to be accept-able to a large section of the Jewish people. There is need, however, to spell out and amplify the ideological implications of these elements as part of an overall approach to contempo-rary Jewry. Indeed, it is necessary to stress that what charac-terizes Zionist ideology is not any one of the elements in isolation but the combination of these elements integrated into a comprehensive view of Jewish life. Such elaboration and amplification would reveal that there are ideological issues in regard to which both confusion of thought and differences of opinion exist.

The Zionist movement allows for the different religious, social, and political emphases reflected in the programs of the political parties which function within its framework. We shall seek to distill out what seems to us to be the essence of a Zionist approach without entering into the various em-phases, however important they may be.

Since we are dealing with a Zionism seen as flowing out of a Jewish identity and shaping its further course, it will be observed that a number of elements in such Zionist ideology link up with the indices we developed in an earlier chapter for testing the compass and the intensity of a Jewish identity.

Elements of a Zionist Ideology

(1) *One people with common history and destiny.* Basic to a Zionist view is the affirmation of Jewish peoplehood; it sees Jews as one people, bound together by a common history and a common destiny.

The recognition of the unity of the Jewish people engen-ders a sense of mutual responsibility and paves the way for an understanding by Jews of the need for united action. It becomes the task of Zionists to show that the Zionist pro-gram represents the most effective form of such concerted action for the creative survival of Jews as a national entity.

(2) *Israel as the Jewish national center.* Zionism has dif-fered from other movements (such as Diaspora nationalism)

affirming Jewish peoplehood in that it regards Israel as the homeland of the Jewish people, as the Jewish national center. It seeks equality of national status for the Jew through the establishment of Israel as the Jewish State. (The antisemitic part of the world denies to the Jewish collective in Israel the equality which it formerly denied the individual Jew.)

(3) *The precariousness of galut.* Zionism looks at Jewish minority existence in the Diaspora in terms of "galut," or exile. Galut has been the condition characterizing Jewish life for a large part of Jewish history and it is a term laden with many associations and meanings.[7] Our use of it here is in accord with the following two definitions taken together: "Galut is the distance of a collective from its homeland; it is marked by a lack of objective possibilities to shape the collective life of a collective unit, to the extent such a shape is humanly possible,"[8] and "Wherever Jews live as a minority, where they are not politically or socially independent, where they rely on the good graces of the non-Jewish majority and are subject to the everyday pressures of its civilization and mode of life, such a place is Galut."[9]

In this sense all Jewish communities outside of Israel are in galut. But there are gradations to galut. A Zionist approach attuned to the realities of contemporary Jewish existence needs to differentiate between the problems of the Jewish minority in a democratic, pluralistic society such as that of the U.S.A. and between the long nightmare of persecutions and expulsions which was the lot of Jews in so many countries in Europe and the Middle East. At the same time, Zionism, while drawing a distinction between parts of the galut, underlines the features common to all the parts: the dependence on the good graces of the non-Jewish majority and the erosion of Jewish identity through assimilation into the majority culture.

While the Jerusalem Program explicitly affirms the unity of the Jewish people—a proposition which is widely accepted even by many non-Zionists—it makes no reference to the issue of exile which is not only unacceptable to non-Zionists

but is also a source of controversy among Zionists themselves, more particularly in the United States. The non-Zionists generally are anxious to avoid a concept which is seen by
them to question their "at homeness" in America, and they
wish to stress the differences rather than the communalities
between their position in the free world and the condition of
Jews in lands where they are subject to persecution or grosser
forms of discrimination. On the part of a number of American Zionists, too, there has been a reluctance to think of
their community as part of galut and they have argued for
the use of the term "tfutzot" (dispersion).[10]

The Zionists who do subscribe to the conception of galut
differ in regard to the policy to be followed in relation to it.
One section urges that a radical approach be taken—the galut
should be "liquidated" as speedily as possible and all Jews be
urged to proceed to Israel. Among the Zionists in this category are those who "negate" the galut ("shlilat hagalut") to
the extent of derogating efforts to stimulate local Jewish
activity and at times (much less so now than in the earlier
years) expressing contempt for many of the manifestations of
Jewish life in the galut.[11] Other Zionists, while they too are
aware of the precariousness of the Jewish minority condition,
hold the view that the galut will continue to exist for many
years to come and maintain that the encouragement of aliya
and the strengthening of the Jewish identity of Jewish communities everywhere should proceed hand in hand. It would
seem that the latter is now the prevailing view, and later in
this chapter we shall turn to its implications.

(4) *Aliya.* The encouragement of aliya is the primary task
of a Zionist movement; it seeks to remove from the golah and
gather into Israel as large a part as is possible of the Jewish
people. A goal of this kind, challengingly difficult but attain-
able, involving so radical a transformation in the life of an
individual is what gives Zionism its peculiar dynamic quality
as a movement—and this it can do even in American society
where popular, self-propelling movements do not easily
arise.[12]

(5) *The historical time perspective: continuity and revolutionary change.* In its political expression Zionism represents the great revolution in Jewish life—the liberation from the shackles of Diaspora existence and the active reshaping of the Jewish condition. It is the essence of the Zionist credo that Jews themselves can and should control their destiny.

At the same time, Zionism reflects continuity as well as change. Only when it is presented as part of the broad stream of Jewish history and tradition can there be a full comprehension of its cultural and spiritual dimensions. Representing as it does a crystallization of longings and strivings rooted deep in the historical consciousness of the Jewish people, it has the capacity to generate forces which it could not easily arouse if it were merely an exotic growth or a strange new phenomenon.

The strength of Zionism lies precisely in the fact that it represents a balance between a past, present, and future orientation to the condition of the Jewish people. A program, which is ostensibly Zionist but does not maintain this balance, is of questionable depth and durability. This may, in part, account for the transient nature of some of the Zionist groups which appeared on the American campus in recent years. While the radical student revolt found some Jewish students in the ranks of the anti-Zionist New Left, others sought to develop Zionist conceptions adapted to the social and political temper of their generation. The weakness in the Zionism they advocated arose in many instances from the excessive present-orientedness which these students shared with other sectors of radical youth.

(6) *Land and people.* Israel is so much at the core of Zionism that a widespread tendency exists to define Zionism as the upbuilding of the Jewish state. This results in a confusion about the aims of Zionism which it is important to avoid. The building of the state has to be seen as only the means, albeit the indispensable means, to the achievement of a goal which relates to the Jewish people in its entirety. It is then more clearly understood that Zionism is concerned with

the fate of Jews everywhere, and a particular community appreciates that Zionism relates also to it and not just to other Jews.

While Zionism exposes, as we have noted, the limitations of Jewish life in the galut, it has to take into account the fact that, even with an increased rate of aliya, considerable sections of the Jewish people are likely to remain in the Diaspora in the foreseeable future. Not only have they to be aided in the protection of their rights—and this the Zionist movement in the Jerusalem Program explicitly undertakes to do—but the communities remaining in the galut have to be stimulated into the active expression of their Jewishness in whatever form the circumstances permit. The issue is clarified by focusing attention on the ultimate aim of Zionism, which may be broadly defined as the redemption ("geulah") of the Jewish people. This in the Zionist view means that as many Jews as possible should settle in the Jewish homeland, and it may also entail a complete exodus of Jews from countries in which danger threatens. In so proposing, Zionism is concerned with the fate of the Jewish people; it is concerned with the whole without overlooking any of the parts, and from the very nature of these aims it cannot neglect any Jewish community anywhere.

A Zionist conception seeks to present land and people in proper perspective; it constantly has to keep within its vision the people for whose sake the land is being built. It mobilizes a Jewish community for action not on a philanthropic basis but as an interdependent part of the Jewish people engaged in a task which relates to the welfare of all its parts.

In terms of such a Zionist approach, there is no balancing up—as do some non-Zionists and anti-Zionists—of the amount of support extended to Israel lest it diminish support for the institutions of the particular Diaspora community. A community cannot be "overcommitted to Israel."[13] In a community acting in terms of this Zionist conception, dynamic forces are liberated, invigorating all phases of its life; while it extends more support to Israel, it also gives more attention to Jewish education and to community organization.

(7) *Pertinence to all facets of communal life.* To see Zionism merely in a general way as affecting the Jewish future is not enough. It has to enter into a number of regions central to the life of a Jew, wherever he may be; it has to result in more than just a peripheral involvement of the Jew. Insufficient attention has been given to spelling out the implications of Zionism for the problems which agitate the Jew of our day in the free countries. It can be shown to involve an approach to the problems of Jewish education, to the organization of the Jewish community, to the fight against assimilation on the one hand and against anti-Semitism on other; it introduces a staunchness and a dignity into the life of the Jew.[14] Such a "holistic" Zionism would be felt by the Jew to be deeply meaningful, and not just an easily discardable appendage to his life.

Many Zionists do play a part in the life of the community, but the form of their participation in its activities often does not differ from that of the non-Zionists. What is important here is whether they participate as Zionists who bring a Zionist approach to bear on the problems of the community.

It should become the task of those students of Zionism who regard it as more than pro-Israelism to elaborate the Zionist approach in the various areas of Jewish life. We shall here briefly indicate the direction in which a Zionist approach points in two such areas—the cultural life of the community and its fight against anti-Semitism.

(a) *Cultural distinctiveness.* Zionism represents a proud, unabashed expression of a Jewish identity, a readiness to be different. In accord with its concern for the creative survival of the Jewish people, Zionism stimulates the cultural distinctiveness of the Jewish community.

One of the clearest expressions of this distinctiveness is the use of Hebrew, which has become the symbol of the Jewish national revival. Quite apart from what the possession of a national tongue does to break down barriers between Jews everywhere, and what it does to provide Jews with a key to the storehouses of their history and literature, it is a bond between the Jew and the center of Jewish life which is Israel.

So, too, Zionists acting in terms of a Zionist approach are more likely than others to encourage the *intensive* forms of Jewish education. This generally means the establishment of Jewish day schools, an emphasis in the curriculum on the teaching of Hebrew and on the role of Israel in Jewish life.

(b) *The fight against anti-Semitism.* Zionism looks at anti-Semitism in the perspective of Jewish history and recognizes that there can be no comprehension of the roots of this endemic hatred unless there is reference to the historical background.[15] In terms of this perspective, a Zionist approach, while not ignoring local variations, sees anti-Semitism in a particular community as part of a problem transcending boundaries of time and space. In contradistinction to the Zionist viewpoint, non-Zionists in the free societies are more likely to regard anti-Semitism in their country as a local aberration differing in kind from anti-Semitism elsewhere and amenable to solution by appropriate measures in the field of interpersonal relations.[16]

It is precisely because of their understanding of the deeper roots of antisemitism that Zionists are less prone than non-Zionists to make the refutation of any and every anti-Semitic allegation a main item in the agenda of Jewish life. When they engage in the fight against anti-Semitism or other forms of prejudice, they are more likely than non-Zionists to boldly assert their role as members of the Jewish group and will be readier to cooperate as a *Jewish group* with other groups on the basis of the common interests involved. Their stance in the fight against anti-Semitism is upstanding and unapologetic, and they are less likely than non-Zionists to attribute anti-Semitism to Jewish behavior or characteristics.

Psychologically Zionism adds a dimension to the Jewish self which enables Jews to meet the non-Jew on a basis of equality. There was unevenness in the encounter as long as the Jewish group was a homeless entity unequal among peoples. It was to this change in the stature of the Jew that a Zionist leader referred when he observed to a non-Jewish colleague, "Zionism is that which enables me, a Jew, to speak to you, a non-Jew, as man to man."[17]

In recent years there has been confusion about how the establishment of a Jewish state has affected anti-Semitism, and in the reinterpretation of Zionism this issue needs to be clarified. The establishment of the Jewish state did not, as some had hoped, put an end to anti-Semitism; it may have changed the stereotype, the perception, of the Jew in some Gentile minds, but it did not eradicate the feeling component, their hatred of the Jew. Indeed, anti-Semitism has found a new focus—an attack on the collective existence of the Jew in Israel. Physical dangers still confront the Jew in Israel; what the Jewish state has accomplished is to radically alter the condition in which the Jew faces up to any attack. He is not a member of a dependent minority subject to the whims and caprices of a non-Jewish majority, but is part of a Jewish majority actively determining its own mode of life and shaping its own destiny.

Facing up to Conflict

A Zionism of the sort we have outlined, boldly facing up to the issues in Jewish life, is bound to sharpen opposition in certain quarters. There is no merit in stirring up unnecessary controversy, but at crucial points Zionism dare not avoid taking a stand. Such ideological conflict is not dysfunctional; on the contrary, it clarifies the issues, defines the lines of battle, and strengthens the dedication of adherents to a cause. Developing a series of propositions originally propounded by the sociologist Georg Simmel, Lewis Coser has drawn attention to the social functions of conflict.

> Internal social conflicts which concern goals, values, or interests that do not contradict the basic assumptions upon which the relationship is founded tend to be positively functional for social structure. Such conflicts tend to make possible the readjustment of norms and power relations within groups in accordance with the felt needs of its individual members or sub-groups. . . . In addition, conflict within a group frequently helps to revitalize existent norms; or it contributes to the emergence of new norms.

In this sense, social conflict is a mechanism for adjustment of norms adequate to new conditions.[18]

While nothing is gained from an unduly vociferous, strident militancy, a silence on the crucial Jewish issues, because of fear lest they become sources of conflict, is distinctly harmful. Such an approach drains Zionism of its vitality, and is a disservice to Jewish life. Assimilation in its many insidious guises is all the more dangerous in our days because there is often no head-on collision between it and Zionism.

On Becoming A Zionist

Zionism derives from Judaism and cannot be separated from it.[19] It finds it fullest expression in the individual for whom it represents the culmination of a sound Jewish education. A leading Zionist thinker, Hayim Greenberg, has summed it up as follows: "Without such education, Zionism may be a doctrine, a convincing theory, a program, a plan, an undertaking of desperate urgency, an appeal to sentiment, a noble humanitarian enterprise, but not a profound creative experience."[20]

"Jewish education" is not necessarily limited to formal schooling or to a systematic course of studies. It may be, and often is, obtained through a variety of informal channels.

While Zionism flows most readily from a Jewish education, many individuals who were minimally Jewish and located on the outskirts of their group have in the past moved in a Zionist direction as the result, for example, of a traumatic event in the life of the Jewish people such as the Holocaust or the attack on Zionism in the international sphere, or as a result of a revealing incident in their own personal experience such as the shock of an unexpected encounter with anti-Semitism. Their Jewish education in such instances began after they entered a Zionist framework. As wrote one such Jew (the French Jewish writer Bernard Lazare), who became a dedicated Zionist: "I awoke to find myself a Jew and I did not know what it was to be a Jew."[21]

In the presentation of a Zionist program, account has to be taken of the developmental level of the community to which it is addressed. In any given sector of a Diaspora community a certain balance or equilibrium exists between the forces making for greater conformity to the norms of the Jewish minority subculture and the forces making for greater conformity to the norms of the general culture. This equilibrium is likely to be established at different levels for different sectors of the Jewish community. The more the balance of forces moves to the Jewish side of the scale, the easier it is to influence the Jews in question in a Zionist direction. The approach to any sector or individual has to be attuned to their place on the scale.

Becoming a Zionist means more than the acquisition of a body of knowledge of Jewish history, of Hebrew, of developments in Israel. Such knowledge is indeed indispensable if Zionist convictions are to have deep roots; moreover, a Zionist attitude may be, and often is, an outgrowth of such knowledge. But the knowledge itself is not sufficient. And, indeed, there are very knowledgeable Jews, and sometimes fluent Hebraists, who are not Zionists. Becoming a Zionist means adopting an action-oriented ideology—a way of perceiving the Jewish people and its problems, a way of evaluating the solutions proposed for these problems, and, in addition, a way of action in regard to their solution. A change from a non-Zionist to a Zionist position involves a change in (a) perception, (b) values and valences (attractions, aversions), and (c) action.

There are problems specific to the change in each of these components. Moreover, although a change effected in one component sometimes leads to change in the others, this does not necessarily always happen.

If we examine Zionist education in terms of these three components, we can appreciate the fallacy in the commonly held view that by simply disseminating appropriate information we make people Zionists. It is true that the provision of new facts where previously there was ignorance or misconception may sometimes set in motion a process leading to a

Zionist viewpoint. The path of Zionist education would be relatively smooth if this were always so. But we know how often the most rational of arguments in favor of Zionism falls on deaf ears. The facts may not be accepted as "facts," and, even if they are accepted as such, they are frequently distorted by the perceiver to fit an existing viewpoint. And even when the change in perception takes place, it does not necessarily lead to a change in likes or dislikes. (A visitor to Israel may acknowledge the achievements of the country, but may still persist in his unfavorable attitude to it.) And when values and valences do change, the appropriate action does not always follow.

The process of educating towards an action-oriented ideology is therefore complex; it often requires a total change, i.e., in all three components we have discussed. Such total change is generally achieved by a person's acceptance of a group with the appropriate ideology as his source of reference.

The Group as Agent of Change

In a study of the attitudes of American Jewish youth to Zionism we found that the Zionists among them did not have Zionist convictions at the time they entered Zionist groups. They joined because they had been approached by a friend or acquaintance to do so; they remained because they found the activities or the company of the other members congenial. They may have been predisposed to join such a group by virtue of home influence or of Jewish education. But at the time of joining they were not Zionists. Gradually they accepted the norms and standards of the group, and these being Zionist norms, they became Zionists.[22]

Similarly in the study we conducted in the United States at a Zionist youth camp, to which both Zionist and non-Zionist campers came, it was found that by the end of their stay, the non-Zionists were moving towards a Zionist standpoint. The camp constituted a "cultural island" with Zionist norms, and the campers who were its inhabitants were influenced by its climate. It was not sufficient to be physically present in the camp; the question was rather whether the camper accepted the group with which he was associated as his reference point. Even then it was necessary to enroll the campers on their departure from the camp in Zionist groups so that their newly acquired attitudes would be buttressed against influences in the environment.[23]

The roots of Zionism are deeper when they are an outgrowth of early socialization processes. A home with an intensive Jewish atmosphere may create a predisposition favorable to later Zionist development; if both parents are Zionists, and are so in more than a merely formal sense, they may exercise a formative influence on Zionist attitudes. Similarly, the Jewish school may provide the foundations of the kind of Jewish education on which, as we have observed, Zionism can most effectively build. But if these influences are to persist and to be extended, the young Jew has to become a member of an organized Zionist group—and this will most appropriately be a group composed of his peers.

There are, of course, cases of individuals who become and remain Zionists without social support. (Even here, the lack of social support is usually more apparent than real—such individuals generally have some source of reference.) The general rule, however, is that Zionist education requires Zionist groups. Becoming a Zionist is, in fact, a process of growing into a group which is Zionist.

While general Jewish organizations may introduce Zionist elements into their programs, they cannot fulfill the functions served by a Zionist organization with clearly defined Zionist norms. Moreover, the very act of joining a group designated as Zionist implies a psychological commitment. Even if the Zionism of the individual has limited content, the commitment is important in that it indicates an identification with certain forces in Jewish life rather than with others.

This does not mean that no Zionist educational effort should be directed towards the members of general Jewish organizations. But this effort will have only limited outcomes unless the organization itself becomes Zionist or the members join Zionist units.

There are Zionists who can be said to have grown up as such, and they almost automatically react in terms of a Zionist orientation in many phases of Jewish life. Weizmann and Herzl have often been contrasted on this score. Weizmann had his roots deep in the Jewish life of Eastern Europe, and his Zionism was an organic growth, with cultural and spiritual dimensions to it. Herzl came late onto the Jewish scene, and his Zionism had more of a purely political character. Weizmann sought to develop a Zionism which would synthesize the practical work of settlement, cultural activities, and the political effort. In fact, in the early years of the century, Weizmann wrote critically of some of the Zionists in Western Europe whose Zionism he described as being "completely devoid of Jewish content, unstable, wavering and hollow."[24]

Ideology does not play a significant role in American life, and there are limitations to the extent to which an ideological Zionist commitment will be embraced by large sections of the community. The possibility does exist, however, of educating small groups to an acceptance of a Zionist ideology. Even in the heyday of Zionism in Eastern Europe, "halutziut," pioneering settlement, was embraced by relatively small groups only, but they gave direction to the movement as a whole and set the sights for wider circles.

A program for the development of Zionist ideology need not, as some fear, disrupt the broad consensus which exists around support for Israel. The presence of nuclei of dedicated Zionists in the community may serve to move this consensus to a higher level, even if it still falls short of the fuller ideological commitment.

A constant interaction between such Zionist nuclei in the Diaspora and parallel groups in Israel around the common unifying theme which their Zionism provides would be to the benefit of both. It could be the task of these groups to restore to Zionist thought the intellectual ferment, the sense of zest and challenge which is necessary to make it the directing force which it could be in Jewish life.

The Zionism of Israel's Youth

Just as in the Diaspora no clear distinction is drawn between Zionism and support for Israel, so in Israel the term Zionism is often used to include all that relates to the upbuilding of the country. The Zionist outlook of the founders of the state bore the imprint of the ideologies they had brought with them from the countries of their origin and the pioneering ("halutzic") immigration from Eastern Europe in particular had a formative influence on the Zionism which developed in Israel. The years following the establishment of the State were years of immersion in the tasks of immigrant absorption, land settlement, and defense, and little attention was given to the ideological implications of Zionism. The Zionism of the generation born in Israel still has a vague, amorphous character, and it becomes necessary to consider what elements enter into it.

It was natural that a people returning to a homeland from which it had been exiled for centuries should place the emphasis on the love of the land in the education of the younger generation. A popular form of such education were the "tiyulim," the excursions into the countryside, exploring every nook and cranny, often with Bible in hand. There is, however, a growing recognition that it is necessary to foster a love not only for the land but for the Jewish people in the countries of the dispersion. The Hebrew literature which had negated the galut has also impaired for the young generation the image of the Jew who remained in what was regarded as a degrading condition. Eloquent expression was given to this problem by the third president of the State of Israel, Zalman Shazar, on the occasion of his inauguration. In the Diaspora, he observed, a people yearned through the centuries for its distant homeland; the young generation of Israelis who have grown up in that homeland are now required to define their relationship to a people in the far-flung lands of the Diaspora.

The feeling of Jewish interdependence which exists among a large section of Israeli youth provides a foundation on which the school, the youth movements, and other educational agencies can proceed to build further. The Ministry of Education is indeed revising curricula to allow for a fuller attention to the study of Zionism and of contemporary Jewry. The extensive educational services of the Israel army are placing special emphasis on the subject of Zionism; their publications, their training courses, their seminars for soldiers of all ranks have Zionism as a key topic. The climate of opinion that now prevails in Israel—further stimulated by the reaction to the U.N. resolution of November 1975 stigmatizing Zionism—constitutes a favorable background for these educational efforts.

Correlates of the Self-Definition as Zionist

The great majority of Israelis regard themselves as Zionists. In a survey conducted during July-September, 1973, by the Israel Institute of Applied Social Research, 82 percent of the urban population over the age of twenty declared themselves Zionists. When the survey was replicated in October, after the outbreak of the Yom Kippur War, 90 percent so declared themselves.[25]

In our 1974 study of a countrywide sample of 1,875 eleventh graders 80 percent declared themselves Zionists. It may be assumed that if the study was carried out after the U.N. resolution of November, 1975, the percentage defining themselves as Zionists would have been even higher.

Our study shows that the percentage of Zionists is higher among the religiously observant (93 percent) than among the nonreligious (72 percent), with the traditionalists (80 percent) occupying an intermediate position. Significant differences appear between students declaring themselves Zionists and their non-Zionist peers in each of the three categories.

The Zionists rank higher than non-Zionists on all criteria of Jewish and Israeli identity. There is, in fact, a close correlation between Jewishness, Israeliness, and Zionism. Thus, the valence of being Jewish and of being Israeli is higher for the Zionists. (Tables S7.1 and S7.2) and they, more than the non-Zionists, regard their Jewishness and Israeliness as interrelated (Table S7.3). Zionists, more than non-Zionists, regard themselves as an inseparable part of the Jewish people, although it should be noted that on this as on other questions a small minority do not subscribe to what is a basic Zionist proposition despite their self-definition as Zionists. (Table S7.4).

Of particular importance is the substantial difference in the strength of the Jewish and Israeli identity of the Zionist students in the nonreligious category as compared with their non-Zionist fellow students in that category. On some of the scales they outrank not only the non-Zionists in their own category but also the non-Zionists in the traditionalist category.

The Zionism of the young Israelis differs from that of their parents or grandparents, many of whom know the galut from personal experience with it. The "revolt against the galut," the desire to terminate their condition of dependence on the goodwill of the non-Jewish majority, was a significant element in the Zionist outlook of the older Zionists. The Zionism of the younger generation is largely Israel-centered. When asked in what way they were Zionists, some of the young Israelis we interviewed in our study replied that they were such by virtue of the fact that they were living in Israel, were ready to serve in the army and fulfill all the duties of citizenship. They were equating Zionism with Israeli patriotism. Others did indeed go beyond this and declared that their Zionism found expression in their desire to see more Jews immigrate to Israel and in their readiness to do what they could to aid in the process of "klita," the integration of the new immigrants. Still others came closer to a more comprehensive definition when they stated that their Zionism was reflected in their conception of Israel as a Jewish state designed to serve as the homeland of all Jews. When asked what Zionism meant in the case of Jews abroad, the majority equated Zionism with aliya and a minority with support for Israel.

The popular impression existed some years ago that Zionism had become a term of derision among Israel's youth. While this impression was an exaggeration of the situation, it did derive from the fact that a number of young Israelis tended to label as "Zionist" any excessively declamatory statement about patriotic intention. There is little trace of this derision at the present time. Zionism has a variety of meanings for Israeli youth but the connotation is generally positive. At times, indeed, the connotation is too broad. It embraces all that is idealistic and patriotic and deprives Zionism of its particular meaning.

The Zionist Perspective

While significance attaches to the declaration of the majority of the young Israelis that they are Zionists, their Zionism generally lacks a clearly defined content and a proper orientation to the Jewish people in the Diaspora. In terms of the analysis we have developed in this chapter, we would submit that what distinguishes a Zionist whose Zionism has this content from a non-Zionist in Israel is the perspective in which the Zionist views the Jewish state; he sees it as part of the Jewish historical continuity, as the homeland of the entire Jewish people, and as having as its primary function the redemption of that people. Nathan Rotenstreich has expressed this view of Zionism in the following words: "Zionism is not the state itself nor even what is done inside its borders, but the historic meaning the state has for Jews."[26]

In recent years Israel's foes have launched a vehement propaganda campaign disputing the right of the Jewish people to its land. By way of reaction, increased attention is being given in the education of the young Israeli to the exposition of the Jewish historical association with the land of Israel. But this has to be seen as only one item in a Zionist education and not as its full substance.

Inside Israeli circles an intense debate is proceeding as to what parts of the land presently under Israel's control should constitute its inalienable possession and what parts, if any, may be ceded as part of a future peace settlement. Without detracting from the importance of this issue or entering into the merits of the arguments advanced by the contending parties, we would state that it does not appear to us to relate, as some maintain, to the essence of the Zionist perspective. Zionists may, and do, range themselves on either side of the debate for reasons which are not incompatible with the Zionist perspective.

What has been said in this chapter about the elements of a Zionist ideology in the Diaspora applies *mutatis mutandis* to Zionism in Israel. Zionism in Israel, like Zionism in the Diaspora, has to be based on a recognition of the unity of the Jewish people and of the central role of Israel as the Jewish state in the life of all sections of that people. The propositions which follow are a restatement of what is in essence contained in the Jerusalem Program as it would apply to the Zionism of a Jew located in Israel.

(a) The Jews of Israel and the Jews of all countries of the Diaspora belong to one interdependent Jewish people and share the responsibility for their common future.

(b) Israel is the homeland not only of the Jews already resident in it but of the entire Jewish people, and the right inheres in every Jew to come to settle in this homeland.

(c) A primary responsibility of Israel as the Jewish state is "the ingathering of the exiles" ("kibbutz galuyot").

(d) Israel represents the continuity in the present and into the future of the Jewish historical tradition and is called upon to develop a Jewish culture which is in accord with that tradition and which should be a source of inspiration to Jews throughout the world.

(e) It is Israel's duty to aid in the preservation of the Jewish identity of communities everywhere and to extend them whatever assistance it can in the development of Jewish education and cultural life.

(f) Israel represents not only its own citizens but the Jewish people in the councils of nations. A threat to the security and welfare of any community is a matter of direct concern to it.

The test of a Zionist in Israel would be the acceptance of, and action in accordance with these propositions.

The Aversion to "Ideology"

In his essay on "Ideology as a Cultural System," Clifford Geertz has properly criticized the tendency of social scientists to adopt an a priori pejorative view of "ideology." It should be the task of the social scientist to subject to scientific examination the function of ideologies as "maps of problematic social reality and matrices for the creation of collective conscience."[27] Instead of projecting a blanket aversion to all ideologies, he should evaluate each ideology on its merits. He may then find—in the light of the value premises which underlie his examination—that while there are some ideologies which are morally repugnant, there are others deserving his commendation.

In our view Zionism is an ideology based on liberal, humanistic principles. Its analysis of the Jewish condition and the course of action it proposed have, moreover, stood the test of historical experience. Geertz has referred to the attempt of ideologies "to render otherwise incomprehensible social situations meaningful, to so construe them as to make it possible to act purposefully within them."[28] We have sought in this chapter to sketch the contours of a Zionist ideology which we believe can provide this purposeful direction in the complex, changing situations which face a Jewish people located in a world in turmoil.

NOTES

1. Cf., B. Halpern, "Zion in the Mind of American Jews," in D. Sidorsky, ed., *The Future of the Jewish Community in America* (New York: Basic Books, 1973), 22-45, pp. 37-38.

2. D. Sidorsky, *The Future of the Jewish Community in America,* a Task Force Report (New York: The American Jewish Committee, 1972), p. 65.

3. Ibid., p. 66.

4. M. Sklare and J. Greenblum, *Jewish Identity on the Suburban Frontier* (New York: Basic Books, 1967), p. 225; C.S. Liebman, *The Ambivalent American Jew* (Philadelphia: Jewish Publication Society, 1973), pp. 93-94; C.I. Waxman, "The Centrality of Israel in American Jewish Life: A Sociological Analysis," *Judaism* 25 (1976), 175-187; L.J. Fein et al., *Reform is a Verb* (New York: UAHC, 1972). In a nationwide Gallup poll of American Jews commissioned by *Newsweek* magazine in 1971, 95 percent responded in the affirmative to the question, "Do you think the U.S. should help Israel with diplomatic support and military equipment?" *Newsweek,* March 1, 1971.

5. D. Sidorsky, "The End of Ideology and American Zionism." Paper presented at a meeting of the Study Circle in the Home of the President of Israel, February 1976, p. 29.

6. For anthologies of Zionist thought, see, A. Hertzberg, ed., *The Zionist Idea: A Historical Analysis and Reader* (New York: Herzl Press, 1960); L. Lewisohn, ed., *Rebirth: A Book of Modern Jewish Thought* (New York: Harper, 1935). A comprehensive historical study of Zionist thought is contained in the volume by Ben Halpern, *The Idea of the Jewish State* (Cambridge, Mass.: Harvard University Press, 1969). An excellent summary of the main trends in Zionist thought is that by I. Kolatt, "Theories of Israel Nationalism," *In the Dispersion* 7 (1967), 13-50. A significant contribution to the understanding of the development of Zionist thought in the latter part of the nineteenth century is a recent book by D. Vital, *The Origins of Zionism* (Oxford: Clarendon, 1975).

7. Y.F. Baer, *Galut* (New York: Schocken, 1947).

8. N. Rotenstreich, "Are We in Exile?" *Dimensions in American Judaism* 5 (1971), 18-19.

9. H. Greenberg, *The Inner Eye: Selected Essays* (New York: Jewish Frontier Publishing Assoc., 1964), Vol. I, p. 71.

10. For an analysis of the differing views on "galut" in American Jewry, see, B. Halpern, *The American Jew: A Zionist Analysis* (New York: Herzl Foundation, 1956).

11. Prominent among proponents of the "negation of the galut" have been the writers Jacob Klatzkin, Micah Joseph Berdichevski, and Joseph Hayyim Brenner. For extracts of their writings in English translation, see, Hertzberg, *The Zionist Idea,* op. cit., pp. 291-327.

12. "The remarkable lack of self-generating, self-disciplined, organized people's movements in America is a significant historical fact usually overlooked by American historians and social scientists." G. Myrdal, *An American Dilemma* (New York: Harper, 1944), p. 712.

13. A.A. Cohen, "Beyond Politics, Visions," *Congress Bi-Weekly* 39 (1972), 33-42, p. 40.

14. This corresponds to what was termed "Gegenwartsarbeit" in the early Zionist congresses. What we are suggesting is that educational and other activities be fostered in terms of a Zionist orientation attuned to the needs of the communities in the Diaspora.

15. B. Halpern, "Anti-Semitism in the Perspective of Jewish History," in C.H. Stember, et al., *Jews in the Mind of America* (New York: Basic Books, 1966), 273-301.

16. For a critical review of the approach reflected in some of the studies of anti-Semitism in the United States, see, L.S. Dawidowicz, "Can Anti-semitism Be Measured?" *Commentary* 50 (1970), pp. 36-43.

17. Selig Brodetsky, a former member of the World Zionist Executive.

18. L. Coser, *The Functions of Social Conflict* (Glencoe, Ill.: Free Press, 1964), p. 151 and p. 154.

19. Cf., Z. Yaron, "Old and New in Zionism," *Betfuzot Hagolah* 56/57 (1971), pp. 7-12. (In Hebrew.)

20. Greenberg, op. cit., p. 83.

21. B. Lazare, "Notes on a Conversion," in Lewisohn, ed., *Rebirth*, op. cit., 47-51, p. 47.

22. S.N. Herman, "Mesilot laZiyonut Hehalutzit" (Pathways to Chalutzic Zionism), in G. Hanoch, ed., *HaZiyonut be-Sha'a Zu* (Zionism in the Contemporary Period), (Jerusalem: Zionist Organization, 1951), 131-137. (In Hebrew.)

23. Ibid.

24. *The Letters and Papers of Chaim Weizmann,* M.W. Weisgal, general ed., Vol. III, Series A, Sept. 1903-Dec. 1904 (London: Oxford University Press, 1972). Weizmann writes in a letter to Ussishkin: "Whereas on our side the political forms of the movement were being continually shaped into an organic force as the result of our Jewish content, for the West Europeans Zionism remained a cliche, completely devoid of Jewish content, unstable, wavering and hollow, finding its highest expression in the so-called diplomacy, and in the 'Jewish Statism' that smells of philanthropy," p. 82. Weizmann was referring to what he terms "the theorizing behind the East Africa project." The "Jewish Statists" are those who would set up a Jewish state anywhere, not necessarily in Eretz Israel.

25. S. Levy and A. L. Gutmann, "The Jewish Identification of Israelis during and after the War," in M. Davis, ed., *Israel and the Jewish People: During and After the Yom Kippur War* (Jerusalem: Hasifriya Hazionit, 1976), 297-308. (In Hebrew.)

26. N. Rotenstreich, "Between the State and Zionism," *Moznaim* 41(1975), 222-228, p. 223. (In Hebrew.)

27. C. Geertz, *The Interpretation of Cultures* (New York: Basic Books, 1973) p. 220.

28. Ibid.

Chapter 8

JEWISH IDENTITY AND THE DECISION

TO SETTLE IN ISRAEL

It can be readily understood why Jews whose existence is threatened or whose freedom is curtailed in their country of origin should immigrate to Israel, whose gates are open to them and where they can live freely as Jews. But what moves Jews to leave a country of freedom and relative affluence, such as the United States, which is not a country of emigration but rather a country which attracts immigrants? Similarly, why do Jews from countries such as Britain or South Africa choose Israel when they have some choice about the country to which they wish to immigrate?

We shall begin by considering the motivational pattern of such aliya from the free countries, with particular attention to the part played by Jewish identity factors. This will bring us to a discussion of the decision process and of the psychological consequences of the act of decision. We shall also examine how Israelis view the attitudes of their fellow Jews towards settling in Israel.

The Motivational Pattern

The analysis of an individual's decision to settle in Israel reveals a complex motivational pattern into which a number of factors enter. Such analysis requires reference—in terms of our field theoretical approach—to the characteristics of the field as a whole.

THE BACKGROUND SITUATION

The problem of how the background of a situation influences behavior in an immediate situation has been the subject of an illuminating study by Barker, Dembo, and Lewin. In seeking to define background and immediate situations they write:

> The regions of the life space which constitute the background are, according to our definition, not a part of the activity regions in which the individual is involved at the time . . . On the other hand the background still influences the behaviour in some way. It cannot be omitted from the life space, if one is to be able to derive the actual behaviour. The individual behaves as if he were in an overlapping situation consisting of both the immediate and the background situation, the background usually having less relative potency.[1]

The decision of the individual about settlement in Israel is taken within a background setting constituted by several situations.

(1) The social, political, or economic conditions prevailing in a particular country may stimulate or may discourage emigration. Emigration from a country is more likely in a period of social unrest or political upheaval or economic depression. In recent years the unstable situation in countries such as Argentina and Rhodesia has resulted in increased emigration, but whether the emigrants choose Israel as their destination has depended upon the presence of other factors in the motivational pattern.

(2) Factors of direct Jewish pertinence may serve as the background against which a decision to settle in Israel is taken. They may relate to the particular community (e.g., the eruption in it of

the more threatening forms of anti-Semitism) or they may be circumstances common to Jewish communities everywhere (e.g., the impact of the Six Day War which reactivated the memory of the Holocaust).

The years following the Six Day War marked an unprecedented increase in aliya from the United States. At the same time, it has been pointed out that "not all the increase can be attributed simply to the Six Day War and its aftermath, since these patterns were emerging well before June, 1967."[2] Indeed, what the climate of these years did in many cases was to precipitate incipient decisions which were in the making for one or other of the reasons we shall discuss.

(3) In the background influencing the individual's decision are also the norms prevalent in the community—or that section of it which serves as his source of reference—on the subject of aliya. There are indications that American Jewish attitudes—both in Zionist and non-Zionist circles—have become more favorable across the years, although there is still evidence of ambivalence on the subject.[3]

THE INTERPLAY OF PSYCHOLOGICAL FORCES IN THE IMMEDIATE SITUATION

The background situation plays an important part in determining the extent of immigration to Israel and the facility with which a decision on the subject is taken. But it becomes necessary to explore why in a given social milieu, such as that of the United States, some individuals take a decision to immigrate while most others do not.

A Zionist ideological commitment, in the fuller sense of the term as we have defined it, implies a readiness to settle in Israel. But the consideration of the pros and cons of aliya may begin at a stage in the development of a pro-Israel orientation when it still falls short of a specific Zionist commitment. Many of the members of Zionist organizations never take the decision, although their pro-Israel orientation may cause them to ponder such decision. Whether a decision is reached by the individual depends upon the outcome of the interplay of three types of psychological forces.

(1) Driving forces moving in the direction of the goal region.
(2) Opposing forces moving in the opposite direction, away from the goal region.
(3) Restraining forces (or barriers) arresting locomotion into the goal region.[4]

The driving forces are of two kinds—those arising from a desire to leave the country of origin (popularly termed "push") and those arising from the attraction of the country to which the individual decides to immigrate ("pull"). When a person is satisfied with life in his country of origin, he usually does not forsake it merely because of the attraction of another country. The study of migrations reveals the existence in all cases of some sort of dissatisfaction which the migrant hopes to overcome by moving to another country.[5]

Is this also the case in regard to the decision of Jews in the United States to settle in Israel? The fact that there is no obvious compulsion on them to leave the United States and that they leave it not for just another country but for one country in particular naturally focuses attention on the pull, the unique attraction Israel has for Jews. A proper understanding of the aliya decision, however, requires that attention be given to the presence of a push, even if it is obscured by the salience of the pull.

When asked for the reasons for their decision to proceed to Israel, American immigrants do not readily mention factors relating to the push; it is regarded as a "negative" reason for aliya and is accordingly seen as less socially laudable than the "positive" reason which the pull constitutes. Moreover, as the time of aliya draws near, the attractiveness of Israel becomes a more dominant factor in his consciousness. This is a known psychological phenomenon; as a person approaches the goal region, both its valence and salience increase.[6]

The Nature of the Push and the Pull

What, then, is the nature of this push?
In our studies of American students in 1965, and again in the 1970s, we found that they were aware of the existence of

anti-Jewish discrimination. The students in 1965 did not take a serious view of such manifestations of anti-Semitism as they had encountered; indeed, the evidence indicates that anti-Semitism in the United States was ebbing in those years.[7] The students in the seventies take a more serious view, and tend more frequently to view manifestations of anti-Semitism against the background of a reactivated memory of the Holocaust. But they, too, rarely speak of a direct encounter with the grosser forms of anti-Semitism, and this problem does not feature with any prominence in their discussions of the motivation for aliya. What is evident in the interviews with them is the more subtle unease which members of a Jewish minority group experience about their position in a non-Jewish majority culture, and which derives from one or more of three sources.

(1) *A desire to live what they describe as a more completely Jewish life,* and consequent dissatisfaction at the impingement of the majority culture on the full expression of their Jewishness. The more important his Jewishness is to him, the more likely is a Jew to be concerned with these incursions of the majority culture. In our studies this source of dissatisfaction is particularly evident among the more religiously observant students. The following remarks by students are typical:

> To me Zionism is the making of a meaningful contribution to the development of a creative Jewish life style in Israel. That doesn't necessarily mean aliyah for everybody, but for me it does. To be consciously involved on a day to day basis, to have everything I do be part of my Jewish expression—that's what's important to me.

*   *   *

> Life in the States is too big, too fast, too confusing, and too, well, hard to keep track of. It's hard to hold on to being Jewish—it gets lost in everything else you're doing. Here you can hold on to it without worrying, because there's no where for it to go. Or maybe I should say, wherever it goes, that's Jewish too.

*   *   *

I want to give fuller expression to my Jewishness—to lead a more religious life and openly proclaim my Jewish pride. I don't want to have to feel self-conscious or apologetic about my being different from everyone else—like I did in the States.

Some of the students look at the situation in terms of a future time perspective. They wish to live in a Jewish society in which they can feel that their children would grow up as Jews and remain in the Jewish fold. The increasing rate of intermarriage in the United States has heightened apprehensions on this score.

(2) *Sensitivity to exclusion at certain points from, or non-acceptance by, the majority society,* even if there has been no encounter with the grosser forms of anti-Semitism. The more sensitive a person a Jew is, the more likely he is to resent a situation of this kind. Moreover, he needs to feel that he belongs, and this nonacceptance undermines his feeling of belonging to the society around him.

I feel Israel is where I belong as a Jew, that is my home in a way no place else in the world can be. I believe it is the only place where a Jew can live a normal self-respecting life without pressures from Gentiles.

* * *

American society never accepted me as a Jew. I can't say I was ever denied anything because of it, but I noticed—especially in my relationships at college—that being Jewish meant being different, and in a negative kind of way too.

(3) *A less frequently mentioned source of discontent is that experienced by some identifying Jews* who are not religious and as a result have difficulty in finding form and content for their Jewishness in the American situation, where the expressions of such Jewishness have a pronouncedly religious character. They do not always find that their activities in the United States in support of Israel substitute for the missing content. In a sense they are in search of a meaningful secular identity.

Here in Israel I don't have to demonstrate my Jewishness by performing rituals or belonging to organizations or attending demonstrations for Israel. My *mere presence* here is an expression of Jewishness that is not only meaningful to me personally, but, in the long run, I think to the Jewish people too.

*   *   *

I never go to a synagogue in Israel, I don't keep kasher or anything, but I know I'm Jewish here and everybody else knows it too. In the States I also wasn't religious at all, but there I didn't have any other way to be Jewish. I could never see the U.J.A. as really a valid way—at least not for myself—of expressing my Judaism, but here, even though right now I'm only a student and not contributing to the society in any tangible way, I feel like I'm helping Israel just by my presence, and that I'm a real part of the people here—a Jewish people.

There are different ways in which a Jew may react to these sources of unease. If he sees them as inherent in the American environment, but not in another environment provided by a Jewish majority, that other environment will gain in attraction for him, more particularly so since it is the Jewish homeland to which he may already have an emotional attachment. It is the convergence of the factor of push in this sense with the factor of pull that produces a decision on aliya.

The push might also be due to idiosyncratic factors in the background of the particular individual, or to economic factors, or conceivably to a distaste for general features of American society (e.g., revolt against the "establishment") which do not relate directly to majority-minority relations. In the groups we studied, however, it was unease about their position as members of a Jewish minority group which stood out as the dominant factor in the push. The satisfactions that they find in Israel constitute the reverse side of the coin to the dissatisfactions they experience qua Jews in the non-Jewish environment. It is these Jewish satisfactions which Israel is in a position to provide. There may be differences of opinion about the extent to which Israel radiates a cultural influence to communities abroad, but it is clear that as a

Jewish majority society Israel renders possible a life as fully Jewish as the individual wishes to lead and gives him the opportunity of self-fulfillment as a Jew.

If the dissatisfaction has its source in something unrelated to the individual's life as a Jew, it is doubtful whether he will find more contentment in Israel than he experienced in the United States. For a small number—by virtue of their training in some of the Zionist youth movements—a major source of satisfaction may be the collective living in a kibbutz not available to them in the United States. But in these cases, too, if there should be disappointment with the kibbutz, it may result in their leaving Israel—unless the Jewish factor also played a part in the motivational background.

The close, mutually reinforcing relationship between the push and the pull has to be borne in mind in any analysis of the aliya decision. The push is not of a kind which would have impelled the immigrants to leave America for a country other than Israel; the material conditions of their lives in the United States were in most cases more comfortable than those which awaited them in Israel. What happens is that the special Jewish quality which Israel is seen to possess as the Jewish homeland and as a majority Jewish society heightens their consciousness of what they lack as a minority living in a non-Jewish majority culture.

The relative weight of the factors of push and pull will vary among individuals. There are some Zionists for whom the desire to participate in the building of a Jewish homeland is so overwhelming that it seems difficult to speak in their case of anything but the pull. And what may be uppermost in the mind of an Orthodox Jew in settling in Israel is that in so doing he is fulfilling a religious commandment. But generally, push and pull intertwine and interact in the motivational pattern.

The Change in the Balance of Forces

In our 1972 study, American students visiting Israel were asked to weight each factor in a list of thirteen (Table 8.1)

Tables 8.1 and 8.2: Factors influencing aliya of American students
(n = 272)
("In considering the question of aliya certain factors play (or have played) a part in one's thinking on the subject both for and against. Listed below are a number of such factors. Please indicate the extent to which each factor plays (or played) a part in your considerations by encircling one of the numbers as follows:

(1) A very large role
(2) A large role
(3) A medium role
(4) A small role only
(5) No role at all"

Table 8.1: Factors which played or play a part in favor of a decision to settle (listed in order of weight attached by students intent on aliya)

	Division of students according to aliya intentions		
	"yes" or "likely"	"possibly"	"unlikely" or "no"
	(means)		
I have a sense of belonging in Israel	1.6	2.2	3.2
I feel at home as a Jew in Israel	1.7	2.2	3.2
I can live a more completely Jewish life in Israel	1.9	2.3	3.4
Israel gives a sense of purposeful existence	2.0	2.4	3.1
I feel Israel needs my services	2.5	2.8	3.3
I am concerned about certain aspects of life in the country from which I come	2.6	2.5	3.0
In Israel I am a part of a majority rather than a minority	2.6	3.0	3.4
I like the people in Israel	2.7	3.0	3.6
There will be no prejudice or discrimination against me as a Jew in Israel	2.8	2.8	2.9
I like certain aspects of life in Israel	2.8	3.2	2.9
In Israel I can lead a fuller religious life	3.0	3.4	3.9
I am concerned about anti-Semitism in the country from which I come	3.2	3.5	3.9
I can live a Jewish life in Israel without being religious	3.6	3.4	4.0

Table 8.2: Factors which played or play a part against a decision to settle (listed in order of weight attached by students intent on aliya)

	Division of students according to aliya intentions		
	"yes" or "likely"	"possibly"	"unlikely" or "no"
	(means)		
I would not like to leave family	2.3	2.1	2.5
I would not like to leave friends	2.5	2.3	2.4
America offers me better educational opportunities	2.9	2.2	2.3
America offers me better occupational opportunities	3.1	2.3	2.6
I feel American Jewry needs my services	3.3	3.2	3.2
I have a sense of belonging in America	3.7	3.1	2.5
I feel at home as a Jew in America	3.7	3.1	2.5
I prefer living with Americans rather than with Israelis	3.8	3.4	2.6
I would not feel at home as an American in Israel	4.1	3.6	3.2
I like certain aspects of life in America	4.1	4.4	4.8
I am likely to have difficulties with Hebrew	4.4	3.9	4.2
America gives a sense of purposeful existence	4.4	4.0	3.5
I feel America needs my services	4.4	4.2	3.5
	N=138	N=86	N=48

according to the part it played in their consideration of the question of aliya. Students intent on aliya (who had responded "yes" or "likely" to a question on aliya intentions) placed at the head of the list three factors representing driving forces of a Jewish character:

I have a sense of belonging in Israel.
I feel at home as a Jew in Israel.
I can live a more completely Jewish life in Israel.

The decision evolves when the driving forces achieve a relatively higher potency than the opposing forces. The implementation of the decision, however, may then depend upon overcoming the restraining forces, the barriers or obstacles in the path. So, when asked to indicate the extent to which a further list of factors played a part against a decision (Table 8.2), students intent on aliya no longer attached importance to the opposing forces of an ideological character but attached most weight to the following restraining forces:

I would not like to leave family.
I would not like to leave friends.
America offers me better educational opportunities.
America offers me better occupational opportunities.

On the other hand, students who had no intention of immigration (who responded "no" or "unlikely" to the question on aliya intentions) gave equal prominence to the role of opposing forces such as the following:

I feel at home as a Jew in America.
I have a sense of belonging in America.
I prefer living with Americans rather than with Israelis.

The Jewish Identity Factors

The subjects of our research were young students, but other studies which include older subjects provide confirmation of our findings. The importance of the Jewish identity factors is reflected in the fact that the proportion of religiously observant—in particular Orthodox—immigrants was appreciably greater than their proportion in the American Jewish community. An analysis of the statistics for the years 1969-1970 shows that 37 percent of the American immigrants defined themselves as Orthodox, 20 percent as Conservative, 22 percent as Reform, and 21 percent as "other." In a comprehensive review of the demographical data for those years, Goldscheider points out that "fully forty-six percent of American olim define themselves either as religious or very religious, and about one-fourth define themselves as not at all religious. Not unexpectedly, a larger proportion defined their parental home as religious or very religious than so defined themselves. Over sixty percent of the American olim came from homes that were in their view religious or very religious, and only 14 percent came from homes that were not at all religious."[8] Despite the trend across generations towards secularization "fully forty-three percent of third generations Americans on aliya define themselves as religious or very religious."[9]

While the number of visiting students at most institutions of higher learning declined during 1975, a survey indicated that the number coming to study at the "yeshivot," the religious academies, had increased. The survey noted that "despite the fact that the most of the Yeshiva students come as visiting students, 50 percent of those who began their studies five years ago have settled in the country."[10]

Individuals with an intensive Jewish education are more likely than others to immigrate to Israel. The statistical analysis by Goldscheider shows that 63 percent of the American immigrants had enjoyed a Jewish education of six or more years; one-third of all American olim attended a Hebrew day school or yeshiva. Goldscheider concludes that "these data suggest that exposure to intensive Jewish education is an important factor determining American aliya—either because intensive Jewish education is an indicator of heightened Jewish-Zionist consciousness and/or because Jewish education imparts the religio-Zionist ideology of aliya."[11]

A study by Horowitz and Frenkel of immigrants in reception centers from the USSR, the Latin American countries, and the English-speaking countries reports that the two factors cited by the immigrants from all three regions as playing a significant part in their decision were the desire to live among Jews and to bring up their children among Jews. While the immigrants from the USSR cited anti-semitism as another factor of importance, the immigrants from the Latin American and the English-speaking countries did not attribute such importance to it.[12]

A variety of motives—some bound up with a developed Jewish consciousness, others not—determine the decision of a Jew to leave the USSR. When the emigrants reach the transit station at Vienna, a number of them are in a position to exercise a choice: They can proceed to Israel or to another country, such as the United States. A study of these emigrants indicates that the stronger the sense of Jewish identity, the more likely they are to make Israel their choice.[13]

The Decision as Culmination of a Process

The chain of attitudinal development leading to an individual's decision to settle in Israel is generally as follows: "Being Jewish" is central in his life space and has positive valence for him, a linkage is established between "being Jewish" and Israel, the individual becomes increasingly aware of the inadequacies of life as a Jew outside of Israel and is attracted by the Jewish satisfactions which life in Israel can provide. The process is expedited, and often even generated, when the attitudes interact with an ideological orientation which points to the importance of the individual's participation in the building of the Jewish homeland. It is, however, generally not sufficient that the individual recognizes that "Israel needs Jews to build it and accordingly needs me;" he has to reach the further conclusion that "I as a Jew need Israel."

The decision is not—and cannot from its nature be—a sudden one. Even in regard to relatively simple decisions, experiments have shown that decision time increases with the importance of the decision.[14] The transplantation of an individual's life from one country to another cannot be decided in a single leap; it is the culmination of a process of development.

The distinction between *intention* and *decision* should be borne in mind. At the stage of intention, which precedes decision, counterarguments or contrary considerations have not yet been definitely dismissed and there may be a certain vacillation between alternatives. The following statement by a student is a characteristic reflection of the dilemma experienced at this stage: "I can't tell whether or not I'm going to live in Israel. Intellectually I know I should, Jewishly it feels better here in Israel—but America, that's where I was born, I know the language and the society, the way things work, and most importantly, that's where my family is. I really don't know where I'll end up—all I do know is that I'll be missing out on something in either place." Decision means that one of the alternatives has acquired dominant potency permanently and vacillation ceases; a choice has been finally made.[15]

In a study of students visiting Israel we found that many of them, favorably disposed to settlement, were still in the stage of intention at the end of their year's stay—there were still obstacles to be overcome and considerations to be weighed up when they returned to the United States.[16] In following over a period of time the progression towards a decision on the part of these students, we were impressed by the gradual step-wise character of this progression.[17] It becomes clear why general exhortations to settle in Israel have so little practical result; a person who has not passed through the prior development which is necessary for the decision is psychologically not in a position to respond to such exhortations.

The decision is not easily reached by the individual alone and unaided. It is greatly facilitated if he enjoys group support. In discussing the protracted process leading to a student's decision to study medicine, Merton has shown how the social context affects the degree of stress attending the decision to specialize in one branch of medicine rather than another. "The student who decides to specialize in psychiatry in one school, where great value is attached to this field, will be in a substantially different social and psychological situation than the *same kind* of student making this decision in another school, in which psychiatry is often derogated. This may serve, if only by way of tentative allusion, to suggest that the same career decisions will have differing psychological significance depending upon the social context."[18] Just as the social context is important in the case of a career decision, it is even more so in the case of an aliya decision. The group support may come from a friendship circle or from an organized group. Where this is an organized group, such as a Zionist organization, it would be unreasonable to demand a declaration about aliya at the time the individual joins. Such a demand precludes the possibility of his passing through the very development which has to precede a decision.

There may be—and should be—groups composed of those who have taken the decision (such as are the "garinim," the nuclei of settlement groups). In these groups they can indeed find the mutual support they need not only at the time of the decision, but after it. Such groups can—and often do—become highly cohesive units making demands on their members and deeply influencing them. But there must also be groups which do not require the person to be a full-fledged Zionist at the time of entry and which do not require of him a declaration of intention to settle in Israel. These groups provide the conditions for the initiation of the developmental process which leads to a Zionist orientation and may eventually lead to aliya. The ideological climate of the group will determine what proportion of its members are likely to take an affirmative decision about aliya.

CONSEQUENCES OF THE DECISION

Once a decision has been taken, the individual will tend to seek out facts which are consonant with his decision. In terms of one of the postulates of the theory of cognitive dissonance, as Festinger has stated it, "post-decision dissonance may be reduced by increasing the attractiveness of the chosen alternative, decreasing the attractiveness of the unchosen alternatives, or both."[19] This means that the individual is more likely to focus on the favorable features of Israeli life. In our studies American students who had decided to settle had a more favorable stereotype of Israelis and were more favorably disposed to Israel and Israelis than were their fellow students who had not taken such decision. (Table S8.3). The favorableness of these attitudes may have contributed to the decision, but it is also conceivable that they are focusing on those features in the situation which are consonant with their decision.[20]

When the decision has been taken and the new immigrant reaches Israel, the pressing problems of absorption in his new abode result in a change in the salience of the immediate satisfactions he seeks to obtain. What particularly matters at this stage may be the satisfactoriness of his job and the housing facilities. The newcomer may often experience many vexations in this area. Whether he perseveres and overcomes them or leaves the country may depend on a variety of factors, but studies indicate that two of these factors generally are of importance: (1) The social support he receives from family or friends. This may account for the fact that the single newcomer is more likely to leave than he who comes with a family. (2) The priority given in his scale of values to the Jewish satisfactions which Israel can provide. So Antonovsky and Katz in their study of the absorption of American immigrants observe: "On investigating the respondents' reasons for immigrating we found the more important the 'Jewish' reasons for immigration—to live a fuller Jewish life' and 'because Israel is where a Jew should live'—the more likely it was that the respondent integrated well."[21]

Seeing Israel in the broad Jewish perspective which a Zionist outlook provides also facilitates the adjustment of the immigrant. Writing of the immigration to Israel in the early days of the State, Shuval notes that "European Zionists are less disappointed with Israel than European non-Zionists. . . . The ideology of the Zionist apparently provided some sort of frame of reference for experiences in Israel, so that it was possible for the Zionist immigrants to balance disappointments against remote and valued goals, rather than against immediate frustrations."[22] And Antonovsky and Katz, summing up their observations on the two groups, observe that "Zionists tend to integrate better than do non-Zionists."[23]

Effect of Aliya on the Community

When asked whether a substantial aliya from the United States would strengthen or weaken the American Jewish community, the majority of students in our study (57 percent) replied that it would weaken the community. The explanation most frequently given for this view in the interviews was that aliya means the departure of the most active, Jewishly involved members of the community. This is obviously a static view of the situation, and our contention would be to the contrary. Aliya both reflects and further stimulates dynamic processes in the community. It represents a clear Jewish commitment, and the fact that some of its members reach this level of commitment affects the Jewish level of the community as a whole. Furthermore, the personal links between settlers and their relatives and friends who remain in the United States strengthen the bonds and heighten the probabilities of mutual influence between Israel and American Jewry.

Aliya from the Israel Vantage Point

Israel sees itself as the Jewish homeland which has the "ingathering of the exiles" as its primary purpose. It was so envisioned in the Declaration of Independence and in the Law of Return, according to which every Jew has the right to enter Israel. All Jews, including the unskilled, the infirm, and the ailing, have been welcomed. This has throughout the years been a dominant feature in Israel's policy, overriding all other considerations.

A broad popular consensus exists on this issue. A small minority have complained about special housing facilities and other concessions given to immigrants, and difficulties in the field of social absorption have led to a sarcastic comment that Israelis welcome aliya, immigration, but not olim, immigrants. About Israel's readiness, however, to receive into its midst all Jews who wish or need to come, there can be no doubt. During the less than three decades of its existence, Israel, whose Jewish population in 1948 numbered six hundred and fifty thousand, has absorbed more than one and a half million immigrants drawn from almost every country of the world in which Jews are to be found.

In answer to questions on the subject addressed in our 1974 study to a representative countrywide sample of eleventh graders, the great majority of students expressed a positive interest in a large-scale aliya from the United States and the Soviet Union. The religious students are more emphatic in the expression of this interest than are the traditionalists and the nonreligious (Tables S8.4 and S8.5).

In regard to Jews from the free countries, their readiness or otherwise for aliya remains a primary criterion of the feeling of closeness Israelis have for them. In our studies the Israeli students rated highest, in terms of closeness, those Jews who were ready to immigrate to Israel, and expressed a sense of distance from those who were not ready to do so. Seventy-seven percent declared themselves "very close" or "close" to Jews willing to immigrate, whereas only 7 percent expressed similar degrees of closeness to Jews unwilling to come (Table 8.6).

Table 8.6:   Closeness to Jews (a) willing (b) unwilling to immigrate

	Closeness to those willing to immigrate	Closeness to those unwilling to immigrate
Very close	44	4
Close	33	3
Moderately close	12	16
Slightly close	7	28
Not close at all	4	49
Total %	100	100
N	697	688

In an analysis of the relations between social groups and non-members, the groups may be classified as (a) open or closed, (b) complete or incomplete, and the nonmembers into (a) those who are regarded as eligible or ineligible, (b) those who aspire to enter, those who are indifferent, and those who are antagonistic.[24] In terms of this classification, Israel vis-à-vis world Jewry may be compared to an open group—it seeks and welcomes the entry into it of Jews from all parts of the world. It is an incomplete group in the sense that there are potential members still outside of it, and the degree of incompleteness is considerable.

When Jews whom it regards as eligible and desirable members are indifferent or opposed to the call to enter it, an ambivalence in the attitude of Israelis towards them becomes discernible. Such an attitude was manifested by Israelis towards American Jews in the years when aliya from the United States was meager. It was their feeling that American Jews who were free to do so had not chosen to become members of the Jewish homeland. When after the Six Day War aliya increased and problems of absorption arose, the focus of attention moved somewhat from a condemnation of those who did not come to a self-examination by Israelis of the extent to which they were facilitating the absorption of those who came.

While Israel is open to all who come, there are differences in the openness of sectors within Israeli society. In the study of visiting American students who spent a period at work in a kibbutz as part of their training we were able to distinguish three types in terms of the degree of their openness among the collective settlements in which the students worked. The settlements were classified as "open," "indifferent," and "closed," according to the replies of the students as to which of a series of statements best characterized the attitude of the kibbutz members towards their group: *Open*: (a) "They went out of their way to make us feel at home"; (b) "They helped in creating contact." *Indifferent:* (c) "They didn't do much in particular to establish contact, but were willing, if we took the initiative"; (d) "They were somewhat reticent."

Closed: (e) "They didn't care much for having contact with us beyond what was necessary during work"; (f) "They didn't care at all for having contact with us."

The satisfaction or dissatisfaction subsequently expressed with the stay at the settlement correlated with its openness or closedness. The students in the open settlements were the most positive in their attitudes to the settlement and its members.[25]

Implications for Policy

(1) While the motivational pattern of any immigrant is composed of a variety of strands, it is clear that basic to the decision to immigrate to Israel from the free countries are the Jewish identity factors. As conditions in Israel become more difficult—the deterioration of the security position after the Yom Kippur War, the increasingly difficult material conditions—the less stouthearted may hesitate about coming to settle in Israel. Whether Jews in such a situation will decide on aliya will depend more than ever on the strength of the Jewish factor in the motivational pattern. A program for encouraging aliya which does not take the ideological factor into account is not likely to succeed.

It would also be a reasonable surmise that the proportion of returnees ("yordim") is lower among those who come with a strong Jewish motivation.

(2) Israelis tend to discuss the push in terms of the grosser manifestations of anti-Semitism. The American students we studied in 1965 reported that many of the Israelis they met during their sojourn in Israel expressed dire prophecies about the spread of anti-Semitism, often drawing an analogy with what had happened in Europe. The students treated the warnings with disdain. They did not view their situation in this light; moreover, they did not regard the Israelis as qualified to talk about the American scene. The warnings were invariably associated with criticism of the reluctance of American Jews to immigrate to Israel, and criticism in this form generally produced defensive reactions on the part of the students.

In our studies almost ten years later the students themselves viewed anti-Semitism somewhat more seriously, and there was less reference to Israeli criticism of American aliya. But even now anti-Semitism is not seen by them as an important factor in their decision on aliya.

An effective approach by Israelis would need to reflect the subtler psychological nuances of the factor of push—to which we have referred above—in a way which will strike a responsive chord instead of merely arousing indignation or derision. While in any exposition of the problem of aliya the linkage between the factor of push and that of pull has to be borne in mind, the Israeli has to focus on the Jewish satisfactions Israel provides which constitutes the response to the dissatisfactions experienced in the American environment. The Israeli is seen as qualified to discuss what happens at the Israel end; in relation to any direct reference to the dissatisfactions at the American end he may be viewed as an "outsider" who knows less about the American scene than the American "insider."

It is advisable to select the "shlichim," the emissaries for the encouragement of aliya, from among American settlers in Israel. They better understand the mentality of the American Jews, the dilemmas which confront them, and such an emissary is more likely to be seen by Americans as "one of us."

(3) There has been disappointment after the Yom Kippur War at the failure of American Jews—and Jews from other parts of the Western world—to respond to the national emergency with a greater aliya. The aliya figures which rose after the Six Day War have, in fact, declined in recent years. The Israelis see themselves as manning the front line in a struggle which concerns Jews everywhere. In the short space of less than three decades they have fought four wars and thousands of families are bereaved of fathers and sons. The emotional intensity of the call for aliya—as well as its objective necessity—is understandable. In view of the problems in the area of "klita" (absorption) this disappointment has not been voiced as loudly as it might otherwise have been.

Thousands of Jews from the countries of the West did indeed volunteer their services during the Yom Kippur War. Such decision to volunteer for temporary service in the hour of crisis is more easily taken than a decision involving permanent transfer to another country. The disappointment of Israelis is not tempered by a proper understanding of the fact that the more radical decision is a gradual step-wise process and not a resolution taken hastily under the impact of a stirring speech. A call to settle in Israel will not evoke a response from those who have not already moved some distance along the path to a decision.

Exhortations to the community at large are therefore of limited efficacy, as an abortive campaign launched in the United States through posters and mass meetings by the Jewish Agency in 1974 demonstrated.[26] It is more important to pinpoint groups in the community who have advanced some way along the path to aliya, e.g., certain religious circles, students who have visited Israel, and concentrate attention on them.

(4) To the extent that there is a call for aliya, it should not be presented merely as coming from Israelis on behalf of the State of Israel. It has to be seen as a common Jewish responsibility extending to Jews everywhere for the sake of a common Jewish future. The process leading to aliya is likely to begin at the point where this sense of responsibility for the Jewish future intersects with the feeling of the individual that his life as a Jew can best be fulfilled in Israel.

(5) It is important to widen the "prosdor," or corridor, leading to aliya. In this corridor are the students sojourning in Israel at its universities and within other educational frameworks. The numbers have increased in recent years, and with proper organization on campuses at the American end coupled with the proper expansion of facilities at the Israel end there is reason to assume that many thousands more would come each year for shorter or longer study visits. This sojourn in Israel deepens their Jewish consciousness and strengthens their ties with the country. While the primary objective is not preparation for aliya, it does in fact serve this

purpose for a number of students. Some will remain to complete their studies and will eventually move into the occupational life of Israel. Many will on their return to the United States constitute a reservoir of potential olim who may in due course reach a decision to settle—particularly if their intentions are buttressed by the social support of groups of others who share their attitudes.

(6) Israel cannot compete with the United States in offering greater material advantages. As long as there is no decision on the ideological level, material inducements will be of little avail. Where, however, a decision has been taken, or is on the verge of being taken, and it is a question of overcoming barriers rather than opposing forces, assistance in regard to matters such as housing and employment will facilitate the coming of the prospective immigrant and will aid in his absorption in the country.

NOTES

1. R. G. Barker, T. Dembo, and K. Lewin, *Frustration and Regression: An Experiment with Young Children* (University of Iowa Studies in Child Welfare 18 (1941)), pp. 138-139.

2. C. Goldscheider, "Sociological and Demographic Perspectives," in M. Sklare, ed., *The Jew in American Society,* op. cit., p. 355.

3. G. E. Johnson, "The Impact of Jewish Community Priorities of American Emigration to Israel," *Analysis* 53 (1975). Published by the Institute for Jewish Policy Planning and Research of the Synagogue Council of America, Washington, D.C.

4. Lewin, *Field Theory in Social Science,* op. cit.: "The forces toward a positive, or away from a negative, valence can be called 'driving' forces. They lead to locomotion. These locomotions might be hindered by physical or social obstacles. Such barriers correspond to 'restraining' forces. Restraining forces, as such, do not lead to locomotion, but they do influence the effect of driving forces." (p. 259.)

5. Cf., the analysis of the motivation to migrate by S. N. Eisenstadt, *The Absorption of Immigrants* (London: Routledge and Kegan Paul, 1954): "We assume that every migratory movement is motivated by the migrant's feeling of some kind of insecurity and inadequacy in his original social setting." (p. 1.)

6. Cf., Lewin, *Field Theory in Social Science,* op. cit.: "The strength of the force toward or away from a valence depends upon the strength of that valence and the psychological distance between the person and the valence." (p. 258.)

7. C. H. Stember et al., *Jews in the Mind of America* (New York: Basic Books, 1966), summarize the findings of public polls over a period of twenty-five

years from 1937 onward. Their conclusion (which relates to the position before 1966) is that "anti-Jewish prejudice obviously is not yet a thing of the past, any more than anti-Jewish discrimination is, but both are unmistakably in a state of decline." (p. 217.) The implications of this observation are debated by several of the contributors to the volume.

8. Goldscheider, op. cit., p. 379.

9. Ibid.

10. *Immigration and Absorption 1970-1975.* A Report prepared by the Planning and Research Division of the Ministry of Immigrant Absorption, Jerusalem, 1975, p. 25.

11. Goldscheider, op. cit.

12. T. Horowitz and E. Frenkel, *Immigrants in Absorption Centers* (Research Report No. 185 of the Henrietta Szold Institute, Jerusalem, 1975) p. 152. (In Hebrew.)

13. A study in progress by Dr. Mordechai Altschuler, of the Institute of Contemporary Jewry, Hebrew University.

14. Lewin, *Field Theory in Social Science,* op. cit., p. 271.

15. K. Lewin, "Intention, Will and Need," in D. Rapaport, ed., *Organization and Pathology of Thought* (New York: Columbia University Press, 1951): "When in a person there are several, simultaneous tension-systems of opposing directions, a decision often amounts to the effecting of some kind of equilibrium among them, or to isolating some of them. At any rate, the internal situation created is one in which a more or less unitary tension-system controls the action. Occasionally in such cases, an internal vacillation is observed before the decision (the so-called struggle of motives)." (p. 137.)

16. S. N. Herman, *American Students in Israel* (Ithaca, N.Y.: Cornell University Press, 1970), pp. 98-101.

17. Cf., E. Ginzberg, *Occupational Choice* (N.Y.: Columbia University Press, 1951).

18. R. K. Merton et al., *The Student Physician* (Cambridge, Mass.: Harvard University Press, 1957), p. 71.

19. L. Festinger, *A Theory of Cognitive Dissonance* (Evanston, Ill.: Row, Peterson, 1957), p. 264.

20. This was one of the questions which was being explored in an uncompleted doctoral dissertation by David Katz, a student in the Department of Sociology of the Hebrew University, who fell in the Yom Kippur War. See, A. D. Katz, "Dissonance Theory and Immigrant Adjustment," in the Memorial Volume *Abraham David Katz: Jew, Man, and Sociologist.* Jerusalem, 1975, pp. 65-84.

21. A. Antonovsky and D. Katz, *Americans and Canadians in Israel: Integration into Israeli Life,* Report No. 3 (Jerusalem: The Israel Institute of Applied Social Research, 1969), p. 10.

22. J. T. Shuval, *Immigrants on the Threshold* (New York: Atherton, 1963), p. 76.

23. Antonovsky and Katz, op. cit., p. 9.

24. R. K. Merton, *Social Theory and Social Structure* (Glencoe, Ill.: Free Press, 1957), p. 292 and p. 314.

25. Herman, *American Students in Israel,* op. cit.

26. Cf., Johnson, "The Impact of Jewish Community Priorities of American Emigration to Israel," op. cit.

PART III

EMPIRICAL STUDIES

Chapter 9

JEWISH IDENTITY IN THE JEWISH STATE

The Land of Israel was the cradle of Jewish civilization, and so the very geographical setting of the Jewish state—and particularly its capital, Jerusalem—evokes Jewish historical associations. A Jewish state in another part of the world could not have aroused the sense of continuity with a Jewish past which echoes through the first sentences of Israel's Declaration of Independence of May, 1948:

> In the Land of Israel the Jewish people came into being. In this land was shaped their spiritual, religious, and national character. Here they lived in sovereign independence. Here they created a culture of national and universal import, and gave to the world the eternal Book of Books. Exiled by force, still the Jewish people kept faith with their land in all centers of their dispersion, steadfast in their prayer and hope to return and revive their political freedom.

In setting out the objectives of the state, the Declaration of Independence begins by stating that "the State of Israel

will be open to Jewish immigration and the ingathering of the
exiles," and it concludes with a call to "the Jewish people
throughout the Diaspora to join forces with us." The Law of
Return, enacted by the Knesset in July 1950 (on the anniver-
sary of Herzl's death), affirms the right of every Jew to settle
in Israel, and the Nationality Law of 1952 extends Israel
citizenship to Jews who come as immigrants under the Law
of Return. In presenting the bill to the Knesset, Prime Minister David Ben Gurion stressed that this was not a privilege
the state was conferring on the Jews abroad; it was affirming
a historical right inherent in every Jew as such. And when
years later he referred to the laws "setting a nation's course,"
he again drew attention to the special nature of the relationship of the Jew to Israel to which the Law of Return gives
expression:

> The Law of Return identified the historical destiny of the State
> of Israel as the ingathering of the exiles. It stipulated that it was
> not the State that gave the Diaspora Jew the right to settle in
> Israel, but that the right was inherently his by virtue of his being
> Jewish. This right had existed prior to the establishment of the
> State and is the foundation on which the State was built and
> renewed.[1]

Not only in the Declaration of Independence, but also in
the minds of the people of Israel, the raison d'être of
the state resides in its function as the Jewish homeland
gathering in Jews from the lands of dispersion. And the flow
of immigrants over the years—from the arrival of the survivors of the European Holocaust and the communities evac-
uated from the Arab countries in the early years of the state
to the recent aliya from the USSR—has provided a constant
reminder of what is the primary purpose of the State.

When danger threatens a Jewish community anywhere, the
plight of the Jews becomes a matter of national concern in
Israel. Although it lays no claim to the civic allegiance of
Jews in other states, Israel sees itself—and is seen by others—
as the state entitled to speak on behalf of the Jewish people

in the councils of nations and before the bar of public opinion. It acted on behalf of all Jews, the living and the dead, when it brought Eichmann to trial in Jerusalem, and as a state it officially commemorates the Holocaust.

There is a reflection not only of a tradition of social justice but of the experience of Jews as a minority in the long years of their dispersion in the assurance clearly enunciated in the Declaration of Independence that the State of Israel "will rest upon foundations of liberty, justice, and peace as envisioned by the Prophets of Israel . . . will maintain complete equality of social and political rights for all its citizens, without distinction of creed, race, or sex . . . will guarantee freedom of religion and conscience, of language, education and culture."

The Jewishness of Israel as a Jewish state expresses itself not only in the special relationship to the Jewish people but also in the public life of the country. The day of rest is the Jewish Sabbath, the holidays the Jewish holidays, the language Hebrew. (How different the position is of a Jewish minority in the Diaspora was illustrated recently when the opening day of schools in France coincided with Yom Kippur, the Day of Atonement, the holiest day in the Jewish calendar, and the pleas of the representatives of the Jewish community to change the date proved of no avail.) The study of the Bible and of Jewish history is part of the curriculum of every school. The food in the army and in all public establishments is prepared in accord with Jewish dietary regulations.

Within a Jewish state a Jewish identity can develop freely without the constraints imposed by fear of alien influences from the surrounding environment. A Jewish majority society indeed allows for a normalization of the Jewish identity in the sense of integrating it fully into the total identity of the individual Jew. In the Diaspora the Jewishness of the individual is often limited to the private spheres of life. The public life of the country is seen as a domain into which the individual enters not in his role as a Jew but as an American or Frenchman, as the case may be. Since in Israel, on the other hand, the public life of the country bears a Jewish character, no sharp demarcation need exist for the Jew between the public and the private domain or between his Jewish and his Israeli identity.

While it enjoys a new-found freedom in a Jewish majority society, the Jewish identity is not shaped *de novo* in the Jewish state. It bears the mark of the Diaspora experience. Thus, when we look at the evolving Israeli Jewish identity in historical perspective, we see how the dominant tone in the life of Israel was set by immigrants from Eastern Europe (particularly those who came at the time of what are known as the second and third aliyot, immigration waves[2]) and how the Eastern European models have influenced in particular the patterns of religious observance. There are still significant differences in the way a Jewish identity expresses itself in the Ashkenazic and in the Oriental sector of Israel's Jewish population, but these differences are becoming less marked in members of the younger generation who move through a unified educational system and share the army training experience.

The Jewish Identity of Israel's Youth

The young Israelis have grown up as members of the Jewish majority society. Unlike many of their parents, who transplanted their lives from the Diaspora, they have no personal experience of life as a Jewish minority. The parents yearned for a Jewish state and strove to achieve it. Their sons and daughters found a Jewish state in existence, and for them the period when Jews were a people without a state of their own belongs to history.

What does "being Jewish" mean for the young generation born in the Jewish state? What is its attitude to the Jewish past and to Jews in the distant lands of the Dispersion? What is the relationship between the Jewishness of the young generation and its Israeliness?

If Jewishness were merely a question of Jewish knowledge, the answer to these questions would be relatively simple. The fact is that Israel's schools impart to their pupils a substantial body of knowledge—more particularly about the Bible and about Jewish history—equalled by only a tiny fraction of the youth in the Diaspora. So on a test of knowledge they would score comparatively well, although even in this area—as we shall have occasion to observe—much remains to be done to provide Israeli youth with a fuller understanding of recent Jewish history and of the contemporary Jewish situation. While there is a relation between knowledge and values, the possession of the requisite body of knowledge does not always in itself ensure the desired values. It is the values which are of the essence of the problem.

Discussions of the Jewish identity of Israeli youth have generally erred in the direction of exaggerating the weaknesses in that identity.[3] Much depends on which sector of what is a heterogenous society attention is centered. Moreover, what excites public notice are the more blatant deviations from Jewish norms on the part of what at times is a minute minority. The discussions are seldom based on systematic investigation; they do not set forth any clear set of criteria as to what constitutes "Jewishness," nor do they indicate what yardstick, if any, is being used for measuring the intensity of the Jewish identity. When the observer comes from outside Israel, such criteria as are implicit in his evaluation are often taken over from the culture of which he himself is a product.

In order to obtain a systematic view of the attitudes of Israel's youth we undertook a study in 1965 of a representative sample of all the eleventh graders (sixteen- to seventeen-year olds) in Israel's schools.[4] These were students who had been born in the year after the state was established, the first generation to be born "Israelis." We replicated the study in 1974, and this enables us to ascertain what changes, if any, have taken place in the intervening decade. (Our study in 1974 was confined to the eleventh graders, while that of 1965 had included their parents and teachers.)

The sample in 1974 was so constituted as to resemble that of 1965 in regard to the main variables—religious observance and communal background (Ashkenazic, Oriental).[5] In regard to religious observance the sample in 1974, as in 1965, was divided into three categories: "dati'im" (religious), "m'sorati'im" (traditionalists), and "lo dati'im" (nonreligious). In referring to these categories we shall as a matter of convenience use the literal translations of the terms. But in the Israeli context the terms relate to degrees of religious *observance*: dati implies a strict observance of religious obligations; m'sorati indicates a positive orientation to Jewish tradition accompanied by varying degrees of laxity and selectivity in regard to observance; lo dati means nonobservant. This last category ranges from those who honor some customs (as the widely observed fast on the Day of Atonement) to those who are antireligious.

The questionnaire was administered during the period from February to April 1974 to 1,875 eleventh graders from 35 schools. The key questions in the 1965 study reappeared in the 1974 version and a number of further questions were added. In view of the large number of questions two overlapping versions of the questionnaire were employed. For questions which appeared in both versions, we have the responses of the entire sample; in regard to other questions, the responses are those of the subjects replying to the particular questionnaire.

We sought to examine the Jewish identity of the Israeli students according to the criteria set forth in Chapter 3 of this volume, and our analysis of the data will proceed in terms of the framework we developed in that chapter. We shall first discuss the relationship of the students to the Jewish people as a membership group, and will then explore the extent to which the Jewish group serves as a source of reference.

Relationship to the Jewish People as a Membership Group

The great majority of young Israelis do not see themselves, as some observers have supposed, as a separate people; they

Table 9.1:* Israelis as part of the Jewish people ("In your opinion are we in Israel . . .")

	All Respondents	Religious	Traditionalist	Nonreligious
an inseparable part of the Jewish people	85	96	87	76
a separate people	15	4	13	24
Total %	100	100	100	100
N	1,865	475	635	755

regard themselves as part and parcel of a worldwide Jewish people (Table 9.1).

While the impressive size of the majority may be reassuring, an educational program designed to strengthen the Jewish consciousness of the Israelis would have to take into account—on this as on other questions—the existence of a dissentient minority whose view reflects a weakness in its Jewish identity. The minority holding the opinion that Israelis are a separate people is drawn mainly, though not exclusively, from the ranks of the nonreligious students (24 percent of the nonreligious, 13 percent of the traditionalists, and 4 percent of the religious students).

THE BASES OF ALIGNMENT: INTERDEPENDENCE AND SIMILARITY

The students are conscious of the common destiny of the Jewish people. To the question whether they feel that their fate is bound up with the fate of the Jewish people, 84 percent of the students in 1974 (the corresponding figure in 1965 was close to this—82 percent) respond either "yes definitely" or "to a large extent," while 14 percent check "to some extent," and only 2 percent say "no" (Table S9.2).

The interdependence is seen to exist not only between a Jew and his fellow Jews everywhere but also between Jewish communities. The majority of students feel that a deterioration in the prestige of Israel adversely affects Jews throughout the world, and similarly that a deterioration in the status of world Jewry has implications for Israel.[6]

The perception of similarity between Jews is less wide-spread than the feeling of interdependence. Fifty-one percent perceive Jews as "very similar" or "similar" in regard to characteristics and behavior; 57 percent perceive such similarity in regard to customs and culture. The tendency to see similarity between Jews was somewhat greater in 1974 than in 1965. The religious students are more prone than the others to observe similarity.

THE SENSE OF MUTUAL RESPONSIBILITY

The feeling of interdependence is accompanied by a sense of mutual responsibility. Our questions on this subject to the students concerned the relations between Israel and the communities of the Diaspora. The students regard it as the duty of the State of Israel to help Jewish communities in time of need and in turn it is the duty of these communities to extend help in time of need to Israel. When it is a question of help to Israel, a greater percentage of students (substantially the same proportion in 1974 as in 1965) feel that such aid should be given "in every case." There is more of a tendency (which increases further in 1974) to qualify the aid to the Jewish communities in the Diaspora with a proviso "only if the help does not result in a serious detriment to the State of Israel."

ALIGNMENT ACROSS TIME

Israelis are in a peculiar position psychologically in terms of the relation to their historical past. As Israelis they have a short past; as Jews they have a past extending over thousands of years. It is, however, not easy for the young Israelis to identify with the nineteen centuries of minority existence in the Diaspora seen by them as so different from the conditions of their own life as members of a Jewish majority society; it is easier to relate to the days of Bar Cochba or earlier Biblical periods when Jews lived in their own land. Do they in the circumstances seek to obliterate the memory of the Diaspora period with the negative connotations it has for them?

The responses of the students show that the majority do not renounce this past. Eighty-five percent see the State of Israel as a continuation of all periods of Jewish history. Only a small percentage (11 percent) view it as a continuation of only those periods in which Jews lived in Israel, while a minute percentage (4 percent) regard it as opening a new chapter with no connection to the Jewish past. The "Canaan-ite" dismissal of a connection with the Jewish past finds few adherents (Table 9.3).

The way the students feel about the different periods of the past is generally determined (as was observed in an earlier chapter) by two criteria which reflect the tenor of their lives, namely, the extent to which the period was one of Jewish activism and not of passivity, and the extent to which it was characterized by efforts at the preservation of identity and opposition to its surrender. There is consequently an ambiv-alence about periods in which they believe Jewish behavior to have been positive on one criterion and negative on the other. We drew attention to signs of such ambivalence in the atti-tudes to the behavior of Jews during the Holocaust. The ambivalence also exists in relation to the "shtetl" in Eastern Europe although what characterizes the attitudes of a sub-stantial percentage of students on this subject is the absence of any marked emotional reaction such as exists in relation to the period of the Holocaust (Table S9.4).

Table 9.3: * State of Israel as a continuation of Jewish history ("In your opinion is the State of Israel a continuation of Jewish history?")

	All Respondents	Religious	Traditionalist	Nonreligious
Yes, of all periods	85	94	85	79
Yes, only of the period when Jews lived there	11	3	12	14
No, it has opened a new page of history	4	3	3	7
Total %	100	100	100	100
N	1,874	473	637	764

When the students were asked to choose which reason
from a list of five most justified the existence of the State of
Israel, a sharp difference was discernible in the scope of the
historical time perspective of the religious and nonreligious
students. While the majority of nonreligious students turned
to recent history for such justification, the religious students
tended more to stress the rights of the Jewish people as based
on a relationship extending back to Biblical times; accordingly, their most frequent choice was "the settlement of the
Jewish people in the land of Israel in ancient times" (chosen
by 47 percent) followed by "the aspirations of the Jews
through the centuries to return to their homeland" (chosen
by 28 percent). Seventy-five percent of the religious students
thus chose either one or the other of these two reasons in
1974, as compared with 50 percent in 1965. These two
reasons were adduced by 51 percent of the traditionalists in
1974 (as compared with 36 percent in 1965) and by 34
percent of the nonreligious students (as compared with 29

Table 9.5: * Reasons justifying the existence of the State of Israel (Presented in order chosen
by all respondents in 1974. Students were asked to select the one most
important reason.)

	All Respondents		Religious		Traditionalist		Nonreligious	
	1974	1965	1974 *	1965	1974	1965	1974	1965
The suffering of the Jews in the Diaspora as a people without a homeland	26	27	14	26	27	27	31	29
The settlement of the Jewish people in the land of Israel in ancient times	26	18	47	28	28	17	14	13
The aspirations of the Jews through the centuries to return to their homeland	23	18	28	22	23	19	20	16
The resettlement of the country in recent times and the War of Liberation	18	23	5	13	17	23	26	29
The recognition by the nations of the world of the idea of a Jewish state	7	14	6	11	5	14	9	13
Total %	100	100	100	100	100	100	100	100
N	744	765	185	165	240	247	319	363

percent in 1965). The emphasis on the Biblical and the other historical associations with the land of Israel has become more pronounced—particularly among religious circles—in the course of the Arab-Israeli conflict and the continuing debate over what territorial concessions Israel should or should not make.

The nonreligious students recorded as their most frequent choice "the suffering of the Jews in the Diaspora as a people without a homeland" followed by "the resettlement of the country in recent times and the War of Liberation." The traditionalists chose "the settlement of the Jewish people in the land of Israel in ancient times" followed by "the suffering of the Jews in the Diaspora as a people without a homeland."

Lowest on the list of reasons (chosen in 1974 by only 7 percent of the students) was "the recognition by the nations of the world of the idea of a Jewish State" (Table 9.5).

ALIGNMENT ACROSS SPACE

The students see themselves aligned with Jewish communities in other parts of the world, but with some communities more closely than with others.

There is general appreciation of the crucial importance of the support extended in the economic and political spheres by the largest Jewry located in the country upon whose friendship Israel is dependent. The relationship of American Jewry to Israel is salient in the minds of the students, and despite criticism of the fact that American Jews do not come to settle in larger numbers, this Jewry stands highest on the scale of closeness.

An attack on Jews qua Jews anywhere emphasizes for Israelis the fact of common fate, and they feel close to such Jews. This is reflected in a greater closeness to the Jews of the USSR and the Arab countries than to the Jews of Latin America, England, South Africa, and France (Table S9.6).

In addition to probing the feeling of closeness to Jewish communities we examined the degree of closeness to various categories of Jews. The students are closest to Jews whom they see as similar to themselves in background or belief. The religious students express a greater closeness than do the nonreligious to Jews whom they regard as similar and at the same time display less distance to Jews of dissimilar views. They are closer to religious Jews in Israel than are the nonreligious students to nonreligious Jews in Israel; they feel less of a distance from nonreligious Jews in Israel than do the nonreligious students from religious Jews in Israel; they are closer to nonreligious Jews abroad than are the nonreligious students. The traditionalist students feel closer to the nonreligious Jews in Israel than they do to the religious, but they feel closer to the religious than to the nonreligious Jews in the Diaspora.

Both nonreligious and traditionalist students feel somewhat closer to religious Jews abroad than to religious Jews in Israel. From the interviews it appears that the relationship to Jews inside and outside of Israel is determined by different criteria. In regard to religious and nonreligious groups of Jews in Israel, the students adopt the criterion of similarity. "They are like me," "I am one of them" were frequent remarks. In this context religious observance (or the lack of it) is salient as the source of the similarity or dissimilarity. When the question is one of closeness to Jews outside of Israel, the frame of reference becomes the relationship of the particular group to the Jewish people and to Israel, and a number of the students adopt another criterion, that of interdependence. They do not feel themselves close to assimilating Jews. Religious Jews are seen by these students as less likely to assimilate than nonreligious Jews and as likely to have a greater attachment to the Jewish people and to Israel. Furthermore, the conflict which exacerbates relations between the religious and nonreligious camps in Israel weighs less heavily when the relationship to Jews abroad is considered.

The students feel close to Jews overseas who support Israel, and experience a sense of distance from those who do not give support. The religious students feel closer than do the other categories to Jews supporting Israel and at the same time are less distant from the nonsupporters.

On questions about closeness to Jews in Israel of the same and of different communal origin ("edah"), the religious students show more closeness than do the other categories to Jews of their own communal group and at the same time less distance than the other categories from Jews of a different communal origin.[7]

ATTITUDES TO THE NON-JEWISH WORLD

When the students think of themselves as "marked off" as Jews, it is as part of a Jewish people in the Gentile world. The Arab minority and other non-Jews living in Israel serve only a limited marking off function. The Arabs serve this function more in relation to the Oriental Jews than in relation to the Ashkenazic Jews; the parents of the students from the Oriental sector have lived in the Arab countries, in many cases the Arabs are the only non-Jews they have personally encountered, and, moreover, in Israel they are anxious to be seen as different from Arabs. At the same time, they too—like the Ashkenazic Jews—are conscious of the wider Gentile world from which they are marked off as Jews.

When the students were presented with the following statement, "We are Jews and they on the other hand are . . ." and were asked to supply the missing word, the most frequent response—on the part of both Ashkenazic and Oriental students—was "goyim" (Gentiles), with a smaller number inserting such terms as "non-Jews" and "Christians." Only a minority of subjects inserted "Arabs"; within this minority the larger proportion were students from the Oriental communities.

When asked whether non-Jews are anti-Semites, the majority of students give the qualified answer "some of them." Suspicion of the non-Jewish world has, however, increased. In 1974 it was seen as significantly more anti-Semitic than in 1965, and the minority of students limiting anti-Semitism to

Table 9.7:* The extent of anti-Semitism ("Are non-Jews anti-Semites?")

	All Respondents 1974* 1965		Religious 1974* 1965		Traditionalist 1974* 1965		Nonreligious 1974* 1965	
Yes, almost all	7	3	18	6	3	3	2	1
A large section	19	11	33	21	18	12	12	6
Some of them	63	56	44	55	68	54	71	58
Only a small section	11	30	5	18	11	31	15	35
Total %	100	100	100	100	100	100	100	100
N	1,862	1,438	471	346	634	451	757	641

"only a small section" decreased from 30 percent in 1965 to 11 percent in 1974. The religious students tended more than the others to view non-Jews as anti-Semitic (Table 9.7).

The students attach varying degrees of seriousness to anti-Semitism in different countries. Most serious, as they see it, is the anti-Semitism in the Arab countries and in the USSR, least serious in the United States and England (Table S9.8).

When asked to indicate what are the major causes of anti-Semitism, a majority attributed it to the position of Jews as a minority among a non-Jewish majority. At the same time, about a third of the students attributed anti-Semitism to the characteristics of the Jews abroad.

In the interviews a number of students stated that the characteristics they regarded as causing anti-Semitism were positive in their eyes, e.g., the maintenance by Jews of their separate identity or the fact that Jews were "a chosen people" and as such evoked a certain jealousy. On the other hand, there were some students who spoke disparagingly of forms of "Jewish behavior and characteristics" (such as "ostentatiousness" and "commercial malpractices") which they believed caused anti-Semitism. Their comments reflect a confusion prevalent in the minds of Jews about a presumedly causal relationship between anti-Semitism and Jewish behavior. The source of anti-Semitism is to be sought in the psychology of the anti-Semite who hates Jews—as history has tragically shown—irrespective of what the Jew does or does not do. What then gives rise to the mistaken view that Jewish behavior is a major contributing factor?

The prevalence of this view among Jews in the Diaspora lends itself more readily to explanation. The Jew sees himself in a distorting mirror held up by the Gentile majority and accepts the generalizations about Jewish characteristics as reflected in that mirror. There is still a further factor operative in the Diaspora. Jews who seek to enter the majority group often cannot do so because of the barriers erected against such entry. The frustration of such Jews leads to aggression, which is directed not against the source of the frustration (the powerful Gentile majority), but is directed inward against their own group, at times reaching the proportions of self-hatred. They blame their failure to gain acceptance in the majority on the behavior of a section of the Jewish group.

What is the source of the confusion among Israelis located in their own majority society? The repudiation of the golah ("shlilat hagolah") by an older generation of Zionists was at times accompanied by contempt for the Jews living in those conditions.[8] It would seem that something of this derogatory view has been transmitted—through the Hebrew literature of the period and in other ways—to the young generation; they have been seeing Jews in what is a distorting Jewish mirror. This, however, is only a partial explanation of the acceptance by some Israelis of stereotypes concerning Jews prevalent in the Gentile world.

The Content of the Israeli Jewish Identity

We move into the more problem-ridden area when we come to explore the position the Jewish group occupies in the life space of the young Israeli, how he feels about the group and its attributes, and the extent to which its norms serve as a source of reference. In view of the interrelatedness of Jewishness and Israeliness our analysis will deal simultaneously with both the Israeli and the Jewish identity.

The Jewish group is perceived by the great majority of Israelis as a religio-national entity (Table 4.1 above). There are occasions when the one or the other of the components is in the foreground, but both elements are present in the conception of most of the students of what being Jewish is.

THE CENTRALITY OF "BEING JEWISH" AND "BEING ISRAELI"

How central is "being Jewish" and "being Israeli" in the eyes of the students? (In our questions we equated "centrality" with "importance" although strictly speaking "centrality" has a wider meaning.) The importance of "being Israeli" is more widely endorsed by the sample as a whole than the importance of "being Jewish" (although in the case of the religious students, "being Jewish" has the wider endorsement). In regard to both "being Jewish" and "being Israeli," the most emphatic response ("plays a very important part") registers an increase in 1974.

Table 9.9: * Centrality of Jewishness ("Does the fact that you are Jewish play an important part in your life?")

	All Respondents 1974* 1965		Religious 1974* 1965		Traditionalist 1974* 1965		Nonreligious 1974* 1965	
It plays a very important part	31	23	73	62	26	18	9	7
It plays an important part	43	45	26	36	59	60	40	39
It is of little importance	21	25	1	1	12	18	40	44
It plays no part	5	7	0	1	3	4	11	10
Total %	100	100	100	100	100	100	100	100
N	1,873	2,980	475	680	638	942	760	1,358

Table 9.10: Centrality of Israeliness ("Does the fact that you are Israeli play an important part in your life?")

	All Respondents 1974* 1965		Religious 1974* 1965		Traditionalist 1974* 1965		Nonreligious 1974* 1965	
It plays a very important part	51	43	56	44	51	43	49	42
It plays an important part	40	47	36	48	40	49	42	48
It is of little importance	7	7	7	5	7	5	7	8
It plays no part	2	3	1	3	2	3	2	2
Total %	100	100	100	100	100	100	100	100
N	1,870	2,980	471	680	638	942	761	1,358

The religious students are—as might be expected—very
much more emphatic than the others about the centrality of
"being Jewish." In 1965 the responses about the importance
of "being Israeli" were almost identical among the three
categories of students; in 1974 the religious students were
more emphatic on this component too than are the other
categories (Tables 9.9, 9.10).

THE VALENCE OF JEWISH AND ISRAELINESS

In order to test the valence, or attractiveness, of "being
Jewish" and "being Israeli," the students were asked to
respond to the following hypothetical situations:

(1) "If you were to be born anew, would you wish to be born
Jewish?"
(2) "If you had to live abroad, would you wish to be born Jewish?"
(3) "If you were to be born anew, would you wish to be born
Israeli?"

The majority of students (80 percent in 1974 as compared
with 70 percent in 1965) express a positive wish to be born
Jews. The feeling of the religious students on this matter is
almost unanimously affirmative (97 percent); the majorities
among the traditionalists (89 percent) and among the nonreligious (62 percent) are larger than they were in 1965 (Table
9.11).

When the question relates to being born a Jew living
abroad, the majority supporting the proposal is reduced (63

Table 9.11:* Valence of Jewishness ("If you were to be born anew, would you wish to be born a Jew?")

	All Respondents 1974* 1965		Religious 1974 1965		Traditionalist 1974* 1965		Nonreligious 1974 1965	
Yes	80	70	97	94	89	76	62	54
It makes no difference to me	17	28	2	6	10	23	32	43
No	3	2	1	0	1	1	6	3
Total %	100	100	100	100	100	100	100	100
N	1,872	2,980	473	680	635	942	764	1,358

percent in 1974; in 1965 it was smaller—54 percent). A substantial majority of religious students (87 percent) would wish to be born Jews even in the circumstances of Diaspora existence; such affirmative desire is also expressed by the majority of traditionalists (69 percent), but only by a minority (41 percent) of the nonreligious. While on the earlier question only a minute percentage expressed opposition to being born a Jew (most of those who did not accept the proposition endorsed "it is a matter of indifference"), an appreciable minority stated that they would not wish to be born Jews if they had to live abroad. For many of the nonreligious students the valence of being Jewish is predicated on living as part of a Jewish majority society in Israel, while for the great number of religious and traditionalist students it is positive under all conditions (Table 9.12).

The majority of students opt for being born Israeli (82 percent in 1974, 81 percent in 1965). In regard to the valence of Israeliness—unlike the valence of Jewishness—no sharp differences exist between the three categories. The

Table 9.12: * Valence of Jewishness in life abroad ("If you were to live abroad, would you wish to be born a Jew?")

	All Respondents		Religious		Traditionalist		Nonreligious	
	1974 *	1965	1974	1965	1974 *	1965	1974	1965
Yes	62	54	87	84	69	57	41	37
It makes no difference to me	17	25	3	8	13	23	29	34
No	21	21	10	8	18	20	30	29
Total %	100	100	100	100	100	100	100	100
N	1,871	2,980	473	680	637	942	761	1,358

Table 9.13: * Valence of Israeliness ("If you were born again, would you wish to be born an Israeli?")

	All Respondents		Religious		Traditionalist		Nonreligious	
	1974	1965	1974	1965	1974	1965	1974	1965
Yes	82	81	86	79	81	78	81	83
It makes no difference to me	13	17	7	17	14	18	16	17
No	5	2	7	4	5	4	3	—
Total %	100	100	100	100	100	100	100	100
N	1,876	2,980	473	680	640	942	763	1,358

religious students register an increased sense of Israeliness in 1974 and their majority is slightly higher than that of the others (Table 9.13).

STRENGTH OF JEWISH AND ISRAELI
FEELING AND THEIR RELATIVE POTENCY

The students were asked to indicate their position on a seven point scale with "strong Jewish feeling" at the one end and "lack of Jewish feeling" at the other. They were similarly asked to locate themselves on a scale designed to measure the strength of the feeling of Israeliness. Sixty-eight percent of the students locate themselves on the first three rungs of the ladder of the Jewish scale. There are marked differences between the religious students (mean position 1.4), the traditionalists (mean 2.4), and the nonreligious students (mean 3.8). Ninety percent of the students locate themselves on the first three rungs of the Israeli ladder. The students of all three categories are high on this scale, but the religious students are slightly higher than the others—their mean position is 1.7 as compared with a mean of 1.8 in the case of both the traditionalists and the nonreligious students.

A positive correlation (r=.20) exists between position on the Jewish scale and on the Israeli scale. We sought, however, to determine the relative strength of the Israeli and Jewish components in the Israeli-Jewish identity when they were presented as counterposed on a scale.

Strictly speaking, relative potency is a function of the relative valence of the two components and their relative salience in a particular situation. Straining the use of the term somewhat, we developed a rough general measure of potency—over and above situations—by asking the students to locate themselves on a seven point scale which we explained to them as follows:

Below is a rating scale, at one end of which appears the word 'Jewish' and at the other end of it the word 'Israeli'. Indicate your position on this scale by placing a checkmark X within the appropriate compartment on this scale. To the extent that the

Table 9.14:[*]   The Israeli-Jewish continuum (mean scores)

| All Respondents | | Religious | | Traditionalist | | Nonreligious | |
1974	1965	1974	1965	1974	1965	1974	1965
4.2	3.5	5.4	5.1	4.4	3.6	3.1	2.6

mark is nearer to 'Israeli' it means that you feel yourself so much more Israeli than Jewish. To the extent that the mark X is nearer to 'Jewish' it means that you feel yourself so much more Jewish. Please note that the mark X should be placed inside the space between the points on the scale.

Israeli   :___:___:___:___:___:___:___: Jewish
                1   2   3   4   5   6   7

Unlike the two previous scales which were included in the 1974 questionnaire only, the Israeli-Jewish scale had appeared in 1965 as well and so we are able to compare the positions of the students in the two periods. The mean position of the entire sample (4.2) in 1974 was just beyond the midpoint slightly to the Jewish side of the scale whereas in 1965 it was on the Israeli side (3.5). The nonreligious students who were on the Israeli side in 1965 (2.6) remained on that side but moved nearer to the midpoint (3.1); the traditionalists who were on the Israeli side (3.6) were on the Jewish side (4.4) in 1974; in the case of the religious students the change was slight (5.1 in 1965, 5.4 in 1974), (Table 9.14).

THE INTERRELATEDNESS OF JEWISHNESS AND ISRAELINESS

It is necessary to go beyond the determination of the relative strength of the Israeli and Jewish components in the Israeli-Jewish identity. What is crucial is whether the two subidentities are seen as overlapping and consonant—whatever their relative weight in the identity of the particular individual. A majority of students (75 percent in 1974 as

compared with 70 percent in 1965) recognize the interrelatedness between their feeling Jewish and their feeling Israeli. The majority is much greater among the religious (86
percent) and traditionalists (80 percent) than among the
nonreligious (63 percent). An appreciable minority of the
nonreligious students (36 percent) view the two as separate
compartments in their life-space, although only a minute
percentage (1 percent) feel that there is dissonance (Tables
9.15, 9.16).

Jewishness and Israeliness are found to be mutually reinforcing in an Israeli-Jewish identity; when they are sundered,
both are weaker. A comparison we undertook on a number
of questions between students who recognize the interrelatedness (we termed them "compatibles") and those who see
Jewishness and Israeliness as things apart ("separatists") reveals that the compatibles in any of the three categories rank
higher on measures of both Jewish and Israeli identity than

Table 9.15:   Overlap and consonance "When I feel more Jewish:

	All Respondents		Religious		Traditionalist		Nonreligious	
	1974*	1965	1974	1965	1974	1965	1974	1965
A also feel more Israeli	75	70	86	83	80	76	63	62
There is no relationship between my feeling Jewish and my feeling Israeli	23	27	12	15	18	22	36	36
I feel less Israeli	2	3	2	2	2	2	1	2
Total %	100	100	100	100	100	100	100	100
N	1,856	2,980	472	680	631	942	753	1,358

Table 9.16:*   Overlap and consonance "When I feel more Israeli:

	All Respondents		Religious		Traditionalist		Nonreligious	
	1974*	1965	1974	1965	1974*	1965	1974	1965
I also feel more Jewish	72	67	87	87	79	72	58	54
There is no relationship between my feeling Israeli an my feeling Jewish	25	29	10	10	19	24	38	41
I feel less Jewish	3	4	3	3	2	4	4	5
Total %	100	100	100	100	100	100	100	100
N	1,865	2,980	474	680	633	942	758	1,358

do the separatists of their category. In the nonreligious category they have a distinctly weaker Jewish identity and also a somewhat weaker Israeli identity than the compatibles. The small minority of religious separatists (12 percent) have a much weaker Israeli identity than the religious compatibles and also fall below them in the intensity of their Jewish identity.

Illustrative of the differences are the responses to the questions determining the centrality of Jewishness and Israeliness. A greater number of compatibles in all three categories regard their Jewishness and Israeliness as playing an important part in their lives than do their fellow students in the same category (Tables S9.17, S9.18). Similarly, the compatibles are more likely than the separatists to view Israel as a continuation of the Jewish history of all periods (Table S9.19).

The correlations between responses on parallel criteria of Israeli and Jewish identity bear out the finding that students who are more "Jewish" are likely also to be more "Israeli." Thus, there is a positive correlation between valence of Jewishness and valence of Israeliness (r=.36) and between centrality of Jewishness and centrality of Israeliness (r=.28).

We have pointed to the differences between those who see their Jewishness and Israeliness as interrelated and those who see them as things apart. When students were questioned how their "being Jewish" and how their "being Israeli" express themselves, significant variations in the degree of perceived overlap became discernible among those who see the two subidentities as interrelated. A number of the religious students view their Israeliness as an extension of their Jewishness. This means that for them Jewishness is the broader, inclusive category embracing Israeliness within it. For the nonreligious students the degree of overlap is generally less. Jewish ritual practices, for example, are seen by them to fall into the nonoverlapping area. At the same time, several of the religious festivals—such as Passover, Shavuot and Succot—are so much a part of the national life that there is a tendency to locate them in the overlapping Jewish-Israeli area. Within this area, too, falls all that concerns relations with world Jewry and events in Jewish history.

COLLECTIVIST V. INDIVIDUALIST ORIENTATIONS

The students were asked to indicate on a seven point "Jewish-private individual" scale whether they felt themselves more of a Jew or more of a private individual. Eighty-three percent of the religious students located themselves on the first of three rungs of the Jewish side as compared with 45 percent of the traditionalists and 24 percent of the non-religious students. As compared with 1965 this represents a significant rise in the Jewish collectivist orientation of the religious students and in the private individual orientation of the nonreligious, while the position of the traditionalists remains approximately the same over the years.[9] On a parallel "Israeli-private individual" scale the response of the religious students again reflects a collectivist rather than individualist orientation, although the differences between them and the other two categories are not as sharp as on the Jewish scale. Sixty-eight percent of the religious students chose the first three rungs on the Israeli side of the scale as did 55 percent of the traditionalists and 50 percent of the nonreligious. As compared with 1965 there was a slight rise in the Israeli collectivist orientation of the religious students and a slight decline in the Israeli collectivist orientation of the traditionalist and nonreligious students (Tables S9.20, S9.21).

THE NORMS OF JEWISH BEHAVIOR: THE ATTRIBUTES OF A GOOD JEW

A list of seven activities was presented to the students and they were asked to indicate to what extent they regarded them as important in order to be a "good Jew" (a) in Israel, and (b) in the Diaspora. A student could check one of the following categories:

(1) Essential in order to be a good Jew;
(2) Very desirable in order to be a good Jew;

(3) Desirable;
(4) Irrelevant in regard to being a good Jew.

The trend in 1974, as compared with 1965, is to upgrade the desirability or necessity of most items as requirements for being a good Jew (Tables S9.22, S9.23).

Ranking highest in 1974, as in 1965, as requirements for being a good Jew in Israel are "to work for the ingathering of Jews from the golah" and "to live an ethical life." Then follow "to take an interest in the fate of the Jews in the world" and "to celebrate barmitzvah." For the good Jew in the golah, the first requirement is "to settle in Israel or to encourage his children to settle," which is accorded a higher rating than in 1965 when it was third on the list. It is followed by the two activities which preceded it in 1965—"to support Israel" and "to take an interest in the affairs of the local Jewish community."

Although there is no item in the list which is rated as completely irrelevant, the general item, "to take an interest in the fate of persecuted peoples," received—in 1974 as in 1965—a relatively low rating as a requirement for a good Jew in the Diaspora and an even lower rating for a good Jew in Israel.

"To be a loyal citizen of Israel" for the Jew in Israel is rated higher than "to be a loyal citizen of the country in which he lives" for the Jew in the golah. In keeping with their perception of Israel as a Jewish state with a special relationship to the Jewish historical tradition and to the Jewish people, the students see a closer connection between being a loyal citizen of Israel and being a good Jew.

The role of the two items of religious observance "to attend synagogue services" and "to celebrate barmitzvah" is stressed more strongly—in 1974 as in 1965—in relation to the Jews of the golah than in relation to the Jews of Israel. Nonreligious students who rated attendance at synagogue services 2.9 for the Jew in Israel (as compared with 3.4 in 1965) rated it 2.4 for the Jew in the golah where it was seen as an act of identification.

The religious students place more stringent demands on the Jew, and their rating reflects the greater importance they attach to all the items in the list as requirements for a good Jew.

The students are interested in the preservation of Jewish identity in the Diaspora and oppose assimilation. When asked whether a young Jew who is not prepared to settle in Israel should assimilate or preserve his Jewishness, 92 percent urge the maintenance of his Jewish identity. A small minority (drawn mainly from the ranks of the nonreligious students) favor assimilation in these circumstances (Table S9.24).

Views on emigration from Israel, "yerida," (a subject of concern and public disapproval) remains substantially the same in 1974 as in 1965. A minute percentage (3 percent in 1974 and 1 percent in 1965) express readiness for such a step, a small minority (10 percent in 1974, and 12 percent in 1965) indicate that they may be prepared to consider such a step, while the great majority register either opposition or disinclination (Table S9.25).

ATTITUDES TO YIDDISH AND LADINO

While Yiddish is still spoken in the homes of many Israeli families who come from Eastern Europe, the main language in Israel is Hebrew which has served as a force unifying Jews from diverse cultural backgrounds. Yiddish is no longer seen as a language competing for the dominant position in Jewish life. Instead, there is a concern in some circles, who cherish highly the language, its literature, and the associations they carry, about the possible disappearance of Yiddish from the contemporary Jewish scene. At the same time there are others who still look askance at Yiddish as one of the symbols of life in the Diaspora, of a "galut existence," although the erstwhile derision of the language seems to have lost its sharpness.

Few members of the younger generation speak either Yiddish or Ladino. The attitude to Yiddish is to a large extent one of indifference—on the part of 54 percent of the

Ashkenazic sector and 70 percent of the Oriental sector. Thirty-one percent of the Ashkenazic students have a positive and 15 percent a negative attitude. Twenty-three percent in the Oriental sector view it negatively. It apparently evokes the feeling in some of them that this is an "ashkenazic" language in which they have no share.

The attitude to Ladino (Judeo-Spanish, the language of the Jewish communities of Turkey, the Balkan countries, and parts of North Africa) is even more pronouncedly one of indifference—on the part of 66 percent of the Oriental sector and 79 percent of the Ashkenazic sector. Very few in either sector express a negative attitude (Tables S9.26, S9.27).

Communal Differences: Ashkenazic and Oriental Communities

The proportion of religious Jews is greater in the Oriental than in the Ashkenazic communities and this produces differences when there is an overall comparison between the two sectors. When, however, the religious observance variable is held constant, no significant differences exist on the basic identity criteria between students from the Ashkenazic and Oriental communities in two of the three categories. Religious students from the Ashkenazic communities hold attitudes corresponding to those of students from the Oriental communities and the same holds true for the nonreligious students of both communities. Differences do, however, exist between the traditionalists of the two sectors. Indeed this category does not admit of strict comparison in the two sectors. Whereas in the Ashkenazic communities a sharp, clear distinction is drawn between the terms "dati" (religiously observant) and "m'sorati" (traditionalist) and the self-classification provides no difficulty, the distinction tends to be blurred among the Oriental communities. Some members of the Oriental communities who are close in terms of observance to the "dati'im" classify themselves as "m'sorati'im." This, in fact, becomes the largest category

Table 9.28:   Religious distribution of students in Ashkenazic and
              Oriental communities

	Oriental	Ashkenazic
Religious	21	28
Traditionalist	56	21
Nonreligious	23	51
Total %	100	100
N	479	1,090

among students from the Oriental sector—56 percent so classify themselves (Table 9.28).

A difference which is not limited to the traditionalist category occurs when Israeliness and Jewishness are counterposed as on the seven point Israeli-Jewish scale. As compared with the religious and traditionalist students from the Ashkenazic sector, the corresponding categories in the Oriental sector move more strongly to the Jewish side of the scale. This is most pronouncedly so in the case of the Oriental traditionalists whose mean position on the scale is 4.7 as compared with 3.8, the mean position of the Ashkenazic traditionalists. The position of the Oriental religious students is 5.9 as compared with 5.3 in the case of the Ashkenazic religious students. There is no difference on this scale between the nonreligious students from the two sectors.

Further differences between the two sectors are expectedly found on specific issues which have direct relevance to the communal factor, such as the attitude to Yiddish and Ladino (Tables S9.26, S9.27), or to the suffering of European Jewry in the period of the Holocaust (Table S6.2) and the suffering of Jews from persecution in the Islamic countries (Table S9.29).

In a number of cases the parents of the students in the Oriental sector came from countries which were technologically backward and they moved into the lower economic strata of Israel's Jewish population. Although efforts are being made, particularly in the educational sphere, to narrow the gap, the socio-economic differences still exist and there is at times a tendency on the part of members of the Oriental communities to regard themselves as an underprivileged sector. Even when there is no objective basis for it, the subjective feeling needs to be taken into account in an analysis of the attitudes of members of this sector.

When we turn our attention to the secularization which is taking place in Israeli society, we observe generational differences in the impact of the process on the Ashkenazic and Oriental sectors. In our 1965 study we compared the religious observance of three generations—grandparents, parents, and their sons and daughters. We found that in the Ashkenazic sector the decline in religious observance had been most marked between grandparents and parents and was slowing down when the parents were compared with their sons and daughters. In the Oriental sector the parents had in large part maintained the traditional practices transmitted by the grandparents, but the sons and daughters were becoming markedly less observant. Our 1974 study confirmed this trend. While 30 percent of the students in the Ashkenazic sector stated that they were less religiously observant than their parents, as many as 56 percent in the Oriental sector so reported. Moreover, in 1974, as compared with 1965, a

Table 9.30: Comparison of religious observance in students and parents —according to communal background

	All Respondents		Oriental		Ashkenazic	
	1974	1965	1974	1965	1974	1965
More religious than parents	10	7	7	7	11	8
As religious as parents	52	51	37	45	59	55
Less religious than parents	38	42	56	48	30	37
Total %	100	100	100	100	100	100
N	1,727	3,636	509	1,116	1,218	2,520

decline was observable in the percentage of students from Ashkenazic families declaring themselves less religious than their parents, but in the case of the students from Oriental communities the percentage increased (Table 9.30).

The young generation in the Oriental sector is moving away from religious practices into a traditionalist and increasingly also into a nonreligious direction. The break with established family patterns in many cases leaves a void which is not filled by other Jewish values, and they are left without anchor and rudder. Their parents had been relatively unaffected by the modernizing trends which have swept the Western world and which have been integrated to some extent into the life of the Ashkenazic sector of Israeli society. The members of the young generation in the Oriental sector are not inured to the challenges of modernity and are less equipped to face them than are their Ashkenazic peers.

While secularization is now having its sharp impact in the Oriental sector, it needs to be observed that the percentage of students declaring themselves nonreligious (23 percent) still remains considerably lower than in the Ashkenazic sector (51 percent), (Table 9.28 above).

Within the Oriental sector differences exist both in regard to the forms of religious practice and the degree of religious observance between the communities which are included under this broad classification. Highest in the scale of religious observance are the Yemenite Jews, and they accordingly have the strongest Jewish identity. When the factor of religious observance is controlled the differences between the subcommunities narrow.

Religious Observance as the Crucial Variable

It will be observed that religious observance is the crucial variable in the determination of the strength of the Jewish identity in Israel as elsewhere. On all criteria of Jewish identity the religious students rank highest, then come the traditionalists, while the nonreligious students stand lowest on all scales. Not only is there—as could be expected—a much greater measure of Jewish content in the lives of the religious students, but their attachment to the Jewish people is stronger. They feel closer to Jews everywhere, whatever their geographical location, their ideology, or their communal background. They have a historical time perspective which is broader in scope and more structured than that of the other categories; they have a strong sense of Jewish historical continuity, and they, more so than members of the other categories, feel that Jews should regard themselves as if they were survivors of the Holocaust. They are more conscious of the interrelatedness between their Jewishness and their Israeliness, and in their case there is a considerable degree of overlap between the two. In 1974 they also stand somewhat higher than the other two categories on criteria of Israeliness. They are also the most Zionist of the three categories. Indeed, they represent the hard Jewish core of Israeli society.

The attitudes of the religious students reflect a crystallized value system fostered in the home and reinforced in the schools and youth movement. It is a value system which enters into many areas of their lives. Their replies to questions in our questionnaire clustered around a particular response category, while those of the traditionalists and nonreligious Jews were more widely distributed. In constrast to the relative homogeneity of outlook within the religious sector, the traditionalists and nonreligious categories are classifications embracing widely differing subcategories. Generalizations about these categories have to be made with due reservation.

Table 9.31: *   Comparison by students of their religious observance with that of their parents

	All Respondents		Religious		Traditionalist		Nonreligious	
	1974*	1965	1974*	1965	1974*	1965	1975*	1965
More religious than parents	10	7	22	16	7	7	5	2
Just as religious as parents	52	51	66	55	42	48	52	51
Less religious than parents	38	42	12	29	51	45	43	47
Total %	100	100	100	100	100	100	100	100
N	1,864	3,626	464	911	635	1,183	765	1,532

A popular impression prevails that the religious fervor of the younger generation of religious Israelis has intensified in recent years. This impression is borne out by the data of our study. Sixty-six percent of the religious students see themselves as being as religious as their parents, and 22 percent regard themselves as more religious. Only a small minority of 12 percent (as compared with 29 percent in 1965) see themselves as less religious (Table 9.31).

1974 and 1965: A Review of Changes

Comparing the responses in 1974 with those of 1965 we find that on the questions concerning feelings about Jewishness and Israeliness, a considerable measure of stability is observable across the period. While no radical changes have occurred in the attitudes relating to the basic elements of the Israeli-Jewish identity, there is somewhat more of a tendency to see Israeliness and Jewishness as interrelated. Where the two are counterposed, as on the seven point Israeli-Jewish scale, a shift occurs towards the Jewish side.

In the 1965 study the religious students ranked highest on all criteria of Jewish identity and stood at about the same level as the other two categories in regard to the strength of the Israeli identity. In the intervening period the Israeli identity of the religious students has further strengthened, and on this component, too, they now rank higher than the other categories. The attitudes of the traditionalists and nonreligious reflect a slight strengthening of their Jewish identity, and they maintain a position similar to that of 1965 on the Israeli identity. The collectivist orientation (both Jewish and Israeli) on the part of the religious students is somewhat stronger than it was in 1965, while there has been no corresponding movement away from the individualist orientation on the part of the nonreligious.

The Process of Secularization

Our sample in 1974 was so constructed as to maintain the same proportions of religious, traditionalist, and nonreligious students as in 1965. To the extent that the proportions have been maintained in the Israeli population at large it may be said that here has been no weakening but rather a strengthening in Jewish identity over the past decade. The process of secularization, however, continues—particularly in what has hitherto been the more religious sector, the Oriental communities—and the proportions are in fact changing. Thus, statistics indicate that there has been a decrease in the enrolment in the religious schools relative to the general enrolment (from 29 percent in 1965 to 25.7 percent in 1974). The weakening of the religious factor brings in its train a weakening of Jewish identity—and also of Israeli identity.

The continuing process of secularization means that an increasing percentage of Israeli Jews falls into the nonreligious category whose Jewish identity is weakest, albeit not as weak as is commonly supposed. Our study shows that the majority of nonreligious Israelis possess a sense of belonging to a Jewish people and see themselves as continuing a Jewish historical tradition—although even on this score a danger signal is provided by the fact that a small minority regard Israelis as a separate people. The main problem, however, lies in the attitude of a not inconsiderable minority to the content of their Jewishness. It has little attraction for them, and Jewish norms play a limited role in their lives. They tend to sunder their Israeliness from their Jewishness.

When we compare the nonreligious Israeli with his parents, the weakness in his Jewish identity emerges sharply. We undertook such a comparison in our 1965 study and the findings demonstrated the stronger Jewish identity of the parents. While the religious students were close to the attitudes of their parents, a considerable gap appeared between traditionalist parents and traditionalist students, and the gap widened between the nonreligious parents and the nonreligious students. The greater proportion of parents had passed through the cauldron of Jewish minority existence and could not be indifferent to the fact of their Jewishness. Many of the nonreligious parents came from Eastern Europe, and even those among them who were in revolt against the religious tradition brought with them a Jewishness which stemmed from an intensive Jewish cultural milieu. The absence of religious observance in the young Israeli had a more pronounced effect on his Jewish identity since it was not buttressed by the peculiar Jewish experience which was the lot of his parents and which in many cases provided the basis for their decision to transplant their lives to Israel.

An acute problem exists in regard to the Jewishness of these nonreligious Israelis as well as that of many traditionalists with whom religious observance is on the decline. The awareness of this problem has stimulated a search in some quarters for paths to an intensified Jewishness which is in keeping with the Jewish historical tradition and yet can be followed by young Israelis who are not strictly observant.

In the exposed non-Jewish environment of the Diaspora, Jews have exercised caution in introducing changes into Jewish life lest the changes result in the infiltration of influences which run counter to the laws of their own Jewish being. It has been a policy of Orthodox leadership to "hedge in" and to criticize groups in the community who in their view have adapted excessively to their environment. In Israel, however, change should be able to proceed more freely in the environment provided by Jewish majority society. But it seems that the inhibitions engendered by the centuries of Diaspora existence still persist. While the need for caution can be understood, there is cogency to the demand frequently heard that there be a more flexible attitude in developing forms of Jewish living which will attract elements in Israeli society who, while not religiously observant in the Orthodox sense, nonetheless seek more Jewish substance in their lives. We would submit that the changes can best come from circles who are themselves rooted in Jewish tradition and are determined to preserve continuity while fostering change.

Countervailing Forces

While the inroads of secularization have serious implications for the future of Jewish identity, there are also countervailing forces. The Six Day War and the Yom Kippur War sharpened the sense of Jewish interdependence among Israel's youth.[10] The memory of the Holocaust which had been simmering at the back of the minds of a generation born after that catastrophe has been activated by the events of these years. Furthermore, Israelis saw how in the testing hour of danger Jews throughout the world spontaneously and unreservedly rallied to their side. The assertion of their identity by the Jews in Soviet Russia and their determined struggle to immigrate to Israel has also had its impact on Israelis as on Jews in the United States and elsewhere.

The growing feeling of a common Jewish destiny and of Jewish solidarity, coupled with a wide acceptance of mutual responsibility, are foundations on which an educational program for the intensification of the Jewishness of Israeli youth can be constructed. The basic attitudes have not fundamentally changed even under the impact of dramatic events, but a psychological climate now exists which is propitious for the deepening of the Jewish consciousness which has been aroused.

The implementation of such a program—even when the climate is favorable—is no easy matter. There has been no systematic evaluation of the program for the strengthening of Jewish consciousness in the secular schools adopted in the Knesset during the 1950s. But few claim that it has been an educational success.

In the case of the religiously observant young Israeli, the home, religious school and religious youth movement interlock to produce an intensity of Jewish identity. When we consider the problem of the nonreligious youth, the school is again just one in a constellation of factors. But in relation to this one factor, which is, at least, amenable to planned change, much remains to be done in terms of curriculum and, even more importantly, the training of teachers.

NOTES

1. D. Ben-Gurion, *Israel: A Personal History* (New York: Funk and Wagnalls, 1971), p. 827.

2. The "second aliyah" denotes the pioneering immigration from the beginning of the century until the outbreak of World War I. Among the immigrants who came during this period were Ben-Gurion and Ben-Zvi, who played a leading role in the establishment of the state. The "third aliyah" refers to the immigration in the nineteen twenties after World War I.

3. Among studies which seem to us to err in this direction are G. Friedmann, *The End of the Jewish People?* (New York: Doubleday, 1967); and M. Spiro, *Children of the Kibbutz* (Cambridge, Mass.: Harvard University Press, 1958).

4. The findings of the 1965 study are reported in S. N. Herman, *Israelis and Jews: The Continuity of an Identity* (New York: Random House, 1970).

5. It should be noted that at the high school level the percentage of pupils from the Oriental communities is below the percentage of these communities in the population at large. The sample furthermore did not include the relatively small number of ultra-Orthodox pupils at schools not within the framework of the Ministry of Education.

6. The tables for these and other questions are contained in a research report submitted by the author to the Memorial Foundation for Jewish Culture on *Studies in Jewish Identity* (Institute of Contemporary Jewry, Hebrew University, Jerusalem 1976).

7. Ibid. for tables on closeness to various categories of Jews.

8. Cf., Y. Kaufman, "Anti-Semitic Stereotypes in Zionism," *Commentary* 7 (1949), 239-245.

9. The implications of the collectivist orientation of the religious sector are discussed in an unpublished doctoral dissertation in the Department of Sociology of the Hebrew University by O. Cohen, *The Conflict Between Religious and Non-Religious Jews in Israel: Solidarity and Social Distance among High School Students* (Jerusalem: 1975).

10. For data on the impact of the Six Day War on the attitudes of university students, see, E. Etzioni-Halevy and R. Shapira, "Jewish Identification of Israeli Students: What Lies Ahead," *Jewish Social Studies* 37 (1975), 251-266. For the impact of the Yom Kippur War, see, M. Davis, ed., *Israel and the Jewish People: During and After the Yom Kippur War* (Jerusalem: Hasifriya Haziyonit, 1975). (In Hebrew.)

Chapter 10

WHEN JEWISH STUDENTS MEET IN ISRAEL

Israel is the meeting ground of Jewish students from all parts of the world. They come every year in the tens of thousands—some for a regular program of studies at one of the universities, others for a year's study, and the largest number for a summer study visit. The Hebrew University has a school for overseas students, and the other universities in Israel provide special facilities as well. The students are to be found not only at the universities but also in the yeshivot, in programs sponsored by the World Zionist Organization and by organizations such as Young Judaea and the Rama Camps. The Hebrew Union College, which trains candidates for the Reform rabbinate in America, makes it a requirement for all its students to spend a year of their studies at its Jerusalem branch, and the Jewish Theological Seminary of America, which trains the Conservative rabbis, similarly provides facilities for its students. The aliya from the USSR brought to the Israeli campus a number of students from that part of the world.

This gathering of students provides an opportunity for a study of the interrelationship between Israelis and their fellow Jews from the Diaspora. What are the expectations of the visiting students and to what extent are these expectations met? How do they perceive their hosts? What is the role of social contact? How does the meeting affect the Jewish identity of the visiting students?

Students from the United States and the USSR

We explored these questions in the course of studies carried out on students from the United States and from the USSR.

Our American subjects were 274 junior-year students who had come to Israel under the aegis of the one year program of the Hebrew University. They were due to return to the United States at the end of the year, but a certain proportion were intent upon immigrating to Israel at a later date. They had been in Israel for just over half the year when the questionnaire was administered at the beginning of 1972.

In a study of reactions to the Yom Kippur War, we administered in February 1974 a brief questionnaire to a random sample (n=100) of junior-year students who had been in Israel during the period of the war. We shall refer to a few of the questions in that questionnaire.

The 443 students from the USSR were all in the category of new immigrants. Through the cooperation of the research division of the Immigrant Absorption Ministry of the Israel government, we were permitted to include a limited number of our questions in a survey which they conducted in 1973 among students from the USSR who had arrived in Israel during the years 1972 and 1973.

In the case of the students from the United States, we were able to supplement the questionnaire with a series of interviews, and a number of students also wrote essays about their stay in Israel as part of a seminar conducted by the author. In regard to the students from the USSR, the data are based on the questionnaires and a limited number of detailed interviews (ten in all). Our discussion accordingly will refer mainly to the reactions of the American students, and we shall introduce the data derived from the responses of the students from the USSR wherever such data are available for purposes of comparison. In making this comparison it is necessary to bear in mind the difference in the time perspective of the two groups of students—the American students are sojourners in Israel, the students from the USSR are immigrants. The former know that soon they will return to the United States and do not need to return to Israel unless they so wish; the students from the USSR realize that they have to reach a permanent modus vivendi with the Israelis.

Neither the students from the United States nor those from Soviet Russia can be regarded as representatives of their Jewish communities. The fact that they chose to come to Israel in itself implies the existence of a selective factor. With this reservation in mind, however, it becomes of interest to observe what is in common and what is different in the reactions to Israel and Israelis on the part of students from two cultures which are so far apart—students from a democratic regime and pluralistic culture who have enjoyed, at least, a modicum of Jewish education and complete freedom of religious worship, and students from a totalitarian anti-religious regime who have been cut off from the wellsprings of Jewish culture.

Limitations of Social Contact

While the problem of social contact is salient in any exploration of the adjustment of the visiting student, it has nonetheless to be seen as just one of a number of factors determining the measure of his satisfaction with the country and his hosts. The popular tendency is to attach exaggerated importance to the role of social contact in shaping the attitudes of a newcomer to Israel and to the Israelis. It does indeed play an important part, but other factors enter as

well. Were it not for the operation of these factors, the
students, who express so much disappointment with the
nature of the social contact, would not leave as satisfied and
as exhilarated with their stay in Israel as they often do.

A distinction should be drawn between two dimensions of
the contact situation, namely its "acquaintanceship potential," i.e., the opportunities it provides for participants to
"get to know" one another, and its "social acceptance implication," i.e., the extent to which the contact implies that the
one participant is willing to accept the other as a social equal
and at least potentially as a friend.[1] Studies conducted on
foreign students in a number of countries show that in regard
to both these dimensions, the area of social contact between
the host society and the student guest is everywhere beset
with problems.

The interest of the guests in meeting their hosts is generally greater than the interest of the hosts in having social
contact with the guests, and the hosts are often preoccupied
with the pursuit of their regular activities. The norms of the
host society are not always easily "visible" to the visitors
located on the periphery, and they often are at a loss how to
act.[2] Furthermore, cultural differences exist in the very process of establishing acquaintanceship and friendship.

In Israel too these problems confront the newcomers.
Thus, in the American culture it is relatively easy to enter the
outer circle of acquaintanceship, but progression towards the
inner circle of friendship is not always easy. In Israel, on the
other hand, the entry into the outer circle is slower and more
difficult, although once the student has surmounted the barriers, the possibilities exist of more rapid progression to the
inner circle of friendship. The American students were taken
aback by the initial barrier, which seemed to them to reflect
an attitude of indifference, or even of rejection, on the part
of the hosts.

The problem of social contact in Israel is complicated by
the high expectations that the visitors have of being welcomed as fellow Jews by the Israelis and the intensity of the

disappointment when this welcome is not readily forthcoming. At the same time, the Jewishness they have in common leads, in a number of cases, to a deeper friendship between the Israeli and the visiting student—and when the Israeli sees the student as a potential immigrant, the feeling of closeness towards him develops further.

The more lasting social contact arises from mutual interests rather than from goodwill or from mere compliance with social etiquette. Friendships grew in cases where there was a discovery of such mutual interests. The orthodoxly religious students found such common interest with religious Israeli students together with whom they constituted a "minyan" for prayer, participated in Sabbath services, were guests at Friday night meals in the homes, and joined in festival celebrations. Students who return to Israel for study in professional courses make friends with Israelis engaged in the same studies.

While it is possible to descern what are the dominant attitudes which prevail in it, Israeli society is not a uniform entity in its approach to the newcomer, whether he is a visiting student or immigrant. Within it are sectors which are more "open," more receptive to entry by the newcomer than others, and much depends on what sector he has occasion to meet.

The semantic differential rating instrument (developed by Osgood and his associates)[3] was administered to the visiting American students to ascertain how they perceived and evaluated the concepts "American Jew" and "Israeli." The students were requested to rate each concept on identical lists of bipolar adjective scales, such as "unsociable-sociable." Each set of adjectives was arranged along a seven point scale (Table S10.1).

The rating of the students reflect the critical view they have of Israelis on some of the traits with a specific bearing on social contact. On the "discourteous-courteous" scale the mean rating for Israelis is 2.6 (on the discourtesy side of the scale), whereas the American Jews are rated at 5.2 (on the

Table 10.2:   Semantic differential: ratings of concept "Israeli" and
              "American Jew" on social contact variables (mean values)

Adjective Pairs	Concepts	
	The Israeli	The American Jew
Unsociable-sociable	4.3	5.3
Cold-warm	3.9	5.1
Discourteous-courteous	2.6	5.2
Inhospitable-hospitable	5.6	5.2

courtesy side). At the same time, the students give the Israelis
a moderately favorable rating for "sociability" (4.3 as compared with 5.3 for American Jews) and a more distinctly
favorable evaluation for "hospitality" (5.6 as compared with
5.2 for American Jews). The ambivalence of the American
students toward the Israelis in the sphere of interpersonal
relations is reflected in the rating on the "cold-warm" variable. They choose a position (3.9) close to the midpoint,
whereas the American Jew is rated as much "warmer" (5.1),
(Table 10.2).

Israel and Israelis—Varying Perspectives

The perspective in which Israel is seen by the visiting
students will influence not only their relationship to the
country, but also their perception of the Israeli.

Israel may have a variety of meanings for the Jewish
student:

(1) He may focus on the geo-political entity, the state in the Middle
    East. He may see the here and now of the state without
    reference to its role in the life of the Jewish people.

(2) The emphasis may be on the Jewish homeland, Eretz Israel, seen
    in a Jewish historical perspective as the land of the Bible, as the
    cultural, spiritual center of the Jewish people.

(3) Israel may be seen primarily in terms of its function in relation
    to the Jewish condition—as the country "gathering in the
    exiles" and ending Jewish wandering and helplessness, its doors

Table 10.3:   Israel as continuation of the Jewish historical tradition
("Is the State of Israel a continuation of the Jewish
historical tradition?")

	USA	USSR
Yes, of all periods	82	75
Yes, but only of those periods when the Jews lived in Eretz Israel	8	15
No, it is somethig new, with no links to the Jewish past	10	10
	n=261	n=439

open to Jews who for one reason or another desire or are
compelled to leave their country of origin.

The majority of the students view Israel in the broader
Jewish contexts. Eighty-two percent of the American students (75 percent of the students from Soviet Russia) regard
the State of Israel as a continuation of the Jewish historical
tradition. At the same time, a minority see it as a continuation of just those periods when Jews lived in Eretz Israel, or
they go further and delimit it as something new with no links
to the Jewish past (Table 10.3).

The majority of students regard Israelis as part and parcel
of the Jewish people. In the eyes of a minority, however,
they constitute a separate people; the minority is significantly larger among students from the USSR than among
students from the United States (Table 10.4).

The American students reported in interviews that when
on their arrival they walked down the streets of Jerusalem
and saw the many variegated types of Israelis drawn from all
parts of the globe, their first impression was of the dissimilarities between American Jews and the Israelis. They remained
conscious, however, of the interdependence binding all Jews
together and of the mutual responsibility that flows from it.
The consciousness of a common fate, although in less emphatic terms, also found expression among students from the
Soviet Union (Table S10.5).

Table 10.4:   Israelis as part of Jewish people
                "Do you think that the Israelis:

	USA	USSR
Are part and parcel of the Jewish people?"	77	66
Constitute a separate people?	23	34
	n=261	n=437

The students from the United States regard it as a duty of
the State of Israel to help the American Jewish community
and in turn see it as a duty of the American Jewish community to extend help in time of need to Israel. When it is a
question of help to Israel, a greater percentage of students
feel that such aid should be given "in every case." There is
more of a tendency to qualify the aid to the American Jewish
community with the proviso "only if the help does not result
in a serious detriment to the State of Israel."

While they express qualifications about the degree of closeness to individual Israelis, the responses of the American
students to a question about their relationship to eight Jewish communities indicate that they feel as close—even slightly
closer—to the Jewish community in Israel as to their own
community in the United States. Then follows the Jewish
community in the USSR, and after it come the Jewish
communities in the Arab countries—communities which are
subject to persecution and in whose support Jews everywhere
have rallied. The degree of closeness to other communities is
lower. The order of attributed closeness approximates that
obtained from the Israeli students on an identical question
(Table S10.6; cf. Table S9.6 for Israeli students).

The Image of the Israelis

Over 90 percent of the students report a favorable impression about Israel. Since they see Israel as the Jewish homeland, the reactions reflected in the interviews with them

indicate a degree of emotional involvement which is not likely to be found among foreign students visiting a country with which they have no such special relationship.

On the whole, the majority of students maintain a favorable view also about Israelis despite the ambivalence to which unsatisfactory social contact gives rise. Their attitudes to Israelis are, however, not as emphatically favorable as is their feeling about Israel, and a minority go further and report an unfavorable impression. This minority is smaller among the students from the Soviet Union than among the students from the United States (Tables 10.7, 10.8).

Our interviews with the American students show that the image of the Israeli appears in two versions in the minds of the students, and the second of these versions is less affected by the experience of social contact than the first.

Table 10.7: Impression about Israel
("What is the general impression you have about Israel?")

	USA	USSR
Very favorable	29	5
Favorable	62	90
Unfavorable	7	5
Very unfavorable	2	0
	n=269	n=432

Table 10.8: Impression about Israelis
("What is the general impression you have about Israelis?")

	USA	USSR
Very favorable	8	3
Favorable	61	84
Unfavorable	28	12
Very unfavorable	3	1
	n=256	n=423

(1) The Israelis may be seen primarily as citizens of the State of Israel. At times they are viewed positively as hospitable hosts, at other times negatively as the bureaucratic officials, or as the rude, uncivil Israeli man in the street, or as the Israeli student who does not seem to go out of his way to become acquainted.

(2) They may be viewed primarily as fellow Jews, the builders of the Jewish homeland, the soldiers defending it, the writers and scientists extending its cultural horizons.

In different settings one or other of these versions becomes more salient. When the students have to contend with "red tape" in a government office or are unceremoniously pushed about in a bus line, the first version dominates. During the Yom Kippur War, on the other hand, the Israelis were seen as fellow Jews defending the homeland, and 77 percent of the American students who were questioned at the time (n=100) reported a more favorable attitude to them than had existed previously. In the interviews with the students, statements such as the following were typical: "I realize they were also fighting the war for me; I realize the pressures and realities they must live with"; and "I am proud of the people who live here and have dedicated their lives to the existence of this country."

An earlier study showed that when the students returned to the United States and the frustrations of daily social contact recede into the background, the Israeli is seen in a more relaxed and broader perspective—and the view of him becomes more favorable.[4]

The students who regard the State of Israel as a continuation of the Jewish historical tradition of all periods have a significantly more favorable view than the others about Israel and Israelis. A more favorable view is also expressed by the students who regard Israelis as part and parcel of the Jewish people rather than as a separate people.[5]

Misperceptions

When asked whether they see themselves first and foremost as Jews or as Americans, 87 percent of the students declared that they see themselves first and foremost as Jews, and a similar percentage (89 percent) stated that they would prefer Israelis to see them in the same way.

Their Jewishness is what they have in common with Israelis; while they may be strangers in the country, they do not regard themselves, and do not wish to be regarded, as foreigners. They get, however, what is for them the disappointing impression that the Israelis see them primarily as the nationals of the country of their origin rather than as Jews. Eighty-eight percent believe Israelis see them first and foremost as Americans, and only 12 percent think they are seen primarily as Jews.

Is this, however, a correct impression of the Israelis' perception? A study conducted in the United States by Bruner and Perlmutter does indeed show that in a meeting with foreigners, the elements of difference between the parties to the encounter are more salient than the similarities.[6] In Israel there are groups of students from so many countries that it is a matter of convenience to differentiate between them in terms of the country of origin (as we are indeed doing in the present study). Under these circumstances, it is all the more impressive to find that when we introduced a question on the subject into a questionnaire administered to first-year students in the Department of Psychology at the Hebrew University and to students at two religious academies in Jerusalem, a substantial percentage declared that they saw the newcomers primarily as Jews. Sixty-six percent of the students at the religious academies—and 52 percent of the Psychology students—so saw them.

The relative salience of the American and Jewish identities will vary from situation to situation both for the American student and for the Israeli in their encounters. But it would seem that the Israelis have a greater awareness of the Jewishness of the visiting students than the latter usually suppose.

A feeling similar to that of the American students is expressed by the students from the Soviet Union. In a questionnaire administered to them a further choice was introduced. They were asked whether they would wish to be seen first and foremost as Jews, Israelis, or Russians. Only a minute percentage (2 percent) would wish to be seen as Russians; the majority (58 percent) would wish to be seen as Jews, and a substantial minority (40 percent) as Israelis. But the majority (63 percent) believed that the Israelis saw them first and foremost as Russians, although the minority who felt they were seen as Jews (35 percent) was greater than in the case of the students from the United States. A mere 2 percent believed they were seen first and foremost as Israelis.

Misconceptions also exist about the extent to which Israelis are religiously observant and about the nature of their Jewishness. On the seven point "irreligious-religious" scale in the semantic differential, the American students located the Israelis on the irreligious side (2.9) while the American Jews were given a significantly higher rating (3.9). A group of American students who were asked the question in 1974 divided equally between those who saw the Israelis as more religious than they would wish them to be and those who saw them as less religious. Among the students from the USSR only 20 percent saw the Israelis as less religious.

While on the semantic differential the American students rated the Israelis as proud of their Jewishness (4.8) and even prouder of their Israeliness (5.8), about half of the group we questioned in 1974 regarded Israelis as less Jewish than they would wish them to be. The students from the USSR who, as we have noted, were not concerned about any lack of religiosity on the part of Israelis, did show concern about their Jewishness—52 percent declared that the Israelis were less Jewish than they wished them to be.

While there are weaknesses in the Jewish identity of the non-religious sector of Israeli society, the Israelis—as our research has demonstrated—are more Jewish than is commonly supposed. What, then, is the source of the inaccurate perception of the extent and nature of their Jewishness? We would suggest that the following factors account for the misconceptions that are to be found among visiting students.

(a) In the United States (and the position is paralleled in other countries of the Diaspora) there is, as we have observed, a sharp demarcation between the areas to which the Jewish role and those to which the American role pertains. In most of his activities, the American Jew is an American; on certain special occasions he acts as a Jew.[7] In Israel being Jewish and being Israeli overlap; the one is not clearly demarcated from the other. Being Jewish is less specific, in this sense less conspicuous, than it is in the United States, but it may be more meaningful in that it pervades a larger number of regions of the life-space.

(b) In the Diaspora Jews are in constant juxtaposition with the non-Jewish groups from whom they see themselves as marked off. This heightens the salience, or awareness, of their Jewishness. In Israel the salience may be lower, but the valence, or attractiveness, of the person's Jewishness is not necessarily less.

(c) In the Diaspora a Jew demonstrates his Jewishness by being different from those around him, and in Israel he is Jewish by being like the others.

(d) The expressions of Jewishness in the majority Jewish society which is Israel do not necessarily conform to the stereotypical conception of what being Jewish is to a Jewish student who has been socialized in America or in another country of the Diaspora.

(e) Not only are these factors not clearly understood, but there is a tendency to generalize on the basis of limited contact with what is a heterogeneous population, and much depends on which sector the Jewish student has occasion to observe.

(f) There may be higher expectations on the part of the newcomer in regard to the Jewishness of Jews in the Jewish state. Furthermore, since this is the common bond between the visitor and his host, between the new immigrant and the veteran, his disappointment may be more marked where the Jewishness is not apparent.

The students also tended to underestimate the extent of religious observance in Israel. When asked to indicate what percentage of Jews in Israel were orthodoxly observant, the mean response was 10 percent, whereas, in fact, the religious sector represents close to 30 percent of Israeli society. The interviews with the students revealed that they were not adequately aware of the heterogeneity of the sector and that they entertained certain stereotyped conceptions about "dati'im." Only gradually is the picture of the ultra-Orthodox Jews throwing stones at passing traffic on the Sabbath replaced by that of the religious soldiers, students of the yeshivot, defending the homeland and showing high morale in doing so.

The Testing out of a Jewish Identity

The students came to Israel because of the interest they had in the country as Jews. Israel for most of them was the Jewish homeland and as such was linked up with their own identity as Jews. In this they differed from students who come to study in foreign countries to which they have no special prior attachment. There is yet another difference. Foreign students may upon the completion of their studies decide to remain in the host country. This generally happens because of the superior professional and other opportunities that the host country has to offer, and many visiting students have remained in a country such as the United States where such opportunities abound. The hosts, however, do not look upon the visiting student as a potential settler. In Israel, on the other hand, the hosts see in the visiting student a Jew whose proper place is as an oleh alongside them.

All the students we interviewed declared that they had been confronted by their hosts with the question, "Do you intend to settle?" Inevitably, aliya becomes a subject of intense discussion between the students themselves. Whatever the direction in which the student resolves the question, it is something with which he has to wrestle. In so doing he clarifies for himself where he stands as a Jew.

The Jewishness of a Jewish state leaves its impress on the visiting students. They live for a year in an environment in which the language is Hebrew and the national celebrations are of a Jewish character; they obtain an insight into the meaning of being Jewish in a Jewish majority society. In the interviews the students reported how deeply impressed they were by the way in which the country as a whole observed the Holocaust Remembrance Day. For the first time the students saw themselves in a Jewish mirror held up by Jews in a Jewish society, and the experience invested their Jewishness with an element of pride. When they left at the end of the year, the majority were more staunchly Jewish than they were when they came.

The following remarks are typical:

> In a curious way I feel more Jewish than when I lived in the U.S. Almost as if I can go home and hold my head up high.

> I had always felt a relationship to the Jews who lived in Israel, but it was always a relationship to a map. This year the relationship has become a real one and one that makes me proud.

> My stay in Israel has deepened my Jewishness—by participating in daily life, by actually *living* as a Jew, in an autonomous, sovereign Jewish state. It has strengthened my resolve to want to live here.

> It has strengthened my desire to enter the field of Jewish education.

And of an American Identity

The sojourn of the students also results in a clarification of their American identity. As soon as the students leave the borders of the United States, they begin to be designated as Americans by all with whom they come into contact. When they are questioned about America, its people, its way of life, and its political policies, they often feel themselves in a representative American capacity in responding to these questions or in affirming or refuting views expressed by others. Their Jewish identity was their distinctive mark in American society. In the Jewish society of Israel, their Jewish identity is what they have in common with others, and their Americanism is the differentiating factor—though not in quite in the same way as their Jewishness was in the United States. They meet not only Israelis but Jewish students from a number of other countries—the USSR, South Africa, Argentina, Britain, and other countries. While they are conscious of the Jewishness they share in common with all these students, they also become aware that each group of students represents and contributes something which is different and special in terms of its particular background. All this heightens the salience of their American identity.

The students also now examine, in the comparative frame of reference which a sojourn in another country provides, many of the elements in their American culture which they had previously accepted unquestioningly, almost as if they were a part of the natural order of things. Such examination leads to different results among different individuals—it may increase or decrease the valence of their American identity. But at the end of their stay they have a clearer view of what being American means to them.

So a student observes: "Of course I felt more American this year than ever before—but I also felt more Jewish too. The difference is that my feeling *more* American didn't make me feel *different* about it, whereas my feeling *more* Jewish made me also feel *prouder and better* about being a Jew." And another student remarks: "I realize America is a pretty good place and I am proud to be an American. I shall be leaving America to settle in Israel, but I will always retain ties with it." They realize that, whatever their feelings now about their American identity, it is an inextinguishable part of their being. The following is a typical remark: "You realize that your Americanism is a permanent part of your past, a part of your personality, it shaped you—you can't ever really run away from it, it is too deep."

NOTES

1. S. W. Cook and C. Selltiz, "Some Factors Which Influence the Attitudinal Outcomes of Personal Contact," *International Social Science Bulletin* 7 (1955), 51-58.

2. For a discussion of the observability or visibility of group norms, see, R. K. Merton, *Social Theory and Social Structure* (Glencoe, Ill: Free Press, 1957), 336-353.

3. C. E. Osgood, G. J. Suci, and P. H. Tannenbaum, *The Measurement of Meaning* (Urbana: University of Illinois Press, 1957).

4. S. N. Herman, *American Students in Israel* (Ithaca, N.Y.: Cornell University Press, 1970), p. 152.

5. The statistical data are contained in the research report on *Studies in Jewish Identity*, op. cit.

6. J. S. Bruner and H. V. Perlmutter, "Compatriot and Foreigner: A Study of Impression Formation in Three Countries," *J. of Abn. and Soc. Psychol.* 35 (1957), 253-260.

7. Cf., I. Chein, "The Problem of Jewish Identification," *Jewish Social Studies* 17 (1955), 219-222.

PART IV

FACING THE FUTURE

Chapter 11

ONE JEWISH WORLD

Jews regard themselves today—as they have in the past—an embattled people. They are confronted with a worldwide resurgence of anti-Semitism spearheaded by a ruthless Arab and Soviet campaign against Israel. In the face of danger there is evident among Jews a heightened sense of interdependence and of mutual responsibility.[1] But are the communities knit as closely together for common action as need to be the members of a people so beleaguered? The question arises when an examination is made of the attitudes of the younger generation. In our research on Israeli students and students from the United States, we found elements of weakness, as well as of strength, in their attitudes to Jews outside of their immediate community.

The Israeli students have been impressed by the support extended so spontaneously and unwaveringly to Israel by Jewish communities throughout the world at the time of both the Six Day War and the Yom Kippur War. While this has resulted in a more favorable attitude to those communities, our interviews with the students reveal that they still lack an understanding of the nature of the Diaspora of today. Their view of this Diaspora is based largely on what they have heard from their parents about the communities from which they came (mainly Europe, the Middle East and North Africa) and on what they have read in the Hebrew literature which they study in school and which in great part relates to the communities of Eastern Europe. There are serious lacunae even in their knowledge of these communities. They do, however, empathize with the plight of Jews subject to persecution or gross discrimination (as in Soviet Russia and in the Arab countries), and they feel closer to such Jews. What they do not comprehend are the subtler dilemmas, the peculiar unease and the Jewish strivings of the communities in the Western democracies. American students visiting Israel sorrowfully reported in the interviews we conducted with them that the Israeli students whom they met did not appear to be interested in, and did not understand, the problematics of Jewish life in the United States. A recent study based on analysis of high school texts and on interviews with 212 history teachers shows how extremely limited and unsystematic is the knowledge transmitted in the schools on the subject of American Jewry.[2] Much remains to be done in and out of the schools to develop a realistic and compassionate understanding—far more than there is at present—of the conditions under which a large part of the Jewish people lives today and will continue to live in the years to come. But it is not merely a matter of empathy. While they recognize the interdependence which exists, Israeli youths do not have an adequate grasp of the full implications of the fact that—whatever the dissimilarities between other Jews and themselves—they and Jews of all parts of the Diaspora belong to the same Jewish world, sharing not only a common history but also a common fate and destiny.

A parallel problem was found to exist among the American students whose attitudes we studied during their sojourn in Israel. While the students have strong Jewish attachments and a favorable attitude towards Israel, our interviews indicate that they generally lack a coherent view of the relationship between Israel and Jews of the Diaspora, or more specifically between Israel and American Jewry. They see them as two different worlds, and they choose to throw in their lot with one or the other. For some, the world of Israel holds the hope of the Jewish future whereas the American Jewish world is doomed to gradual dissolution. For others, the American Jewish community contains within itself the potential for creative development, and they have a vague idea about the inspiration which Israel can supply. But essentially they remain two separate worlds in the minds of the students.

A Model for the Israel-Diaspora Relationship

We would submit that a close and mutually fructifying Israel-Diaspora relationship can most readily develop if it is based on the conception of one Jewish world of which all the Jewish communities are interlocking, interdependent parts. Israel and the Diaspora are often needlessly juxtaposed in a way which undermines this conception of one Jewish people and one Jewish world.

Erikson has distinguished two types of relationships that exist between parts of a whole: "As a gestalt ... wholeness emphasizes a sound, organic mutuality between diversified functions and parts within an entity, the boundaries of which are open and fluid. Totality, on the contrary, evokes a gestalt in which an absolute boundary is emphasized; given a certain arbitrary delineation, nothing that belongs inside must be left outside, nothing that must be outside can be tolerated inside."[3]

The view of the Israel-Diaspora relationship we propose is that of a "wholeness" made up of freely intercommunicating parts. Such an approach does not obscure the differences between the parts of the whole, between the position of a Jewish majority society in Israel and the situation in which the Diaspora communities as minorities find themselves. Galut remains galut, with all the limitations attached to that condition. As long, however, as any part of the Jewish people remains in the Diaspora, there is merit to every effort to sustain the Jewish life of such communities.

While we would contend that Israel is *the* center of the Jewish world, the centrality of Israel does not mean that the other Jewish communities are to be regarded as mere append-ages. There is need to stimulate a vigorous communal life and to encourage every community to develop its institutions and make its contributions to the common Jewish weal. The transmission of influence would have limited effect if the Diaspora communities were simply passive recipients. They should be active partners making their contribution in the course of constant interaction with one another and with the center which is Israel; this would allow for an interpenetra-tion of mutual influences. In an earlier chapter we have advanced the view that a Zionist ideology, serving as a com-prehensive approach to Jewish life, could give coherence and direction to the joint activities.

Such a conception sees Israel and the Diaspora as gaining strength from one another. While it is our view that the situation demands that as many Jews as possible should be encouraged to move as soon as possible to the national center, we believe that this objective can most effectively be accomplished by injecting positive forces into Jewish life everywhere and by stimulating the processes which eventu-ally culminate in aliya. Such policy should not, however, mean a perception of the Diaspora as just a reservoir for aliya.

A Common Language

The absence of a common Jewish language limits the communication that should take place between all sectors of the Jewish world.[4] Since the Holocaust, the role of Yiddish, at one time a major unifying language, has tragically declined; the current role of Ladino is even more limited.

The revival of Hebrew as a living language was a major Zionist achievement but, while it is now taught everywhere in the Diaspora, only a small number of Jews acquire an adequate reading and speaking knowledge of Hebrew. American Jewry, largest of the Jewish communities, is unilingual. The closer linking together of Jews everywhere in a cultural consensus requires that Hebrew become the second language of Jews in the Diaspora, and this needs to be a major goal—even if one difficult to attain—of a Jewish education seeking to play its part in fostering the conception of one Jewish people and of one Jewish world.

While such a Jewish education would give special attention to the role of Israel in Jewish life, it would include in its program the study of Jewish communities in other parts of the globe. There should also be an extension, wherever feasible, of the geographical locale in which the education takes place; a Jewish education in the Diaspora should be seen as incomplete unless complemented by a study visit to Israel. High school students and university students have come in considerable numbers on such study visits; boys have journeyed to Jerusalem to celebrate their barmitzvah at the Western Wall. All this should in increasing measure become a regular practice for a Jewish education.

The Status of Israel

A conception of one Jewish world should not obscure but rather project into proper perspective the special status and quality of that part of it which is the Jewish state. Trends of thought which have developed among Jewish communities, particularly since the Yom Kippur War, make necessary a clarification of the subject.

Since the Yom Kippur War, many Jews have become perturbed by the apparent vulnerability of Israel and its excessive dependence on the United States. There is a tendency to think of Israel as "another Jewish community in need of aid." While Israel does indeed require support in the task which it has undertaken on behalf of the entire Jewish people, it is necessary to differentiate between the situation of a sovereign Jewish state, beset with grave difficulties but shaping its own future, and between the situation of dependence in which a Jewish minority finds itself in the Diaspora.

The term Holocaust (in Hebrew, "Sho'ah") is increasingly extended to apply to a contingency which might develop in Israel. Here again, while the apprehension of Jews is understandable, it is desirable to avoid the confusion of thought which such an extension of the term Holocaust reflects and to draw a clear distinction between the danger confronting Israel and the position in which European Jewry found itself or the position in which a defenseless Jewish minority threatened with destruction might again find itself. The Jewish state faces grave perils and it has no illusions about the intentions of its enemies. It is not, however, in the position of being helplessly subject to the malevolence of the non-Jewish majority; it is precisely such a situation which the Jewish state was set up to avoid.

While the feeling of interdependence brings with it a sense of mutual responsibility among Jews throughout the world, the respective responsibilities need to be more clearly defined. The failure to understand the extent of the responsibility is evidenced by the form in which some Jews in the Diaspora criticise "the quality of life" in Israel. Israel aspires to develop a just, liberal, democratic Jewish society, but it still falls far short of being a society of this kind. It has to be understood, however, that the many deficiencies are to a large extent reflections of the social ailments which the various groups who comprise Israel's population have brought with them from their countries of origin—just as some of the meritorious qualities reflect the contribution of these groups. And so, if American Jews, or any other Jewry, would wish the country to be built more fully in their own image, they can only hope this to be so if they come in large numbers. At the time of the Yom Kippur War, the Jewries of the free countries did indeed give expression to their sense of mutual responsibility by unreservedly extending their aid. But this expression of solidarity did not go beyond a certain point—it did not express itself in a large-scale aliya which would have made so significant a difference to the position of a hard-pressed Israel and to the future of the Jewish people. We have pointed out in Chapter 8 why no amount of exhortation is likely to produce such large-scale aliya from the free countries and why the aliya will be limited to those with a developed sense of Jewish identity. And so changes in the "quality of life" will be a slow process, their pace determined by the measure of reinforcement which Israelis receive in their efforts from such idealistic olim as do come to join them in the common task.

Israel, in its turn, has responsibilities which need to be more effectively implemented. It has indeed given evidence of its concern for the well-being of Jewish communities wherever they are. As a Jewish majority society in the Jewish homeland it has the possibility and the obligation—which it is not yet fulfilling adequately—to serve as the spiritual and cultural powerhouse of the Jewish world, as a reflector moreover of Jewish social ideals. If Hebrew is to become the second language of the Diaspora, Israel will have to join the communities concerned in the development of an imaginatively conceived educational program designed for this purpose. It will need to share with communities abroad the responsibility of extending the scope and depth of Jewish education, and it will have to render special support to the smaller communities. It will need to extend its role in providing opportunities for the training of Jewish teachers and rabbis and in encouraging study visits by students of all categories. The first university established in the country, the Hebrew University of Jerusalem, was intended to serve as the university of the Jewish people, and together with the other institutions which have grown up it is in a position to make Israel the study center of the Jewish world.

The Non-Jewish World

The Jewish world is not an island to itself—it is set within the wider non-Jewish world. Jews need to know what they have in common with this wider world and in what they differ.

The Holocaust shattered illusions about the Jewish position in a Gentile world. In the hour of Jewry's greatest agony that part of the world which was not antagonistic was largely indifferent. The feeling, as we have noted, is widespread among Jews that they cannot rely upon Gentile goodwill. This does not mean a withdrawal from contact with the Gentile world wherever cooperation with it is feasible. Not only have they made a contribution to the wider world, but Jews have always been ready to accept any hand outstretched in friendship, and no people has so honored those who have helped it as Jews have honored the "righteous Gentiles." But bitter experience has made Jews conscious of the fact that they must perforce rely upon themselves. "Today it is basic knowledge that Jews are isolated—and together" observes a Jewish historian.[5] In the face of danger Jews realize, more acutely so after the Holocaust, that they must stand together—as one united people. And they realize, moreover, that if the existence of any section of their people is threatened, no one among them dare rest or be silent.

The Jewish people are—and should continue to see themselves—a nation of survivors. It was the intention of the Nazi regime to root out the entire Jewish people, every Jew, wherever he could be found. The Jews who are alive today are among the living because of the fortuitous circumstance that they or their parents were outside the zone of destruction. They will stand more firmly together if they do so in the consciousness that they are all survivors of the Holocaust, and that as such they have the special obligation to dedicate their energies to what is a continuing struggle of their people for a creative survival and for a better future.

In the Aftermath of the Yom Kippur War

The Yom Kippur War led to a closing of Jewish ranks. The indications are that Israel may face a new Arab attack, and the sense of overhanging danger from this and other quarters continues to emphasize the need for Jewish solidarity. At the same time, the Jews of Israel—and also Jewish circles outside of Israel—have subjected themselves to much heartsearching in the wake of the war.

The victory in the Six Day War was swift and clear and the elation considerable. The Old City of Jerusalem and the Western Wall were again in Jewish hands, and Israeli forces had occupied the Golan Heights and the Sinai Peninsula. There was no such sense of elation after the Yom Kippur War—rather a mood of painful reflection and a sober awareness of the perils still ahead. Although the Egyptian and Syrian forces, which had made initial gains in the surprise attack, were at some points driven back beyond the October 5 lines, the cease-fire came before a conclusive Israeli victory could be achieved. There have subsequently been recriminations about the responsibility for Israel's initial unpreparedness; a large proportion of its manpower has had to remain mobilized and the regular functioning of its economic life has been severely impaired. A bitter debate has continued about the extent of the territorial concessions Israel should make in its efforts to move towards peace with its neighbors. The prospects for such peace—in the light of the intransigent Arab hostility to the existence of a Jewish state—seem dubious. All the while the entire country continues to mourn the young lives lost in the war. The crisis is likely to be a prolonged one and constitutes a serious test of the psychological stamina not only of the Jews in Israel but also of the Jews in the Diaspora who view the future of Israel with increasing apprehension.

The daring commando operation at Entebbe in Uganda ("Operation Jonathan"), in which units of the Israeli army rescued the passengers of the plane hijacked by terrorists, produced an uplift of morale throughout the Jewish world. But it did not diminish the feeling Jews have of being an embattled people.

Time Perspective and Morale

The cohesiveness of the Jewish people and the readiness to extend mutual support represent an important contribution to the staying power required in this crisis. A further determinant of such psychological stamina is a meaningful time perspective.

Kurt Lewin refers to the reactions of Zionists in Germany shortly after Hitler came to power as an indication of how morale may be heightened by such time perspective: "They had a time perspective which included a psychological past of surviving adverse conditions for thousands of years and a meaningful and inspiring goal for the future. As a result of such a time perspective, this group showed high morale— despite a present which was judged by them to be no less foreboding than by others."[6] Morale in the difficult situation in which the Jewish people finds itself will depend in no small measure upon whether the present condition is viewed within a Jewish historical time perspective as part of a continuing, and as yet uncompleted, struggle moving forward from stage to stage through a series of trials and tribulations. The burdens and obstacles ahead will then be more readily faced as challenges to be overcome by dint of steadfast effort and perseverance as have the difficulties of the past. The strivings must be infused with a sense not only of the attainability, but also of the worthwhileness of the goal to be achieved in the future.

Observers have frequently drawn attention to the impressively high morale of the religious soldiers in the Israeli army, many of them students of the yeshivot. Army commanders vie with one another in attracting them to their units. Among the constituents of such morale are a deep faith and a highly developed Jewish historical time perspective.

Across the centuries it has been nuclei of this kind, possessed of a sense of historical continuity and a sense of hopeful purpose, who have maintained Jewish morale undimmed amid the vagaries of Jewish existence and who have preserved a vibrant Jewish identity when less steadfast elements in the Jewish community succumbed to the pressures or allurements of the surrounding society.

NOTES

1. M. Davis, ed., *The Yom Kippur War: Israel and the Jewish People* (New York: Arno, 1974).

2. R. Surkis, *The Teaching of American Jewry in the Israeli High School.* Report prepared on behalf of the Israel office of the American Jewish Committee, Jerusalem, 1976.

3. E. H. Erikson, *Insight and Responsibility* (New York: W. W. Norton, 1962), p. 92.

4. For the function of language in various social contexts, see, J. A. Fishman, ed., *Readings in the Sociology of Language* (The Hague: Mouton, 1968).

5. B. Halpern, *Jews and Blacks* (New York: Herder and Herder, 1971), p. 124.

6. K. Lewin, *Resolving Social Conflicts,* G. W. Lewin, ed. (New York: Harper, 1948), p. 104.

A NOTE ON THE TABLES

The tables are numbered consecutively according to chapter and number within chapter. Where the table is not inserted in the text itself and appears only in the list of supplementary tables, the letter S is prefixed to the number of the table.

An asterisk next to the number of the table indicates a significant difference between the responses of the three main categories into which the Israeli students are classified—religious, traditionalist, and nonreligious. The significance of the difference is at the $p < 0.05$ level according to the X^2 test.

The significance of differences between the averages of responses of the 1965 and 1974 samples, or between Zionists and non-Zionists, or between students from the Ashkenazic and those from the Oriental (Sephardic) sector, or between "compatibles" and "separatists," are indicated by an asterisk next to the particular item in the table. The differences, calculated by the T test, are at the $p < 0.002$ level unless otherwise indicated.

SUPPLEMENTARY TABLES

CHAPTER 6

Table S6.2: Identification with suffering of Jews in Holocaust
(according to communal background)
("Do you identify with Jews who suffered in the
Holocaust?")

	Ashkenazic *	Oriental
Yes, to a large extent	52	41
Yes	37	45
Only to a slight extent	10	11
No	1	3
Total %	100	100
N	1,099	644

CHAPTER 7

Table S7.1: Valence of Jewishness
(differences between Zionists and non-Zionists)
("If you were to be born all over again, would you wish to be born a Jew?")

	All Respondents		Religious		Traditionalist		Nonreligious	
	Z *	non-Z	Z	non-Z	Z	non-Z	Z *	non-Z
Yes	85	64	98	94	90	84	68	49
It makes no difference to me	13	30	1	3	9	13	28	42
No	2	6	1	3	1	3	4	9
Total %	100	100	100	100	100	100	100	100
N	1,366	340	410	33	462	110	494	197

Table S7.2:   Valence of Israeliness
(differences between Zionists and non-Zionists)
("If you were to be born again, would you wish to be born an Israeli?")

	All Respondents		Religious		Traditionalist		Nonreligious	
	Z*	non-Z	Z*	non-Z	Z*	non-Z	Z*	non-Z
Yes	86	69	87	75	83	71	88	67
It makes no difference to me	10	22	7	10	12	18	10	27
No	4	9	6	15	5	11	2	6
Total %	100	100	100	100	100	100	100	100
N	1,368	341	412	32	462	113	494	196

p $<$ .05

Table S7.3:   Overlap and consonance
(differences between Zionists and non-Zionists)
When I feel more Jewish:

	All Respondents		Religious		Traditionalist		Nonreligious	
	Z*	non-Z	Z	non-Z	Z*	non-Z	Z*	non-Z
I also feel more Israeli	79	58	87	79	84	64	68	52
There is no relationship between my feeling Jewish and my feeling Israeli	20	40	11	21	14	33	31	46
I feel less Israeli	1	2	2	—	2	3	1	2
Total %	100	100	100	100	100	100	100	100
N	1,352	337	410	33	454	112	488	192

Table S7.4:   Israelis as a continuity of the Jewish people
(differences between Zionists and non-Zionists)
"In your opinion, are we in Israel:

	All Respondents		Religious		Traditionalist		Nonreligious	
	Z*	non-Z	Z	non-Z	Z	non-Z	Z*	non-Z
An inseparable part of the Jewish people throughout the world?	87	76	96	94	88	82	80	68
Do we belong to a separate people formed here—Israelis?"	13	24	4	6	12	18	20	32
Total %	100	100	100	100	100	100	100	100
N	1,361	334	411	32	459	111	491	191

CHAPTER 8

Table S8.3:   Semantic differential[**]   The Israeli in the eyes of
American students differing in aliya intentions

	Improbably and No	Possibly	Probably	Yes
Unsociable-sociable	3.2	4.2	4.5	4.9
Unpleasant-pleasant	3.5	4.3	4.5	4.7
Weak-strong	4.6	4.8	5.7	6.1
Stubborn-yielding	1.8	2.0	2.0	1.8
Impractical-practical	4.2	4.4	5.3	5.5
Conservative-progressive	3.0	3.0	2.9	3.7
Cold-warm	3.2	3.9	4.2	4.5
Discourteous-courteous	2.0	2.7	2.8	2.8
Irreligious-religious	2.9	2.9	2.8	3.0
Ashamed of his Jewishness- proud of his Jewishness	4.9	4.7	4.7	4.7
Intolerant-tolerant	2.6	3.1	3.1	3.5
Ashamed of his Israeliness- proud of his Israeliness	5.7	5.9	6.8	6.8
Lacking roots in his Jewishness- with roots in his Jewishness	4.6	4.4	4.6	4.5
Lacking self respect-self respecting	5.6	6.1	6.1	6.3
Inhospitable-hospitable	4.9	5.7	6.0	6.0
Narrowminded-broadminded	1.5	1.9	3.1	3.2
Materialistic-idealistic	1.8	2.1	3.2	3.6
Lacking in intellectual alertness- intellectually alert	3.7	4.4	4.4	4.4
N	48	86	60	76

[**]Each set of adjectives was arranged along a seven-point scale. In the table
the adjective pairs have been rearranged so that the adjective with the unfavorable
connotation appears on the left and the adjective with the favorable connotation
on the right. The higher the mean, the greater the measure of favorableness.

Table S8.4:[*]   Interest in immigration from the United States
("To what extent are you interested in a large-scale aliya from the United States?")

	All Respondents	Religious	Traditionalist	Nonreligious
Very interested	39	60	35	31
Interested	50	36	56	54
Indifferent	9	3	8	12
Opposed	2	1	1	3
Total %	100	100	100	100
N	1,863	465	636	762

Table S8.5: *   Interest in immigration from the U.S.S.R.
                ("To what extent are you interested in large-scale aliya from Soviet Russia?")

	All Respondents	Religious	Traditionalist	Nonreligious
Very interested	35	65	25	23
Interested	43	28	50	48
Indifferent	19	5	22	26
Opposed	3	2	3	3
Total %	100	100	100	100
N	777	206	246	325

CHAPTER 9

Table S9.2: *   Common fate of Jewish people
                ("Do you feel your fate is bound up with the fate of the Jewish people?")

	All Respondents		Religious		Traditionalist		Nonreligious	
	1974	1965	1974	1965	1974	1965	1974	1965
Yes, definitely	52	48	85	58	53	41	30	50
To a large extent	32	34	13	35	36	47	40	22
To some extent	14	14	2	7	11	10	25	21
No	2	4	0	0	0	2	5	7
Total %	100	100	100	100	100	100	100	100
N	1,872	776	468	166	639	242	765	368

Table S9.4: Attitudes towards "shtetl" in Eastern Europe (n=775)

	Pride		Neither Pride nor Shame		Shame		Lack of Knowledge		Total Percentage	
	1974	1965	1974	1965	1974	1965	1974	1965	1974	1965
	35	27	49	46	12	18	4	9	100	100

Table S9.6:   Closeness to Jewish communities
              (The communities are listed in order of closeness)
              ("Below is a list of a number of Jewish communities. Indicate to what extent you
              feel close to each of these communities by encircling one of the following five
              numbers.")

		USA	USSR	Arab Countries	Latin America	England	South Africa	France
(1)	Very close	23	21	19	7	6	6	35
(2)	Close	27	24	21	16	11	11	8
(3)	Moderately close	30	27	24	28	29	28	25
(4)	Slightly close	12	15	16	24	30	23	29
(5)	Not feel close to them	8	13	20	25	24	32	33
	Total %	100	100	100	100	100	100	100
	N	698	678	679	674	673	675	675
	Mean	2.5	2.7	2.9	3.4	3.5	3.6	3.7

Table S9.8: Danger of Antisemitism
(Countries listed according to order of attributed danger)
("How would you estimate the danger of anti-Semitism in the following countries?")

	Very Great Danger	Great Danger	Slight Danger	No Danger At All	%	N
Arab countries	57	24	12	7	100	692
USSR	34	34	26	6	100	688
South America	5	18	46	31	100	671
France	4	20	50	26	100	681
South Africa	4	15	54	27	100	670
USA	4	10	42	44	100	693
England	2	9	46	43	100	682

Table S9.17: Centrality of Jewishness: differences between compatibles and separatists
("Does the fact that you are Jewish play an important part in your life?")

	Religious Compatibles*	Separatists	Traditionalist Compatibles*	Separatists	Nonreligious Compatibles*	Separatists
It plays a very important part	75	70	29	18	13	14
It plays an important part	25	28	61	51	55	19
It is of little importance	0	2	8	25	28	57
It plays no part	0	0	2	6	4	20
Total %	100	100	100	100	100	100
N	409	50	494	120	434	283

Table S9.18: Centrality of Israeliness: differences between compatibles and separatists
("Does the fact that you are an Israeli play in important part in your life?")

	Religious Compatibles*	Separatists	Traditionalist Compatibles*	Separatists	Nonreligious Compatibles*	Separatists
Plays a very important part	60	28	55	40	54	42
Plays an important part	34	48	41	36	42	44
It is of little importance	5	20	3	19	3	11
It plays no part	1	4	1	5	1	3
Total %	100	100	100	100	100	100
N	405	50	494	120	435	286

Table S9.19: State of Israel as a continuation of Jewish history: differences between compatibles and separatists
("In your opinion is the State of Israel a continuation of Jewish history?")

	Religious Compatibles*	Separatists	Traditionalist Compatibles*	Separatists	Nonreligious Compatibles*	Separatists
Yes, of all periods	96	81	88	74	87	68
Yes, but only of those periods when Jews lived here	2	13	10	18	10	21
No, it has opened a new page of history and has no connection with the past of the Jewish people	2	6	2	8	3	11
Total %	100	100	100	100	100	100
N	409	48	490	121	435	285

Table S9.20:   The Jewish-private individual continuum

		All Respondents		Religious		Traditionalist		Nonreligious	
		1974	1965	1974*	1965	1974	1965	1974*	1965
Jewish	(1-3)	46	45	83	75	45	47	24	29
Midpoint	(4)	18	18	10	16	23	20	17	20
Individual	(5-7)	36	37	7	9	32	33	59	51
Total %		100	100	100	100	100	100	100	100
N		757	2,980	202	680	237	942	318	1,358

Table S9.21:   The Israeli-private individual continuum

		All Respondents		Religious		Traditionalist		Nonreligious	
		1974	1965	1974	1965	1974	1965	1974*	1965
Israeli	(1-3)	57	57	68	65	55	61	50	54
Midpoint	(4)	22	24	15	16	25	21	24	27
Individual	(5-7)	21	19	17	19	20	18	26	19
Total %		100	100	100	100	100	100	100	100
N		757	2,980	201	680	238	942	318	1,358

Table S9.22:* "Good Jew" in Israel
  (Activities listed in the order rated by students in 1974. Mean values)

	All Respondents		Religious		Traditionalist		Nonreligious	
	1974	1965	1974	1965	1974	1965	1974	1965
To work for "the in-gathering of the exiles"	2.2	2.3	1.6	1.9	2.2	2.2	2.5	2.5
To lead an ethical life	2.2	2.4	1.4	1.7	2.2	2.3	2.6	2.7
To be interested in the fate of Jews around the world	2.3	2.6	1.8	2.2	2.4	2.5	2.5	2.9
To celebrate bar-mitzvah	2.3	2.7	2.0	2.1	2.1	2.4	2.6	3.0
To attend synagogue services	2.4	2.9	1.6	2.0	2.4	2.8	2.9	3.4
To be a loyal citizen of Israel	2.4	2.6	1.9	2.1	2.4	2.6	2.7	2.7
To take an interest in the fate of persecuted peoples	3.2	3.1	2.9	2.9	3.3	3.2	3.2	3.2

Table S9.23: *   "Good Jew" abroad
            (Activities listed in the order rated by students in 1974. Mean values)

	All Respondents		Religious		Traditionalist		Nonreligious	
	1974	1965	1974	1965	1974	1965	1974	1965
To settle in Israel or to encourage his children to settle	1.7	2.1	1.4	2.0	1.7	2.2	1.9	2.1
To take an interest in the affairs of the local community	1.9	2.0	1.5	1.8	1.8	2.1	2.1	2.1
To support Israel	1.9	2.0	1.5	1.8	1.9	2.1	2.1	2.4
To attend synagogue services	2.1	2.2	1.5	1.8	2.0	2.2	2.4	2.4
To celebrate bar-mitzvah	2.1	2.2	1.9	2.0	1.9	2.1	2.3	2.4
To live an ethical life	2.1	2.3	1.4	1.8	2.1	2.3	2.5	2.4
To take an interest in the fate of other Jewish communities	2.2	2.4	1.8	2.2	2.2	2.4	2.4	2.5
To take an interest in the fate of persecuted peoples	3.1	2.8	2.9	2.6	3.0	2.9	3.1	2.9
To be a loyal citizen of the country in which he lives	3.2	3.0	3.0	2.8	3.0	2.9	3.4	3.0

Table S9.24: *   Assimilation or preservation of Jewish identity in Diaspora
            ("A youth abroad who is not prepared to settle in Israel—what should he do?")

	All Respondents		Religious		Traditionalist		Nonreligious	
	1974	1965	1974	1965	1974	1965	1974	1965
He should maintain his Jewishness abroad	92	88	99	99	95	93	84	82
He should assimilate	8	12	1	1	5	7	16	18
Total %	100	100	100	100	100	100	100	100
N	1,754	767	459	166	618	241	677	360

Table S9.25: *   Emigration from Israel
            ("Would you be prepared to emigrate from Israel?")

	All Respondents		Religious		Traditionalist		Nonreligious	
	1974	1965	1974	1965	1974	1965	1974	1965
I would not be prepared under any circumstances	52	52	62	57	51	50	46	53
I think that I would not be prepared	14	15	9	22	15	20	17	18
Only under very special circumstances	21	20	23	10	17	17	22	17
Perhaps I would be prepared	10	12	4	10	15	13	11	11
I am prepared	3	1	2	1	2	—	4	1
Total %	100	100	100	100	100	100	100	100
N p < .01	772	767	205	169	246	246	321	352

Table S9.26: Attitude towards Yiddish of students from Ashkenazic and Oriental sectors

	All Respondents		Religious		Traditionalist		Nonreligious	
	Ashkenazic*	Oriental	Ashkenazic*	Oriental	Ashkenazic*	Oriental	Ashkenazic*	Oriental
Very positive	7	1	10	4	7	0	5	1
Positive	24	6	31	7	30	8	20	3
No particular feeling	54	70	49	68	48	73	58	63
Negative	11	16	8	15	10	12	13	23
Very negative	4	7	2	6	5	7	4	10
Total %	100	100	100	100	100	100	100	100
N	1,101	642	292	136	237	362	572	144

Table S9.27: Attitude towards Ladino of students from Ashkenazic and Oriental sectors

	All Respondents		Religious		Traditionalist		Nonreligious	
	Ashkenazic*	Oriental	Ashkenazic*	Oriental	Ashkenazic*	Oriental	Ashkenazic*	Oriental
Very positive	4	12	2	15	6	11	4	8
Positive	12	18	11	13	17	22	10	16
No particular feeling	79	66	84	65	71	64	81	71
Negative	3	3	2	5	4	2	3	3
Very negative	2	1	1	2	2	1	2	2
Total %	100	100	100	100	100	100	100	100
N	1,092	645	289	136	235	364	568	145

p < .02

Table S9.29: Identification with Jews who suffered from attacks in Islamic countries
("Do you identify with Jews who suffered from attacks in Islamic countries?")

	Ashkenazic*	Oriental
Yes, to a large extent	34	40
Yes	43	45
Only to a slight extent	18	13
No	5	2
Total %	100	100
N	1,099	639

CHAPTER 10

Table S10.1:   The Israeli and American Jew: Ratings on semantic differential by students from USA (mean values) n=270

	Concepts	
Adjective Pairs	*The Israeli*	*The American Jew*
Unsociable-sociable	4.3	5.3
Unpleasant-pleasant	4.3	4.9
Weak-strong	4.8	2.8
Stubborn-yielding	1.9	4.4
Impractical-practical	4.4	3.6
Conservative-progressive	3.2	5.1
Cold-warm	3.9	5.1
Discourteous-courteous	2.6	5.2
Irreligious-religious	2.9	3.9
Ashamed of Jewishness-proud of Jewishness	4.8	3.3
Intolerant-tolerant	3.1	5.1
Ashamed of his Israeliness-proud of his Israeliness	5.8	—
Ashamed of his Americanism-proud of his Americanism	—	3.9
Lacking roots in his Jewishness-with roots in his Jewishness	4.5	3.8
Lacking self-respect-self-respecting	6.1	4.6
Inhospitable-hospitable	5.6	5.2
Narrowminded-broadminded	1.9	1.2
Materialistic-idealistic	2.2	2.6
Lacking in intellectual alertness-intellectually alert	4.3	5.9

Table S10.5:   The sense of interdependence (students from USA and
from USSR)
("Do you feel that your fate and future is bound up with
the fate and future of the Jewish people?")

	USA	USSR
Yes, definitely	67	48
To a large extent	21	40
To some extent only	11	10
No	1	2
N	265	440

Table S10.6:   **Feeling of closeness on part of American students to Jewish communities. N=264.**
(In the table the communities are listed in order of attributed closeness.)

"Below is a list of a number of Jewish communities. Indicate to what extent you feel close to each of these communities by encircling one of the following five numbers:
(1) I feel very close to them.
(2) I feel close to them.
(3) I feel moderately close to them.
(4) I feel only slightly close to them.
(5) I do not feel close to them."

	Means
Israel	2.0
USA	2.1
USSR	2.7
The Arab countries	3.3
England	3.5
South America	3.6
South Africa	3.7
France	3.7

GLOSSARY OF HEBREW TERMS

aliyah: (literally, "ascent") immigration to Israel

Ashkenazim: descendants of Jews originally settled in Northwestern Europe

barmitzvah: religious celebration of the thirteenth birthday by a boy at which time he is initiated into full religious duties

dati (pl. dati'im): religiously observant

edah (pl. edot): community; "edot hamizrach": Jewish communities originating from the Oriental countries (mainly the Middle East and North Africa)

Eretz Israel: Land of Israel

Galut, Golah: exile

garin: nucleus of settlement group

goy (pl. goyim): Gentile

halacha: Jewish religious law

Hasid (pl. Hasidim): a member of the Hasidic religious movement which developed in the Jewish communities of Eastern Europe in the latter part of the eighteenth century

kibbutz (pl. kibbutzim): collective settlement

kibbutz galuyot: (literally, "ingathering of the exiles") ingathering of Jews from the Diaspora

Kiddush Ha'chayim: sanctification of life

Kiddush Ha'Shem: sanctification of God's name, martyrdom

klal Yisrael: the totality of the Jewish community

klita: immigrant absorption, the integration of immigrants into Israeli society

le'om: nationality

lo-dati (pl. lo-dati'im): nonobservant

minyan: the congregation of at least ten males required for communal prayer

Mitnagged (pl. Mitnaggedim): a term originally applied to the opponents of the Hasidim. The Mitnaggedim, reflecting an intellectual tradition, place more emphasis on the study of the Talmud, while the emotional aspects of Judaism find greater expression among the Hasidim

mitzvah (pl. mitzvot): religious obligation, commandment

m'sorati (pl. m'sorati'im): traditionalist

oleh (pl. olim): immigrant

prosdor: corridor

Sephardim: descendants of Jews who lived in Spain before the expulsion of 1492

shaliach (pl. shlichim): emissary, usually emissary from Israel to the Diaspora for Jewish education of youth or encouragement of aliya

shlilat hagalut: "negation" of the galut

sho'ah: (literally, calamitous event) the Holocaust, the destruction of six million Jews in Europe during the Nazi regime

shtetl: (from the Yiddish) Jewish village in Eastern Europe

Shavuot: the Festival celebrating the Giving of the Law

Simhat Torah: the festival of the Rejoicing of the Law (on completion of the reading each year of the Pentateuch)

Succot: the festival of Tabernacles, commemorating the wanderings of the children of Israel in the desert

Tisha Be'av: ninth day of the month of Av, commemorating the destruction of the Temple

tiyul (pl. tiyulim): excursion

Torah: Pentateuch; also used more broadly to refer to the teachings of Judaism

tsabar (pl. tsabarim): local-born Israeli

yerida: (literally, "descent") emigration from Israel

yeshiva (pl. yeshivot): religious academy

Yidishkayt: (from the Yiddish) Jewishness

Yishuv: the Jewish community in Israel

Yom Kippur: Day of Atonement

yored (pl. yordim): an emigrant from Israel

BIBLIOGRAPHY

Antonovsky, A., and Katz, D. *Americans and Canadians in Israel: Integration into Israeli Life*. Report No. 3, Jerusalem: The Israel Institute of Applied Social Research, 1969.

Baer, Y. F. *Galut*. New York: Schocken, 1947.

Barker, R. G., Dembo, T., and Lewin, K. *Frustration and Regression: An Experiment with Young Children*. University of Iowa Studies in Child Welfare, 18 (1941).

———, and Wright, H. F. *Midwest and its Children: The Psychological Ecology of an American Town*. Evanston, Ill.: Row, Peterson, 1954.

Barth, F. *Ethnic Groups and Boundaries: The Social Organisation of Cultural Difference*. Bergen, Norway: Universitetsforlaget, 1969.

Bauer, Y. *Flight and Rescue: Brichah*. New York: Random House, 1970.

Bell, D. "Reflections on Jewish Identity," *The Ghetto and Beyond*, ed. P. I. Rose. New York: Random House, 1969.

Ben-Gurion, D. *Israel: A Personal History*. New York: Funk and Wagnalls, 1971.

Berkowitz, L., and Daniels, L. R. "Responsibility and Dependency," *Journal of Abnormal and Social Psychology*, LXVI (1963), 429-436.

Berlin, I. "Benjamin Disraeli, Karl Marx and the Search for Identity," *Midstream*, VII (1970), 29-49.

Bogoraz, L. "Do I Feel I Belong to the Jewish People?" *I Am a Jew: Essays on Jewish Identity in the Soviet Union*, ed. A. Voronel and V. Yakhot. Academic Committee on Soviet Jewry and A.D.L., 1973.

Bruner, J. S., and Perlmutter, H. V. "Compatriot and Foreigner: A Study of Impression Formation in Three Countries," *Journal of Abnormal and Social Psychology*, 35 (1957), 253-260.

Chein, I. "The Problem of Jewish Identification," *Jewish Social Studies*, 17 (1955), 219-222.

Cohen, A. A. "Beyond Politics, Visions," *Congress bi-Weekly*, 39 (1972), 33-42.

Cohen, O. *The Conflict Between Religious and Non-Religious Jews in Israel: Solidarity and Social Distance among High School Students*. Unpublished doctoral dissertation, Dept. of Sociology of the Hebrew University, Jerusalem, 1975.

Cook, S. W., and Selltiz, C. "Some Factors Which Influence the Attitudinal Outcomes of Personal Contact," *International Social Science Bulletin*, 7 (1955), 51-58.

Coser, L. *The Functions of Social Conflict*. Glencoe, Ill.: Free Press, 1964.

Dashefsky, A., ed. *Ethnic Identity in Society*. Chicago: Rand McNally, 1976.

Davis, M. *Beit Yisrael Be-Amerikah (From Dependence to Mutuality: The American Jewish Community and World Jewry)*. Jerusalem: Magnes Press of the Hebrew University, 1970. (In Hebrew.)

―――. "Centres of Jewry in the Western Hemisphere: A Comparative Approach," *The Jewish Journal of Sociology*, 5 (1963), 4-26.

―――, ed. *Israel and the Jewish People: During and After the Yom Kippur War*. Jerusalem: Hasifriya Haziyonit, 1975. (In Hebrew.)

―――. *The Jewish People in Metamorphosis*. Syracuse University: The B. G. Rudolph Lectures in Judaic Studies.

―――, ed. *The Yom Kippur War: Israel and the Jewish People*. New York: Arno Press, 1974.

Dawidowicz, L. C. "Can Anti-Semitism Be Measured?" *Commentary*, L (1970), 36-43.

Dawidowicz, L. S. "Can Anti-Semitism Be Measured?" *Commentary*, L (1970), 36-43.

―――. *The War Against the Jews 1933-1945*. New York: Holt, Rinehart and Winston, 1975.

Deutsch, M., and Hornstein, H. A., eds. *Applying Social Psychology*. New York: John Wiley, 1975.

―――. *The Resolution of Conflict*. New Haven, Conn.: Yale University Press, 1973.

Eisenstadt, S. N. *The Absorption of Immigrants*. London: Routledge, 1954.

Elazar, D. J. "The Reconstitution of Jewish Communities in the Post-War Period," *The Jewish Journal of Sociology*, 11 (1969), 187-226.

Elon, M. *Chakikah Datit* (Religious Legislation). Tel Aviv: Hakibbutz Hadati, 1968. (In Hebrew.)

Erikson, E. H. *Childhood and Society*. New York: W. W. Norton, 1950.

―――. "The Concept of Identity in Race Relations: Notes and Queries," *The Negro American*, ed. T. Parsons and K. B. Clark. Boston: Beacon: The Daedalus Library, 1965, 227-253.

―――. *Insight and Responsibility*. New York: W. W. Norton, 1962.

―――. "The Problem of Ego Identity," *Identity and Anxiety*, ed. M. R. Stein, et al. Glencoe, Ill.: Free Press, 1960.

Esh, S. *Studies in the Holocaust and Contemporary Jewry*. Jerusalem: Institute of Contemporary Jewry, Hebrew University, Yad Vashem, and Leo Baeck Institute, 1973. (In Hebrew.)

Etzioni-Halevy, E., and Shapira, R. "Jewish Identification of Israeli Students: What Lies Ahead," *Jewish Social Studies*, 37 (1975), 251-266.

Fackenheim, E. "Jewish Faith and the Holocaust," *Commentary*, XLVI (1968), 30-36.

Fein, L., et al. *Reform Is a Verb*. New York: UAHC, 1972.

Festinger, L. *A Theory of Cognitive Dissonance*. Evanston, Ill.: Row, Peterson, 1957.

Fishman, J. A., ed. *Readings in the Sociology of Language*. The Hague: Mouton, 1968.

Frank, L. K. "Time Perspectives," *Journal of Social Philosophy*, 4 (1939), 293-312.

Friedmann, G. *The End of the Jewish People?* New York: Doubleday, 1967.

Geertz, C. *The Interpretation of Cultures*. New York: Basic Books, 1973.

Ginzberg, E. *Occupational Choice*. New York: Columbia University Press, 1961.

Glazer, N., and Moynihan, D. P. *Beyond the Melting Pot*. Cambridge, Mass.: M.I.T. Press, 1963.

———, and ———, eds. *Ethnicity: Theory and Experience*. Cambridge, Mass.: Harvard University Press, 1975.

Glock, C. Y., et al. *The Apathetic Majority*. New York: Harper and Row, 1966.

Goldscheider, C. "American Aliya: Sociological and Demographic Perspectives," in M. Sklare, ed., *The Jew in American Society*. New York: Behrman, 1974.

Gould, J., and Kolb, W. L., eds. *A Dictionary of the Social Sciences*. Glencoe, Ill.: Free Press, 1964.

Greeley, A. M. and McCready, W. C. *Ethnicity in the United States: A Preliminary Reconnaissance*. New York: John Wiley, 1974.

Greenberg, H. *The Inner Eye: Selected Essays*, Vol. I. New York: Jewish Frontier Publishing Association, 1964.

Halpern, B. *The American Jew: A Zionist Analysis*. New York: Theodore Herzl Foundation, 1956.

———. *Jews and Blacks* New York: Herder and Herder, 1971.

———. "Anti-Semitism in the Perspective of Jewish History,'" *Jews in the Mind of America*, ed. C. H. Stember, et al. New York: Basic Books, 1966, 273-301.

———. *The Idea of the Jewish State*. Cambridge, Mass.: Harvard University Press, 1969.

———. "Zion in the Mind of American Jews," in D. Sidorsky, ed., *The Future of the Jewish Community in America*. New York: Basic Books, 1973, 22-45.

Herman, S. N. *American Students in Israel*. Ithaca, N.Y.: Cornell University Press, 1970.

———. *Israelis and Jews: The Continuity of an Identity*. New York: Random House, 1970.

———, and Schild, E. O. "Ethnic Role Conflict in a Cross-Cultural Situation," *Human Relations*, 13 (1960), 215-228.

———. "Mesilot laZiyonut HeHalutzit" ("Pathways to Chalutzic Zionism"), ed. G. Hanoch, *HaZiyonut be-Sha'a Zu* (Zionism in the Contemporary Period). Jerusalem: Zionist Organization, 1951. (In Hebrew.)

———, Peres, Y., and Yuchtman, E. "Reactions to the Eichmann Trial in Israel: A Study in High Involvement," *Scripta Hierosolymitana*, 14 (1965), 98-118.

———. *Studies in Jewish Identity*. Research Report. Institute of Contemporary Jewry, Hebrew University, Jerusalem, 1976.

Hertzberg, A., ed. *The Zionist Idea: A Historical Analysis and Reader*. New York: Herzl Press, 1960.

Horowitz, T., and Frenkel, E. *Immigrants in Absorption Centers*. Research Report No. 185 of the Henrietta Szold Institute, Jerusalem: 1975. (In Hebrew.)

Information Department of the Israel Office of Foreign Affairs report, *The Image of Israel in the Eyes of French Students*. Jerusalem: June 1971. (In Hebrew.)

Johnson, C. E. "The Impact of Jewish Community Priorities of American Emigration to Israel," *Analysis* 53 (1975). Institute for Jewish Policy Planning and Research of the Synagogue Council of American, Washington, D.C.

Judgment of Israel Supreme Court in the case of Dr. George Tamarin v. State of Israel. (C.A. 630/70.)

Kariv, A. *Lithuania, Land of My Birth*. New York: Herzl Press, 1967.

Kastenbaum, R. "The Structure and Function of Time Perspective," *Journal of Psychological Researches*, 8 (1964), 1-11.

Katz, A. D. "Dissonance Theory and Immigrant Adjustment," *Abraham David Katz: Jew, Man, and Sociologist*. Jerusalem: 1975.

Katz, J. *Out of the Ghetto*. Cambridge, Mass.: Harvard University Press, 1973.

Kaufman, Y. "Anti-Semitic Stereotypes in Zionism," *Commentary*, 7 (1949), 239-245.

Kaznelson, B. "Youth and Jewish Fate," *Molad*, 10 (1949), 226-229. (In Hebrew.)

Kelman, H. C. "The Place of Jewish Identity in the Development of Personal Identity." Working paper prepared for the American Jewish Committee's Colloquium on Jewish Education and Jewish Identity, November 1974.

Klineberg, O. "The Multi-National Society: Some Research Problems," *Social Sciences Information*, 6 (1967), 81-99.

Kluckhohn, C., and Murray, H. A., eds. *Personality in Nature, Society, and Culture*. New York: Alfred A. Knopf, 1953.

Kolatt, I. "Theories of Israel Nationalism," *In the Dispersion*, 7 (1967), 13-50.

Lamm, N. "Teaching the Holocaust," *Forum*, 24 (1976), 51-60.

Landau, A. F., and Elman, P., eds. *Selected Judgements of the Supreme Court of Israel*. Special Volume. Jerusalem: Ministry of Justice, 1971.

Lazare, B. "Notes on a Conversion," *Rebirth: A Book of Modern Jewish Thought*, ed. L. Lewisohn. New York: Harper, 1935.

Levin, S. *The Arena* (transl. by M. Samuel). London: Routledge, 1932.

Lewin, K. *Field Theory in Social Science*, ed. D. Cartwright. London: Tavistock, 1952.

–––. "Intention, Will, and Need," *Organization and Pathology of Thought*, ed. D. Rapaport. New York: Columbia University Press, 1951.

–––. "The Research Center for Group Dynamics at M.I.T.," *Sociometry*, 8 (1945), 126-136.

–––. *Resolving Social Conflicts*, ed. G. Lewin. New York: Harper, 1948.

Lewisohn, L., ed. *Rebirth: A Book of Modern Jewish Thought*. New York: Harper, 1935.

Levy, S., and Gutman, A. L. "The Jewish Identification of Israelis During and After the War," *Israel and The Jewish People: During and After the Yom Kippur War*, ed. M. Davis. Jerusalem: Hasifiya Hazionit, 1976, 297-308. (In Hebrew.)

Liebman, C. S. *The Ambivalent American Jew*. Philadelphia: Jewish Publication Society, 1973.
———. "Israel in the Ideology of American Jewry," *Dispersion and Unity*, 10 (1970), 19-26.
Lipset, S. M. "The Study of Jewish Communities in a Comparative Context," *Jewish Journal of Sociology*, 5 (1963), 157-166.
Litvin, B. *Jewish Identity: Modern Responsa and Opionions on the Registration of Children of Mixed Marriages*, ed. S. B. Hoenig. New York: Feldheim, 1965.

Marrow, A. J. *The Practical Theorist: The Life and Work of Kurt Lewin*. New York: Basic Books, 1969.
Memmi, A. "Does the Jew Exist?" *Commentary*, XLII (1966), 5, 73-76.
Merton, R. K. *Social Theory and Social Structure*. Glencoe, Ill.: Free Press, 1957.
———, et al. *The Student Physician*. Cambridge, Mass.: Harvard University Press, 1957.
Miller, D. R. "The Study of Social Relationships: Situation, Identity, and Social Interaction," *Psychology: A Study of a Science*, Vol. 5, 639-738, ed. S. Koch. New York: McGraw-Hill, 1963.
Myrdal, G. *An American Dilemma*. New York: Harper, 1944.

Near, N., ed. *The Seventh Day*. London: Deutsch, 1970.
Newcomb, T. N., Turner, R. H., and Converse, P. E. *Social Psychology*. New York: Holt, Rinehart and Winston, 1965.
Niebuhr, R. "Jews After the War," *The Nation*, Feb. 21, 1942.
Novak, M. *The Rise of the Unmeltable Ethnics*. New York: Macmillan, 1973.

Osgood, C. E., Suci, G. J., and Tannenbaum, P. H. *The Measurement of Meaning*. Urbana: University of Illinois Press, 1957.

Parsons, T. "Full Citizenship for the Negro American? A Sociological Problem," *The Negro American*, ed. T. Parsons and K. B. Clark. Boston: Beacon: The Daedalus Library, 1965, 709-754.
Planning and Research Division of the Ministry of Immigrant Absorption report, *Immigration and Absorption 1970-1975*. Jerusalem: 1975.

Rotenstreich, N. "Are We in Exile?" *Dimensions in American Judaism*, 5 (1971), 18-19.
———. "Between the State of Israel and Zionism," *Moznaim*, 41 (1975), 222-228. (In Hebrew.)
Ruppin, A. *The Jewish Fate and Future*. London: Macmillan, 1940.

Samuel, M. *In Praise of Yiddish*. New York: Cowles, 1971.
Sartre, J. P. *Antisemite and Jew* (transl. by G. J. Becker). New York: Schocken, 1965.
Scheffler, I. "How Can a Jewish Self-consciousness Be Developed," *The Study of Jewish Identity: Issues and Approaches*, ed. S. N. Herman. Jerusalem: Institute of Contemporary Jewry, Hebrew University, 1971.
Shuval, J. T. *Immigrants on the Threshold*. New York: Atherton, 1963.
Sidorsky, D. "The End of Ideology and American Zionism." Paper presented at a

meeting of the Study Circle in the home of the President of Israel, February 1976.

———, ed. *The Future of the Jewish Community in America,* New York: Basic Books, 1973.

———. *The Future of the Jewish Community in America.* Task Force Report. New York: The American Jewish Committee, 1972.

Sklare, M. "Lakeville and Israel: The Six Day War and its Aftermath," *Midstream,* 14 (1968), 1-19.

———, and Greenblum, J. *Jewish Identity on the Suburban Frontier.* New York: Basic Books, 1967.

———, ———, and Ringer, B. B. *Not Quite at Home.* New York: Institute of Human Relations Press, A.J.C. Pamphlet Series, No. 11, 1969.

Spiro, M. *Children of the Kibbutz.* Cambridge, Mass.: Harvard University Press, 1958.

Steg, A. "France: Perspectives," *The Yom Kippur War: Israel and the Jewish People,* ed. M. Davis. New York: Arno Press and Herzl Press, 1974, 206-213.

Stember, C. H., et al. *Jews in the Mind of America.* New York: Basic Books, 1966.

Surkis, R. *The Teaching of American Jewry in the Israeli High School.* Report prepared on behalf of the Israel office of the American Jewish Committee, Jerusalem: 1976.

Tajfel, H. "Aspects of National and Ethnic Loyalty," *Social Sciences Information,* 9 (1970), 119-144.

———. "Social Identity and Intergroup Behaviour," *Social Sciences Information,* 13 (1974), 65-93.

Talmon, J. L. "European History as the Background to the Holocaust," *Hasho'ah Vehatekumah* (The Holocaust and the Revival). Proceedings of a symposium, Jerusalem: Yad Vashem, 1975, 11-48. (In Hebrew.)

Talmon, Y. "Pursuit of the Millenium: The Relation between Religious and Social Change," *European Journal of Sociology,* 3 (1962), 125-148.

Vital, D. *The Origins of Zionism.* Oxford: Clarendon Press, 1975.

Voronel, A. "The Social Pre-conditions for the National Awakening of the Jews in the U.S.S.R.," *I am A Jew: Essays on Jewish Identity in the Soviet Union,* ed. A. Voronel and V. Yakhot. Academic Committee on Soviet Jewry and A.D.L., 1973.

Waxman, C. I. "The Centrality of Israel in American Jewish Life: A Sociological Analysis," *Judaism,* 25 (1976), 175-187.

Weber, M. "The Ethnic Group," *Theories of Society,* Vol. 1, ed. T. Parsons, et al. Glencoe, Ill.: Free Press, 1961.

Weinreich, M. "Yidiskayt and Yiddish: On the Impact of Religion on Language in Ashkenazic Jewry," *Readings in the Sociology of Language,* ed. J. A. Fishman. The Hague: Mouton, 1968.

Weizmann, C. *The Letters and Papers of Chaim Weizmann,* Vol. 3, Series A, Sept. 1903-Dec. 1904, general ed. M. W. Weisgal. London: Oxford University Press, 1972.

Wittgenstein, L. *Philosophical Investigations* (transl. G.E.M. Abscombe). Oxford: Blackwell, 1963.

Yaron, Z. "Old and New in Zionism," *Betfuzot Hagolah*, 56/57 (1971), 7-12. (In Hebrew.)

Zavalloni, M. "Social Identity: Perspectives and Prospects," *Social Sciences Information*, 12 (1973), 65-91.

SUBJECT INDEX

ABOUT THE AUTHOR

Simon N. Herman is Professor of Social Psychology at the Hebrew University of Jerusalem and teaches in its Department of Psychology and Institute of Contemporary Jewry.

A graduate of the University of Cape Town and of the University of the Witwatersrand in South Africa, he continued his studies in the United States at Harvard University and at the Research Center for Group Dynamics (then at MIT) where he worked under the late Professor Kurt Lewin.

His papers in the social science journals have been on subjects relating to ethnic identity, sociolinguistics, and cross-cultural education. He has devoted particular attention to the application of the theories and methods of social psychology to the problems of contemporary Jewish life. He is the author of *The Reaction of Jews to Anti-Semitism; American Students in Israel;* and *Israelis and Jews: The Continuity of an Identity*.